Costi Hinn has seen close-up the hyping [...] gain. Acutely aware of the dangers of fals[e ...] *Knowing the Spirit* in God's Word. If you're looking for a biblical and pastoral treatment of the Holy Spirit, his person, his works, and his importance in the Christian life, you've found it!

—RANDY ALCORN, author, *If God Is Good*
and *The Promise of the New Earth*

The Holy Spirit has become the forgotten member of the Trinity. Never has a right understanding of his divine person and sovereign ministry been more needed—and more important—than today. That is why this book by Costi Hinn, *Knowing the Spirit*, is so strategic. Here is a straightforward, doctrinally sound, and readable book on this vital subject. Drawn from the wells of Scripture, these pages are sure to revitalize your Christian life.

—STEVEN J. LAWSON, president, OnePassion Ministries;
professor, The Master's Seminary; teaching fellow, Ligonier
Ministries; lead preacher, Trinity Bible Church of Dallas

Rarely has a book come along in recent years that exemplifies Jesus' "grace and truth" approach (John 1:17) more than this one. As I read it, I marveled at the Spirit-bestowed gifts given to my brother Costi Hinn: his ability to handle tough doctrinal questions, his clarity and concision of expression, his joyful passion for Christ and his church, and his pastoral warmth and care. As Calvin said, the faithful pastor has two voices: one to call the sheep, and one to call off the wolves. Costi has both voices, and the overall work here will help to make disciples even as it protects the church through wise biblical counsel. I do not say this lightly: this is a wonderful book.

—DR. OWEN STRACHAN, provost, Grace Bible Theological
Seminary; author, *Awakening the Evangelical Mind*

This is such a helpful book! Costi has done a great job of teaching on a subject that is often misunderstood. His writing is profound but still clear, straightforward, and practical. I will be referencing this book for many years, because it has deepened my understanding of who the Holy Spirit is and how I can know him better.

—JINGER VUOLO, *New York Times* bestselling
author, *Becoming Free Indeed*

When I first heard that Costi Hinn was writing a book on the Holy Spirit, my heart leaped in my chest. I am thankful to see this book in print not only because of its excellent content but also because of the nearness of the doctrine to Costi's heart. If you know his story, you know what I'm talking about. In *Knowing the Spirit*, Costi aptly follows in the footsteps of J. I. Packer and Mark Jones, offering up a biblical, doctrinal, practical, and pastoral treatise on the often-misunderstood member of the Godhead. Costi writes in a clear and engaging way; you can almost hear his heart beating between the sentences. I'm so thankful for this book and I sincerely pray that God will use it to correct and comfort his people as they walk by the Spirit.

—NATE PICKOWICZ, pastor, Harvest Bible Church, Gilmanton
Iron Works, New Hampshire; author, *How to Eat Your Bible*

The Holy Spirit remains a mystery to many in the church. What role does he play? How do we know he's working? How can we ensure we're following him? When these questions go unanswered, Christians are vulnerable to false teaching and unbiblical doctrines. In this book, Costi provides so much comfort and clarity as he paints a biblical picture of who the Spirit is and how he works in the believer's life.

—ALLIE BETH STUCKEY, host, *RELATABLE*;
author, *You're Not Enough (and That's Okay)*

Burdened by the fact that the Holy Spirit is the most misunderstood and abused person of the Trinity in the church today, Costi writes to clarify the person and work of the Spirit. He focuses on Scripture's emphasis on the Spirit's presence and power in every believer's life while also navigating the minefield of aberrations that create confusion about him. The book provides much-needed discernment and clarity for the believer to express genuine worship of the Holy Spirit.

—JOHN MACARTHUR, pastor, Grace Community Church, Sun Valley, California; chancellor, The Master's University and Seminary

Once again, Costi has offered an extraordinary service to the church by taking aim at misrepresentations of the Holy Spirit and pointing us all to the Spirit's majesty, value, and transforming power. Whenever Christianity faces a threat to the purity of doctrine, God raises a generational voice to platform truth and confront error. That is what we have here—a gracious yet meticulous and robust clarification of the third member of the Trinity that will stand the test of time and bless Christ followers for decades.

—DR. TONY WOOD, pastor-teacher, Mission Bible Church, Orange County, California

*Knowing the Spirit* is an incredibly insightful and impressively accessible survey of the person and work of the Holy Spirit. Even if you disagree with some of Hinn's conclusions, his biblical arguments, both reasonable and pastoral, will challenge and encourage you to greater faithfulness to God and his Word.

—JARED C. WILSON, assistant professor of pastoral ministry and author in residence, Midwestern Seminary; author, *Supernatural Power for Everyday People* and *Friendship with the Friend of Sinners*

Costi's history with the prosperity gospel has provided him a front-row seat to the abuse and misuse of the Holy Spirit, lending credence to his assessment of those wrong ideas and the importance of properly interpreting Scripture on the person and work of the Holy Spirit. I appreciate how Costi graciously and biblically deals with differing positions regarding the work and gifts of the Holy Spirit and the importance of unity in the body of Christ even when we differ. In our experientially driven church culture, Costi calls us to be grounded in the authority and truth of God's Word and to use it as our sole, objective guide to the very important, but often neglected, third person of the Trinity. The book is written in a style accessible to all believers while still relating biblical truths, providing not just head knowledge but also knowledge of how to live out those truths in our everyday lives.

—DR. GEORGIA PURDOM, PhD, vice president of educational content and director of Answers for Women Conferences, Answers in Genesis

Winston Churchill once referred to Russia as "a riddle wrapped in a mystery inside an enigma." Sadly, that's how most Christians think of the person of the Holy Spirit. Because of the wild misrepresentation of many and the unintentional overreaction of others, many believers fail to fully appreciate and enjoy the unspeakable gift of the Holy Spirit, whom God has given to be with us and live in us.

In this refreshing, insightful, and encouraging study, Costi Hinn combines his unique spiritual background and journey with a relentless desire to be biblical. The result is a gracious and balanced explanation of the person and work of the Holy Spirit filled with rich, practical application. On such a debated issue, you might not agree with every detail, but as you read and meditate on the truth, you will grow in your knowledge of, dependence on, and love for the Holy Spirit.

—TOM PENNINGTON, pastor-teacher, Countryside Bible Church, Southlake, Texas

Christians cannot know God or understand his Word apart from the person of the Holy Spirit. Apart from this blessed third person of the Trinity, we cannot be saved, sanctified, equipped to serve, and sustained in trials, experience answers to prayer, and be united to other members in the family of God. Simply stated, you cannot live a single moment of faithfulness to Jesus Christ apart from the Spirit. In light of this, you need to know the Holy Spirit—who he is, what he does, and how he can transform your life. I can commend to you no greater resource than the one my friend Costi Hinn has written.

—JONNY ARDAVANIS, pastor, Stonebridge Bible Church, Franklin, Tennessee

# KNOWING

## *THE*

# SPIRIT

# OTHER BOOKS BY COSTI W. HINN

*God, Greed, and the (Prosperity) Gospel:*
*How Truth Overwhelms a Life Built on Lies*

*More Than a Healer: Not the Jesus You*
*Want, but the Jesus You Need*

# KNOWING

## *THE*

# SPIRIT

WHO HE IS, WHAT HE DOES,
AND HOW HE CAN TRANSFORM
YOUR CHRISTIAN LIFE

# COSTI W. HINN

ZONDERVAN BOOKS

*Knowing the Spirit*
Copyright © 2023 by Costi W. Hinn

Requests for information should be addressed to:
Zondervan, *3900 Sparks Dr. SE, Grand Rapids, Michigan 49546*

Zondervan titles may be purchased in bulk for educational, business, fundraising, or sales promotional use. For information, please email SpecialMarkets@Zondervan.com.

ISBN 978-0-310-36679-9 (audio)

Library of Congress Cataloging-in-Publication Data

Names: Hinn, Costi W., author.
Title: Knowing the Spirit : who he is, what he does, and how he can transform your Christian life / Costi W. Hinn.
Description: Grand Rapids : Zondervan, 2023.
Identifiers: LCCN 2023015300 (print) | LCCN 2023015301 (ebook) | ISBN 9780310366775 (trade paperback) | ISBN 9780310366782 (ebook)
Subjects: LCSH: Holy Spirit. | Baptism in the Holy Spirit. | Gifts, Spiritual. | Christian life. | BISAC: RELIGION / Christian Theology / Pneumatology | SELF-HELP / Spiritual
Classification: LCC BT121.3 .H566 2023 (print) | LCC BT121.3 (ebook) | DDC 231/.3—dc23/eng/20230522
LC record available at https://lccn.loc.gov/2023015300
LC ebook record available at https://lccn.loc.gov/2023015301

Published in association with the literary agency of Wolgemuth & Associates, Inc.

*Cover design: Studio Gearbox*
*Cover illustrations: Marylia / Shutterstock*
*Interior design: Sara Colley*

*Printed in the United States of America*

23 24 25 26 27  LBC  5 4 3 2 1

*To the beloved members of Shepherd's House Bible Church:*
*May the Spirit transform us year after year for the glory of Christ.*

# CONTENTS

# ACKNOWLEDGMENTS

BY THE TIME THIS BOOK GETS PUBLISHED, IT WILL have been more than one year since the Lord made a way for us to plant Shepherd's House Bible Church in Chandler, Arizona. When we launched in February 2022, I wasn't sure whether I would be able to write as much, though I love to study, write, and meditate on God's truth. A church plant requires a level of attention that could make a project like writing this book unlikely. But in God's providence, it came to fruition. Without the loving support of my wife and our church staff, I wouldn't be able to take time to write. Beyond that, they don't just support me, they push me to keep writing so that our church can benefit from resources like this book. Ultimately, we are all focused on the same things: the glory of God and the good of his people. I am the undeserving recipient of much grace. Jesus gets the credit, and I want to thank some people he has used in special ways.

First, Christyne. You are my love, my beauty, my wife, my teammate, and my best friend. Only heaven will reveal how you've blessed my life and how behind every book I've written was a wife who selflessly held down the fort and took on extra so I could serve with my pen. Our conversations about the Spirit's work have been woven into the fabric of this book in countless ways. Thank you for anchoring our home, pouring into our children, encouraging me, and receiving my sermons from the pulpit and still living so graciously with the preacher. Next to salvation, you are God's greatest gift to me.

Second, Brett McIntosh. Your brotherhood and friendship are a gift from the Lord. Planting a church together has been the adventure of a lifetime, and you've been there every step of the way. Thank you for encouraging me to write this book and loving our church so faithfully. It's an honor to shepherd the flock with you, and Shepherd's House is blessed in countless ways because of your servant leadership.

Third, staff and leaders of Shepherd's House. Diana Riggins, thank you for taking so much off of my plate so I could focus on this project at key moments. Ryan Shackelford, thank you for always jumping in at a moment's notice to help with whatever was needed as we structured budgets, planned logistics, and took care of numerous other details to plant Shepherd's House at the same time that I needed to write this book. To the rest of our staff, core team, and members who have made the heavy lifting of a church plant lighter in countless ways: thank you!

Fourth, For the Gospel leadership team and staff. Brett Skinner, your leadership at FTG and love for gospel work moves us forward in so many ways. Justin Bond, every video and podcast you edit matters in eternity. Thank you for going all in every day. Thank you for all you do to get resources in front of people who need truth and want to grow. Ashley Brodeur, your dedication has been a difference maker, and I know that without Matt's support you couldn't do what you do.

Fifth, Erik Wolgemuth. Your name is in every book I've written, and I hope it stays that way for years to come. You are a friend and gospel partner in so many ways. Thank you for being steady and consistent. You're the best there is.

Sixth, Carolyn McCready. There is a joy and comfort in having the same editor every step of the way. I am so thankful that you've continued to put your heart into every project we do together. Your questions, feedback, and encouragement are like nitrous oxide injected into the book. You get me thinking and seeing things from so many different angles and always have both my and the reader's best interests in mind.

# INTRODUCTION

# *Holy Who?*

YEARS HAVE PASSED SINCE I WAS SAVED AND BEGAN studying the Holy Spirit with the curiosity of Sherlock Holmes, but one trend continues to be prevalent: the Holy Spirit is quite possibly the most used and abused member of the Trinity. Confusion and disillusionment abound because of the abuses and poor theology, but it doesn't have to be this way. I wrote this book to spur us all, regardless of background, onward to a genuine and thriving relationship with the real Holy Spirit. If you've come from a place of confusion, this book will bring clarity. If you have never experienced abuse and chaos regarding his work, you'll have little to deconstruct, but I hope this book will serve you in a foundational way as well.

## A DISTURBING TREND OF IGNORANCE

Fifty-eight percent of people who identify as Christian do not believe the Holy Spirit is real. At least that is what the Cultural

Research Center at Arizona Christian University found in a study done in 2021. Nearly 70 percent of US adults self-identify as Christian, but many of them express a deeper reliance on their feelings, experiences, family, and friends than on the Bible. Their moral guidance comes from somewhere other than the origin of all morality—God. George Barna concluded in one recent study that only a small minority (6 percent) of professing Christians actually possess a biblical worldview.[1]

Research like that breaks my heart. If the Holy Spirit is real (he is), if he is the Comforter like Jesus says in John 14:26 (he is), if he takes up residence inside of every believer like 1 Corinthians 6:19 teaches (he does), and if he bears fruit like love, joy, peace, patience, kindness, goodness, faithfulness, gentleness, and self-control like Galatians 5:22–23 says (he does), then the vast majority of the next generation of professing Christians do not know the God they desperately need. Another shocking statistic I read in *USA Today* reports a nearly 60 percent increase in suicide by young people ages ten to twenty-four over the past ten years.[2] A generation is lost in depression, despair, and anxiety. We can all relate to that, can't we? We're seeing it everywhere, or perhaps you're experiencing those feelings right now. You need peace. You need love. You need joy. You need comfort. We all need the God who can meet our deepest spiritual needs. Guess what? The Holy Spirit is the God who can meet your needs. Even if you believe in him, do you know him? Do you have a relationship with him? Do you understand him?

I want you to encounter the Holy Spirit and know this lesser known person of the triune God like never before. But before we go

---

1. Tracy Munsil, "CRC Report Finds Nearly 70% of Americans Claim to Be 'Christian,' but What Does That Mean?" Arizona Christian University, August 31, 2021, www.arizonachristian.edu/2021/08/31/crc-report-finds-nearly-70-of-americans-claim -to-be-christian-but-what-does-that-mean/.

2. Alia E. Dastagir, "More Young People Are Dying by Suicide, and Experts Aren't Sure Why," *USA Today*, September 11, 2020, www.usatoday.com/story/news/health/2020 /09/11/youth-suicide-rate-increases-cdc-report-finds/3463549001/.

on this journey together, I have three confessions and three promises to make that will set the stage for the rest of the book.

# THREE CONFESSIONS

*Confession 1: I used to believe in a version of the Holy Spirit that was wholly unholy.* If you don't already know the full story, I used to believe and teach a version of the Holy Spirit that was twisted. The hard truth is that much of what I believed was based on a false version of the Holy Spirit. That was many years ago now, but one day, God in his grace and mercy opened my eyes, crushed my pride, and showed me how spiritually misled I was. He showed me that I was abusing the Holy Spirit, misrepresenting the Holy Spirit, and even lying about the Holy Spirit. After repenting of my sin and being transformed by God's power, I spent a number of years being privately discipled and not speaking or teaching publicly. I went to counseling, graduated from seminary, and studied what the Bible reveals about the Holy Spirit, determining never to lie about him again. You can read about my experiences and how Jesus changed my life in another book I wrote titled *God, Greed, and the (Prosperity) Gospel.*

While none of my past has a bearing on the truth I believe now, it's important for you to know what God has saved me from.

*Confession 2: The subject of the Holy Spirit can be controversial at times, but it shouldn't be all the time.* This book is not meant to be controversial, and I don't think it is. But there are three controversial debates about the Holy Spirit that I do cover in this book.

First, some believe that certain gifts the Holy Spirit gives are not as active today as they once were. Others believe that certain gifts he gives are for everyone and that anyone can possess all of his gifts. I'll try to deal with these views in a fair, balanced, and biblical way. I'll also explain what I believe, but don't assume you have to agree with me. I want you to weigh everything I write against Scripture.

Second, some people believe that you must have a "second blessing" from the Holy Spirit to really experience his power in your life. I will explain what this means in the chapter about the baptism of the Holy Spirit. Again, you don't have to agree with me, but I'll do my best to present positions that are clearly based on Scripture.

Third, there is debate over whether the Holy Spirit speaks to people today. Some teach that he speaks with a "still small voice," others claim they hear from God audibly, and still others express that he speaks to their hearts or their minds. I'll address all of this in the chapter "Does the Spirit Speak?"

I hope you will find my presentation to be well argued from Scripture, even if you disagree with my interpretation.

*Confession 3: There are mysteries we might never completely understand until we get to heaven.* The rationalist in me would like to say that if you study hard enough, you can uncover every mystery about the Holy Spirit and you'll never have questions. The truth is, you and I have to be humble about how mysterious some aspects of his work are. Thankfully, Scripture has made many things clear about him so that we don't stumble into serious error. But God's sovereignty and divine providence mean that the Spirit is working in infinite ways at once in billions of lives. No one can honestly say they have a lock on the Holy Spirit, that they can predict everything he is doing or going to do. That kind of control is reserved for him alone. If we compare the Holy Spirit's work in human lives to the amount of invisible data whizzing around the digital airwaves, the Holy Spirit's work would make digital data look like nothing more than the old dial-up version of the internet. The Holy Spirit is making moves, influencing minds, and changing lives at speeds that make lightspeed look like a snail's pace. For a follower of Jesus, it's so important to discern what is and isn't the Holy Spirit's work. The last thing I want for you is a life of confusion or ignorance because you never got to know him truly and deeply. If you take a moment to think about it, I'm sure you've had moments when you wondered, *Was that the Holy Spirit? Is this situation from the Holy Spirit? Did this event occur because of the Holy Spirit? Are my feelings from the Holy Spirit? Was that thought from the Holy Spirit?* Many times, that *is* him at work, transforming us from the inside out, while other times you will need to remember what Scripture teaches so that you can discern when another spirit or influence is at work.

No matter how far you plumb the depths of his work, there will always be a mysterious element to all that he is doing. You know what that means? God is an infinite God that you can't fully comprehend or predict, a God far greater, far more powerful, and far more knowledgeable than you or me.

## THREE PROMISES

*Promise 1: You are going to finish this book with a far greater understanding of the Holy Spirit than when you started.* I am going to cover the most important questions asked about the Holy Spirit and provide you with answers straight from Scripture. I will take you on a deeper dive into certain topics, along with explaining various views on some misunderstood and sometimes controversial areas, like the gifts of the Spirit and how they are in use today. You'll need your Bible-student hat on when we get to those points, and I'll provide you with a number of quotes and references from trusted theologians. Whether you're a longtime churchgoer or new to Christianity, you are going to understand the Holy Spirit if you finish this book.

*Promise 2: You are going to learn how to apply truths about the Holy Spirit.* Putting your knowledge into practice is key to your growth. My friend and fellow pastor Adam Bailie once said, "People and preachers need to remember that we don't just learn to learn. We learn to live!" He's a gifted expositor and preacher who includes a final section in every sermon called "Learning to Live" in which he boils the sermon down into actions you can take immediately to live out the truth you just learned from Scripture. Practical application is such a priority at his church that when I preached for him one weekend, he made me include Learning to Live in the final section of my sermon—even as a guest! I loved it so much that I've borrowed his approach and put it into the final section of every chapter in this book. You and I will not just learn about the Holy Spirit, we will learn to live in light of what Scripture says about the Holy Spirit.

*Promise 3: This book is only just the beginning of your knowing and loving the Holy Spirit.* Remember this: The Holy Spirit is not a topic you conquer and move on from. He is someone you walk with every day for the rest of your life. It's incredible to think that you will never be able to plumb the depths of the Holy Spirit or his power, nor can you ever fully predict his movement in someone's life. In John 3:8, Jesus describes the Spirit's work in salvation saying, "The wind blows wherever it pleases. You hear its sound, but you cannot tell where it comes from or where it is going. So it is with everyone born of the Spirit" (NIV). You will learn much about him from this book, but you'll still need to remain humble and be open to continuing to grow and learn. Depend on him through prayer. Ask him to do the things contained in this book to you and through you. Tell him even now as you read these words, "Holy Spirit, I want to be yielded and surrendered to you. Please do a mighty work in me for Jesus' glory."

Are you ready to deepen your understanding of and relationship with the Spirit? Let's walk together to that end.

# WHO IS THE
# HOLY SPIRIT?

*Therefore go and make disciples of all nations,*
*baptizing them in the name of the Father*
*and of the Son and of the Holy Spirit.*
—MATTHEW 28:19 NIV

I CLICKED THE PLAY BUTTON ON THE VIDEO OF A woman sitting in a chair on a stage, microphone in hand, seemingly ready to share something from the Bible to a crowd of eager listeners. She was a well-known singer and songwriter, so the crowd undoubtedly was on the edge of their seats in anticipation. The video began: "The Holy Spirit, to me, is like the genie from Aladdin."

The crowd responded immediately with laughter, engaged with her right from the start. I tried hard to fully understand what she was saying and not be hasty to judge her. Perhaps she was just attempting to have a little fun and bring levity to a theological subject. As

7

she went on, however, no well-intentioned motive could account for what she said, and my concern deepened because of how much confusion abounds in the church today when it comes to the Holy Spirit.

She continued, "That's who he is to me. He's funny, and he's sneaky, and he's silly. He's wonderful. He's like the wind. He's all around."

When studies show that only 6 percent of professing Christians have an accurate Christian worldview, and nearly 60 percent of those who identify as Christians do not believe the Holy Spirit is real, likening him to a chaotic Disney character is the last thing a professing Christian with a microphone should be doing.

The truth is that the Holy Spirit is not funny and definitely is not silly. If he is sneaky, it's because you can't predict him or because in his sovereign power he does incredible things that you never see or know about. He's not at all like the genie from Aladdin, for he's not some magical force you can coerce and control with just the right phrase. He is active and powerful, and Scripture has made it possible for you and me to know enough about him that we need not be lured away from the truth by comical versions of him.

When it comes to the Holy Spirit, we need to make sure everything we believe lines up with Scripture. I've often heard this quote attributed to Charles Spurgeon (though I can never find the original source) that says, "Discernment is not knowing the difference between right and wrong. It is knowing the difference between right and almost right."

You and I must get our understanding of the Holy Spirit right if we love the truth and want to glorify Jesus Christ with our lives.

## THE HOLY SPIRIT IS GOD

First and foremost, we need to understand that the Holy Spirit is God and that he is an equal and active part of what we call the Trinity. While few people who claim to be Christians would argue against God the Father or Jesus the Son being God, there is widespread confusion among us regarding the divinity of the Holy Spirit. Is he just an expression of Jesus in spirit form? Is he a less than divine force that God uses to express his power? Is he an angel?

The Bible answers these questions with absolute clarity.

Several key passages from both the Old and New Testaments give us evidence that the Holy Spirit is an equal part of the Trinity: which is God the Father, God the Son, and God the Holy Spirit. In Christianity we understand that God is one, yet he exists in three persons. This may seem a bit confusing to the human mind, but God is infinite, beyond our comprehension, and outside of the limits that creation is bound by. That God is three in one is possible because he is God, though it's a mystery to us. When you think that such teaching is a contradiction to logic, remember the words of renowned theologian R. C. Sproul, who wrote, "The doctrine of the Trinity is not a contradiction but a mystery, for we cannot fully understand how God can exist in three persons."[1] The word *trinity* is not found in the Bible, but we use the word to describe the tri-unity of God because in the Bible we clearly see the three persons of God in action, equally divine and unified.

The Holy Spirit is seen as operating as God in a number of passages in the Old Testament, including:

1. Hovering over the waters before creation (Gen. 1:2)
2. Filling certain men under Moses (Exod. 35:30–35)
3. Empowering Joshua to lead Israel (Num. 27:18)
4. Coming upon Gideon (Judg. 6:34)
5. Coming upon Samson (Judg. 13:25)

---

1. R. C. Sproul, *What Is the Trinity?* Crucial Questions, vol. 10 (Orlando, FL: Reformation Trust, 2011), 58–59.

6. Rushing upon David when he was anointed as king
   (1 Sam. 16:13)
7. Departing from Saul (1 Sam. 16:14)
8. Carrying along the word of the prophets (2 Peter 1:21)
9. Enabling Ezekiel to prophesy (Ezek. 2:2)
10. Prophesied to one day rest upon the Messiah (Isa. 61:1)

Anyone confused about where the Holy Spirit was in the Old
Testament can rest assured that he was very much present and active
before what is commonly known as Pentecost (Acts 2). While Jesus
did promise that the Holy Spirit would come and move powerfully
in the life of the church from Pentecost onward, that incredible
moment was not the first time the Holy Spirit was revealed as an
equal part of the Trinity.

In the New Testament, the Holy Spirit is undeniably present
and divine. He moves from coming "upon" believers in the Old
Testament to entering "into" believers under the new covenant
through Christ. The Holy Spirit is God, and we can see this in a
number of passages in the New Testament, including:

1. He is mentioned almost one hundred times in Matthew,
   Mark, and Luke.
2. He conceived Jesus in Mary's womb (Matt. 1:20).
3. He was present at Jesus' baptism (Matt. 3:16).
4. He was sent by the Father (John 14:16).
5. He teaches the disciples all things and reminds them of
   what Jesus taught (John 14:26).
6. He is God, and believers are baptized in his name
   (Matt. 28:19–20).
7. He is eternal (Heb. 9:14).
8. He has the power to seal believers so that nothing can steal
   their salvation (Eph. 4:30).

9. He dwells within believers and makes them his temple
   (1 Cor. 6:19–20).
10. He has the power to make believers new and washes
    away sin (Titus 3:5).

It's not hard to find in Scripture the Holy Spirit operating as God. The Holy Spirit is everywhere. You could probably add twenty more items to each list in no time at all.

One of my favorite slam-dunk pieces of evidence for the Holy Spirit being God is in Acts when a husband and wife named Ananias and Sapphira put on an elaborate show of generosity when actually they had lied to God about the money they were giving to the church. The apostle Peter confronts them, saying, "Ananias, why has Satan filled your heart to lie to the Holy Spirit and to keep back some of the proceeds of the land?" Peter goes on to say, "You have not lied to men, but to God" (Acts 5:3–4). If the Holy Spirit is not equally God, why would Peter say that Ananias lied to the Holy Spirit and refer to him as God?

These passages were pivotal to my understanding of the Holy Spirit years ago, and I hope they help you grasp the remarkable truth about who he is. According to Scripture, our God is three in one, the Holy Spirit is equally God, and the Holy Spirit is distinctly God (meaning that he is not merely an expression of Jesus in spirit form). As you study what the Bible teaches about the Holy Spirit, you will find that this is essential doctrine, which is why I want you to know the Spirit in a deeper way.

## THE HOLY SPIRIT IS A PERSON

As an equal part of the Godhead, the Holy Spirit is a person and personal. The Father loves you and calls you his own (1 John 3:1), the Son died for you and calls you to believe (John 11:25–26), and the Spirit fills you and transforms you as you follow Jesus (1 Cor. 6:11; Eph. 5:18). Obviously, there is more to God's work than this short summary, but picture those truths as brushstrokes beginning to paint a picture of how God in three persons operates.

That the Holy Spirit is a person means he is most certainly not an "it." I have lost count of how many times I have heard people and even pastors refer to him this way. I'm certain not everyone means to depersonalize him, and some may think I am splitting hairs, but this is an important truth. When we refer to the Holy Spirit as an "it," we are treating him more like a mystical force or a distant power than a relatable person. We would never call the Father an "it." We would never call Jesus an "it." Likewise, it is not respectful or biblical to call the Holy Spirit an "it."

In John 16:1–15, Jesus is preparing his disciples for his departure back to heaven after the resurrection. In this passage, he tells them that he is going to leave, but it's to their advantage that he should go because he will send the Holy Spirit to be their advocate, comforter, and helper. When Jesus describes the Holy Spirit in this passage, he refers not to a mystical force but to a person. Thirteen pronouns point to a person who functions in a personal, powerful, and relatable way. I'll unpack more of what the Holy Spirit does in the next chapter, but for now, rest assured that Jesus says who he is. He is sent from heaven to continue the work of God on earth through the disciples.

Throughout church history, confusing teachings have twisted the simple reality I just showed you. One such teaching is called Sabellianism, and its namesake, Sabellius, taught that the Holy Spirit is not a person but an impersonal force and just an expression of God. According to him, God is one person who simply expresses himself in three different ways. Sabellianism holds that God the Father was expressed in creation, God the Son was expressed through redemption (Jesus redeeming sinners), and God the Spirit was expressed in sanctification (the act of making us more holy). Eventually, this belief was declared a heresy because it denied the personhood of the Holy Spirit.

Another view that confused the early church was Arianism, which denied the deity of both Jesus and the Holy Spirit. Arianism taught that Jesus and the Holy Spirit were both created beings and not of the same substance or nature as God the Father. This dangerously heretical view demeans both Jesus and the Holy Spirit. If Jesus and the Holy Spirit are not divine persons and equally God, how can they be worshiped? Arianism was such a devastating doctrinal threat to the understanding of God in the early church that Emperor Constantine called together a council of around three hundred church leaders to discuss and clarify what all Christians should believe about God, including Jesus and the Holy Spirit. This is known as the Council of Nicaea and it is one of the hallmarks of church history. Out of this council came the Nicene Creed, which many churches still use to clarify biblical doctrines.

The truth is that the Holy Spirit is a person and he is someone we should want to have a relationship with as God. We only need to think about the words Jesus used to describe the Holy Spirit and how the New Testament speaks about him to realize that he is a person. Here is a quick list to help you understand this clearly:

1. Jesus refers to the Holy Spirit as Comforter, Helper, and Advocate to reveal that the Holy Spirit is active as a person and part of the Trinity who was sent to us (John 14:26; 15:26).
2. He has feelings (Eph. 4:30; Heb. 10:29).
3. He reveals (1 Cor. 2:10).
4. He searches (1 Cor. 2:11).
5. He indwells (1 Cor. 2:12).
6. He teaches (John 14:26; 1 Cor. 2:13).
7. He helps and prays (Rom. 8:26–27).

8. He speaks (Acts 13:2).
9. He has a will (Acts 15:28).
10. He bears witness to our spirits that we're children of God (Rom. 8:16).

All of the activities on this list are marks of personhood. God the Holy Spirit is a person. So, since Scripture reveals that he is a person, what does that mean for you and me?

## HE IS APPROACHABLE

If the Holy Spirit is God (and he is), and if the Holy Spirit is a person (and he is), then we can have a relationship with him and interact with him. Even though he is God and ought to be feared (in a healthy way) and respected, Scripture presents him as approachable, relatable, and personal. After all, the Bible says that believers are filled with him (1 Cor. 6:19), so we ought to experience a close relationship with him. The Holy Spirit is not a mystically distant deity. You can pray to him, ask him for help, be honest with him about your desperate need for strength, wisdom, healing, holiness, and growth in your spiritual life. It is good to remember that he is God and can be depended on in your greatest hour of need. Approach him, seek him, implore him, and trust him. Like a relationship with Jesus as your savior, and like a relationship with the Father as a perfect one who loves you, approach the Spirit as you do any member of the Trinity and depend fully on him. It may take you some time to see him that way, but the more you understand him, the more your relationship with him can develop.

Perhaps you're a bit confused by the doctrine of the Holy Spirit or feel uneasy because, like me, you have seen some of the irreverent—and even blasphemous—antics of preachers who make the Holy Spirit a wild, sensational show. I remember going through a season when relating to the Holy Spirit was difficult because my context for his work was my family members acting drunk and falling all over platforms, blowing on people and laughing uncontrollably, and pacing back and forth in a pulpit, breathing as heavily as a marathon runner and shouting that anyone not getting fired up in church needs a "Holy Ghost enema up their rear." (Yes, that's a true story.)[2]

After becoming disillusioned by the lunacy of what I had grown up in, I needed to deconstruct. And by the grace of God and with his guidance, I was able to also *re*construct—but really, it was the Holy Spirit doing it. Wiser and older Christians told me to build my beliefs on Scripture alone, like building a house on rock instead of on sand. I needed to put experiences in the back seat and not let impersonal and blasphemous antics influence my relationship with the Holy Spirit and my view of him. I could approach him and receive answers from the Bible. When you and I build our doctrinal beliefs on Scripture, we will find that truth is never far from our reach.

Have you been confused, frustrated, or indifferent about building a relationship with the Holy Spirit? Approach him, learn about him, and ask him for help. Turn off the opinions and foolish fantasies that some televangelists conjure up to manipulate their cultlike followings. Turn on the voice of God through the Bible. The Holy Spirit has made himself knowable and approachable. The rest of the chapters of this book will make that a reality for you. But first, let's apply what we've learned so far.

---

2. Scott Hutcheson, *Suzanne Hinn—Holy Ghost Enema*, YouTube, December 5, 2006, www.youtube.com/watch?v=2jhw_5ye8Qo.

# LEARNING TO LIVE

## 1. Worship the Holy Spirit as God

If the Holy Spirit is everything we've covered so far, then he is God and we are to worship him. Include him in your worship, acknowledge him in your worship, and remember that he is essential to your worship. This could be as simple as praising the Holy Spirit for his work in your life during a time of worship in your church or including him in your conversations about God with your family. The Holy Spirit typically gets neglected because of ignorance, but also sometimes out of fear. Finally, be reverent in your worship. The word *worship* in the original language of the New Testament is the Greek word *proskuneo*, and it means to "kiss the hand in reverence" or "to bow down." When we worship God, we are to have a heart (and even a body) posture of bowing down out of respect and honor for God Almighty.

## 2. Seek a Relationship with the Holy Spirit as a Person

One way to apply what we've learned is by living with a resolve to see the Holy Spirit as a person. Remove "it" from your spiritual vocabulary for the Spirit. Like any person you have an important relationship with, talk about him, think about him, consider his thoughts and feelings, consider what pleases him, and consider what he would want for you and from you. In the chapters ahead, I've made sure to explain what grieves him, what blasphemes him, and what pleases him so that you will have clarity on what the Bible says about those things. For now, relish this truth: the Holy Spirit is a person and personal.

### 3. Pray to the Holy Spirit as God

When is the last time you addressed the Holy Spirit in your prayers? Chances are, you have addressed the Father and Jesus the Son, but how should you address the Holy Spirit? Based on what we've covered so far, I hope you are already experiencing an impulse to pray to him as God. Ask him to fill you; he will (Eph. 5:18). Ask him to bear fruit through your life; he will (Gal. 5:22–23). Ask him to use your spiritual gifts to bless others; he will (1 Peter 4:7–11). Ask him to help you glorify Jesus today; he will (John 16:14). One of the most incredible truths that we'll cover later in this book is that the Holy Spirit actually prays for you, and he also helps you when you don't know what to pray for or how to pray. John Bunyan, author of *Pilgrim's Progress*, wisely wrote, "Prayer is a sincere, sensible, affectionate pouring out of the soul to God, through Christ, in the strength and assistance of the Spirit, for such things as God has promised." Here's a great idea: Take a few minutes right after finishing this chapter to pray to the Holy Spirit. If you don't know what to pray, ask him for help. He'll be there for you.

## Questions for Reflection

1. Why do you think so many people either do not believe in the Holy Spirit or seem ignorant of his work and ministry?
2. List three ways the Holy Spirit was active in the Old Testament and three ways he was active in the New Testament.
3. If someone were to say they believe in the Holy Spirit but do not believe he is God, what would you say to them to prove his deity?
4. Have you ever seen antics in church that a leader claimed to be the Holy Spirit's work but instead confused you or even angered you? What are some constructive responses you could have to these situations, rather than only remaining frustrated?

5. As we covered in this chapter, worship of the Holy Spirit
   is biblical, and we should maintain a heart of reverence
   even in our personal and authentic relationship with him.
   What does reverence look like to you?

## 2

# HOW DO YOU ENCOUNTER THE HOLY SPIRIT?

*Repent and be baptized, every one of you, in the*
*name of Jesus Christ for the forgiveness of your sins.*
*And you will receive the gift of the Holy Spirit.*
—ACTS 2:38 NIV

YOU'VE SPENT HARD-EARNED MONEY BUYING THIS book and precious time reading chapter 1, so I'm not going to make you wait even another page for the most important answer in this book. There are plenty of important questions we still need to cover, but none more vital to your soul than this: How do you encounter the Holy Spirit and experience the power of his life-changing, destiny-altering, eternity-securing work?

You can ask this question of several different pastors or people and get several different, even confusing, answers. Here are just a few I have heard:

- When you speak in tongues
- When the hands of an anointed leader are laid on your head
- When you get around people who are experiencing the power and presence of God
- When you go to the right church or conference
- When you listen to music that makes you feel the presence of God

All of these miss the mark. Some of them are troubling and weigh people (maybe even you) down with guilt, shame, and failure because they never think they have done enough to encounter the Holy Spirit.

I remember a young woman from our church approaching me with tears in her eyes. She was a new Christian and said that she was spiritually exhausted. I asked her what was the matter, to which she responded, "I just don't feel the Holy Spirit. A friend I met invited me to an event where we were supposed to encounter the Holy Spirit. The speaker laid out the things we needed, and one of them was to get prayed over and to speak in tongues. I genuinely tried, and it didn't work for me. When I asked some questions, I was labeled as having a critical spirit. One of the leaders at another event said that I needed to be set free from that critical spirit before I could encounter the Holy Spirit. I have spent this past year looking for more experiences so that I could encounter him. Now I feel exhausted and more confused than ever."

As a pastor, few things stir up my zeal to speak truth more than people striving to be "good enough" to encounter the Holy Spirit. Why? Because the answer is so simple and requires no tongues or hands being laid on you, and you do not need to attend the best conferences with celebrity preachers to find it.

How do you encounter the Holy Spirit? By believing the gospel of Jesus Christ, placing your faith for salvation wholly on him, abandoning your works and human strivings, repenting of your sin, and relishing in his perfect ability to save you from a life of destruction here on earth and in eternity. Want to encounter the Holy Spirit? Do less! Yes, you read that correctly. Stop chasing encounter after encounter, conference after conference, and feeling after feeling. The Holy Spirit invades your life not through feelings but through faith. Feelings undoubtedly will be a byproduct of faith, but faith is the foundation.

My answer may seem simplistic and even anticlimactic, but maybe that's because we're conditioned to crave emotional experiences as evidence of the Holy Spirit's residence in our lives. In this chapter, I'll explain clear biblical steps to encountering the Holy Spirit, but first, I want to help you understand why my answer might be seen as too simple. I want you to understand that the modern church has done something to all of us and the way we think about the Holy Spirit.

## HYPING UP THE HOLY SPIRIT

In 2012 the *Christian Post* ran a story that perfectly illustrates how our consumer-driven church culture hypes things up, only to leave us scrambling for the next emotional high. This approach is catalyzed by leaders who try to convince people that the next Sunday is the "Super Bowl of all Sundays" or the next sermon is "the megamonster of all sermons." People are bombarded with church marketing messages that sell the next big experience that will lead to their breakthrough or encounter with God. Is there anything wrong with being excited about the next Sunday service or wanting people to experience life-changing messages or resources? No. The problem was described in the *Christian Post* article this way:

"It would be easy to blame church congregations for the madness that has consumed our gatherings these days, except that from what I see from their pastors, we're *conditioning* them to behave this way. We hype and promote and position and tweet and inadvertently create pews full of consumers instead of devoted worshipers of God," [pastor Brady] Boyd stated.

"We hyp-ers are setting up our people to expect an experience, instead of teaching them to *encounter* their Lord." . . .

"We're adopting the world's model to build God's Church; it's not a sustainable model," he said. "[These churches] are built on marketing principles and not the Holy Spirit, in many cases. Or they're built on both and you can't combine them. It's like oil and water."

The Colorado pastor said he doesn't want to be preoccupied with how to keep consumers happy. That's not his goal. His goal each weekend is to "display passion that comes from having been in the presence of God, instead of the slickness that always surfaces when you've been sucked into the latest trend."

Boyd offered a recipe for hype-free pastoring: prayer, reading Scripture, and giving spiritual direction to people in need. This forces the pastor to rely on the Holy Spirit and not on big personality.[1]

What I love about this article is that the pastor is someone I differ with on some aspects of the Spirit's work. Boyd is charismatic theologically, and I am not. He pastors a church of ten thousand, and I pastor a church much smaller than that. Yet truth is truth when we all simply let the Book talk. Boyd expresses what I long for so many people and leaders from various theological backgrounds to return to. We must go back to the basics of prayer, and reading

---

1. Lillian Kwon, "Colo. Megachurch Pastor: Hype vs. Holy Spirit," *Christian Post*, October 19, 2012, www.christianpost.com/news/colo-megachurch-pastor-hype-vs-holy -spirit.html.

and meditating on Scripture, and do away with the consumer-driven hype being sold as the work of the Spirit. With the Spirit as our guide, we must find direction and give direction from the holy Word of God, not the hype of consumer-driven church strategies.

You and I have been conditioned to believe that we need a hyped-up experience to encounter the Holy Spirit. This is why when the feelings aren't there or the experience isn't emotional, people's confidence wavers. We've traded spiritual confidence in the truth of Scripture for man-made ideas that change with the winds of culture. We don't need another emotionally charged encounter, we need the simplicity of the gospel to make our jaws drop with awe and wonder again and again. We also need to understand that everyone in the universe crosses paths with the Holy Spirit at some level. How they respond determines whether they will experience the fullness of who he is. When we study what the Bible says about the most important encounter that anyone could have with the Holy Spirit, we find that it has little to do with marketing, emotionalism, and consumer-driven hype, and everything to do with the gospel powerfully changing lives.

## THE UNIVERSAL ENCOUNTER

In John 16:8–11, Jesus provides insight regarding the Holy Spirit and his work in the lives of every single individual in the world. Jesus explains, "When he comes, he will prove the world to be in the wrong about sin and righteousness and judgment: about sin, because people do not believe in me; about righteousness, because I am going to the Father, where you can see me no longer; and about judgment, because the prince of this world now stands condemned" (NIV).

The word "prove" can also translate from the Greek language as "convict" or "expose," making it clear that the Holy Spirit is active in drawing lines of truth in the hearts of all people. In just three short verses, we can see that every person in the world will encounter the Holy Spirit in three ways. Let's break these down.

## 1. HE CONVICTS THE WORLD ABOUT SIN

Jesus promised that when the Spirit comes, he would convict the world about their sin because they do not believe in him (vv. 8–9). Even if people are not Christians, the Spirit will convict their hearts regarding their unbelief. He will impress upon their hearts the truth that they are great sinners and that Jesus is a greater savior. This will undoubtedly be a great moment of joy for many who are convicted and put their faith in Jesus, while others will respond with hardheartedness because, though they are convicted about sin and unbelief, they do not want to surrender to Jesus.

I saw this hardheartedness unfold before my eyes after preaching in Hume Lake at a young adults retreat. I had just finished preaching a tasteful message on what the Bible teaches on God's beautiful design for sexuality. Like many people who grew up in church, I have spent countless hours listening to preachers beat the next generation over the head with guilt-laden statements about sex and all kinds of spiritualized threats to make them refrain from sex until marriage. I also, like many people who sat through those sermons, went completely off the rails between the ages of eighteen to twenty-five, and no amount of browbeating could have solved my sinful heart issue. Now when asked to preach on the topic, I was determined to paint a beautiful and biblical picture of sexuality that wasn't taboo, while explaining the scars that remain when we take God's design and use it however we want, hopefully leaving my listeners with a clear sense that without the gospel and belief in Jesus Christ, they'd never be fulfilled. After the message, a line formed of people who wanted to ask me questions or to ask for prayer. I'll never forget one particular girl who was so brutally honest, our encounter stood out from all the others.

She said, "I really enjoyed that message, and I believe everything you said is true, but what if I really love my sin? Like, what if I don't want to do the things you spoke about even though I know they are true, because I really enjoy my life of sin?"

I was taken aback. Her honesty was refreshing, but my heart broke because she was also serious. I asked why she was even at a retreat on this topic if she felt that way.

She said, "My mom paid for me to come and said it would be good for me."

After a brief explanation that a love for sin is not the mark of genuine faith, and that her soul was most certainly in peril if she continued to reject Jesus and embrace her sinful lifestyle, I prayed with her. She said she would seriously consider what I had said, but she also said that she was looking forward to going home after the retreat to continue in her ways.

That heartbreaking conversation is a sobering example of how people can come under the conviction of the Holy Spirit but not respond with repentance and faith. Still, it's important to realize that that girl did have an encounter with the Holy Spirit, like many people will as the truth comes to bear upon their souls. Even in their unbelief, they will experience conviction.

Have you ever wondered why people get really uncomfortable when you talk to them about their sin? Have you ever noticed the way some people lash out with anger or even violence when confronted with their evil actions? Defensiveness, aggression, anger, and denial are all universal responses when people get called out on their sin. In contrast, many Christians can think back to a moment when they were confronted with their sin and broke down in humility and repentance. No matter what the response of our human hearts, the Holy Spirit's convicting work is universal. He presses in on every human conscience regarding morality, and especially does so when the truth of Scripture is put in front of them.

But what about people who have never heard the gospel or who have their own cultural moral standards? Yes, even they get convicted and either run to God or away from God when the Spirit presses in on them concerning sin, righteousness, and judgment. My friend Brooks Buser is a missionary and the president of Radius International. Brooks and his wife, Nina, when their son Beau was two years old, moved to the remote jungles of Papua New Guinea to reach an unreached people group. They left their American dream life, complete with the San Diego coastline, a high-paying corporate job, and all the comforts that money could buy.

After years of training and preparation, they landed among the YembiYembi tribe and began to form relationships, learn the language, and help the Yembis develop a written version of their language. Along the way, Brooks, Nina, and their team began sharing the gospel, something the YembiYembi described as the "God-talk." Eventually, there came a time when all of the Yembi had heard the gospel. Just like John 16 says, all were convicted (or proven wrong) by the Scriptures as Brooks proclaimed the truth about the origin of humanity, original sin, the righteousness of God, and judgment upon those who reject Jesus. Some believed and put their faith in Christ, while others suppressed the truth in unrighteousness (Rom. 1:24) and continued in their own ways. In a number of cases, those who did not want to believe lashed out in anger, ransacked the homes of others in the tribe who had become Christians, and developed a strong hatred for Brooks and his God-talk. They had encountered the Holy Spirit through the convicting message of the gospel and rejected it.

No matter who people are or where they are from, the Holy Spirit's conviction of sin is a universal experience, and those who do not believe in Jesus Christ will be convicted of the greatest sin of all: the sin of unbelief and refusing to have faith in Jesus for salvation.

## 2. HE CONVICTS THE WORLD ABOUT RIGHTEOUSNESS

Everyone has a standard of what they consider to be righteous, but the righteousness of God is the perfect standard. Only Jesus can cover our sin and present us as righteous before the Father (2 Cor. 5:20–21). In John 16:10, Jesus says that the Holy Spirit will convict the world concerning righteousness "because I am going to the Father, where you can see me no longer" (NIV). This is a loaded statement that takes a little bit of digging to understand. I want to give you two things to consider.

First, Jesus' going to the Father means that he truly is the Son of God. Scripture teaches that no one can go to the Father except through Jesus (John 14:6). Jesus repeatedly told people that he was the Son of God and one with the Father (John 10:30). Therefore, the Spirit convicts the world in their hearts about Jesus being the Son of God, because only God could be righteous. One must ask, If everything Jesus said about himself is true, will I believe in him or not? Do I accept that he is God or not? Such convicting questions have eternal results.

Second, Jesus' going to the Father means that he truly was righteous and perfect, and we are not. You may have heard preachers speak about how God cannot look upon sin or allow sin into his presence; therefore, he had to sacrifice his own son to save us (John 3:16). One of the primary places that idea is found is in Habakkuk 1:13, where the prophet declares, "Your eyes are too pure to approve evil, and you can not look on wickedness with favor" (NASB 1995). The Spirit convicts all people of this reality and causes them to ask, Do I have a righteousness that goes beyond my good works (Matt. 5:20)? Am I covered by a perfect righteousness because I can never be perfect enough to atone for my sin (1 Cor. 1:30)? If no one can come before the Father unless they are righteous, do I have faith in Christ to be reckoned as righteous (Rom. 4:5)?

## 3. HE CONVICTS ALL PEOPLE ABOUT JUDGMENT

In John 16:11, Jesus says that the Holy Spirit convicts the world of judgment "because the ruler of this world has been judged." This means that the Holy Spirit is pressing in on human hearts about the coming judgment of God on all those who reject Christ and have not repented of their sin. All must choose whom they will serve and worship. The "ruler of this world" is a term used for Satan, and since he now stands condemned by God, all those who follow after his kingdom of darkness will also be condemned. Now think of the incredible contrast between that reality and Romans 8:1, which reminds us that there is no condemnation for those who are "in Christ Jesus." Jesus was victorious at the cross, and Satan was defeated. The devil's days are numbered! If you have put your faith in Jesus, you're on the winning side. If not, your end will be exactly as Satan's. You might think that choosing the winning side is an easy decision for people to make, but many people want their rebellious way. They refuse to submit to the convicting work of the Holy Spirit and obey Jesus.

Did you know that the Bible contains an illustration of people whom the Holy Spirit has pressed in upon with conviction, yet they openly rebelled against God even in the midst of clear judgment? Revelation 16:21 describes this horrifying scene in which God judges the earth during the tribulation and people blaspheme God in response. The Bible says, "From the sky huge hailstones, each weighing about a hundred pounds, fell on people. And they cursed God on account of the plague of hail, because the plague was so terrible" (NIV). At this stage in the tribulation, the earth is under intense judgment and people would be smart to concede to God. Yet like so many today, their hearts harden toward him, and instead of surrender, they opt for insurrection.

All people will encounter the Holy Spirit. The question is whether such an encounter will be a triumphant moment of salvation or a tragic moment of rejecting him. Whatever the case, God has put eternity in the hearts of all people (Eccl. 3:11). Everyone is searching for the "more" that can be found only in God.

## EVERYONE IS SEARCHING, BUT FOR WHAT?

In a June 2005 interview by Steve Kroft on *60 Minutes*, NFL quarterback and modern-day sports legend Tom Brady expressed his wonderings about there being more to life than his championship rings and global star status. He says, "Why do I have three Super Bowl rings, and still think there's something greater out there for me? . . . I think: God, it's gotta be more than this. I mean this can't be what it's all cracked up to be. I mean, I've done it. I'm twenty-seven. And what else is there for me?"

Kroft asked, "What's the answer?"

Brady answered the best way he could, saying, "I wish I knew. I wish I knew. . . . I love playing football, and I love being a quarterback for this team, but, at the same time, I think there's a lot of other parts about me that I'm trying to find. I know what ultimately makes me happy are family and friends, and positive relationships with great people. I think I get more out of that than anything."[2]

It doesn't matter who someone is or how successful they are in earthly circles of influence, the greatest influencer is the Spirit of God, and without him, every human soul will remain empty and in search of lasting satisfaction.

When someone responds to the Spirit's work positively and in

---

2. Daniel Schorn, "Transcript: Tom Brady, Part 3," CBS News, November 4, 2005, www.cbsnews.com/news/transcript-tom-brady-part-3/. For video of this interview, see "Tom Brady on Winning: There's 'Got to Be More Than This,'" *60 Minutes*, June 2005, www.youtube.com/watch?v=-TA4_fVkv3c.

faith, they encounter the most miraculous chain of spiritual events that will ever take place in a human life. In the next chapter, we're going to look at three life-altering ways the Spirit transforms the lives of those who put their faith in Jesus Christ. But first, let's apply what we've covered in this chapter.

# LEARNING TO LIVE

## 1. Identify the Sources of the Spirit's Conviction in Your Life

The Holy Spirit works in our hearts primarily through the declaration of God's Word to us.

We hear it, read it, think about it, remember it, and respond to it. Make a list of the sources he uses in your life to bring conviction upon your heart. Here are several to consider to get you started:

- A friend who consistently speaks the truth to you and dares to make you uncomfortable because they challenge you spiritually (Prov. 27:17)
- A pastor who doesn't shrink from preaching the whole counsel of God to you (Acts 20:27)
- A small group that presses in on your comfort zone, speaking the truth and asking you hard questions about faith, obedience, worship, and personal holiness
- A podcast that hits your heart with convicting realities about living for Jesus
- A conference that sends you home feeling it's time to change for the better
- Social media pages and friends who post clear, unapologetic truths from God's Word and inspire you to live unashamed
- Exemplary people who are more spiritually mature than you in their daily disciplines, marriages, relationships, words, work ethic, godliness, parenting, spending habits, and more

Why identify these sources of conviction? Because they are gifts to you from the Holy Spirit. He puts people in your path who will be faithful ambassadors for Jesus. If you'll learn to identify these sources, you will be in the perfect position to grow stronger in your faith and apply the next step.

## 2. Commit to Loving Correction, Not Rejecting It

If you've made a list of what the Spirit uses to convict you, the next step is deciding how you're going to view those sources—and the discomfort they cause you—who speak truth, correction, and encouragement into your life. To put it plainly, you need to commit to loving correction. Billionaire entrepreneurs and top-level athletes will tell you that to accomplish something great or to grow in a skill, you must commit to facing hard truths and addressing your weaknesses. This means that you need to embrace correction. I had a college coach who used to say, "Do not feel bad or get down on yourself if we [the coaching staff] are picking on your swing, pushing you harder in the gym, and pointing out your weaknesses. It may seem like we're always on you, because we are! We want to help you, so we highlight these things. It may feel better never to be critiqued, but you should be *very* concerned if we ignore you because it likely means you don't listen to correction and we're not able to develop you as much." These approaches are really just expressions of a biblical concept called conviction. Think of it in spiritual terms: the worst form of judgment on this side of heaven is to be left to your own devices, lost in sin—for God not to even bother to intervene. That is the scene in Romans 1:24, where the Bible says that "God gave them over in the lusts of their hearts to impurity" (NASB 1995). People who ignore the conviction of the Spirit are left stuck in the muck of their love for sin. In contrast, people who live with conviction go farther, grow faster, and get results more than those who live without conviction, because they are living for something bigger than themselves. People with principles know who they are and why they are here on earth. If you're going to grow as a believer in Jesus and take full advantage of the Spirit's powerful work, commit to loving his conviction, loving the discomfort of hard truth, loving the disruption of correction, and loving the pain that comes with spiritual progress.

If you wanted to get into good shape physically, you'd fire a gym trainer who didn't make you a little bit sore and push you to your limits. If you were a sports fan and your favorite team's coach let players just go through the motions, you'd call for him or her to be fired. We love strong and clear correction when we want results. So why not commit to loving the avenues through which the correction and conviction of the Spirit come into your life?

I always love to tell folks in our church, "God does love you the way you are, but he also loves you too much to leave you the way you are." He lovingly saves us while we are still dead sinners (Rom. 5:8; Eph. 2:1–3), then makes us alive in Christ and transforms us to do good works and live for his glory (Eph. 2:4–10). God will use your determination in powerful ways. Commit to loving the Spirit's conviction and watch as truth penetrates your heart and transforms every area of your life. Like getting your teeth cleaned even though it can be uncomfortable, learn to say, "It hurts so good!"

### 3. Run toward the Spirit's Conviction, Not from It

This one is easier said than done, but if you identify the sources that bring conviction on your life, then commit to loving the correction and conviction, you're ready to run, and not away. The temptation to run from conviction is an ever-present threat to your spiritual growth, and no one is immune. It may even be that the older and more mature we get in the faith, the stronger the temptation to give in to pride and resist wise counsel. I remember talking to an older mentor who said that too many people head for the exits when truth infringes on their comfort zones. Instead, run toward the sources of conviction like you've been in the desert for three days without water and you've discovered an oasis. The waters of Spirit-led conviction will wash over your soul and cleanse you. Divine truths will shape you like an artist chiseling away at a marble masterpiece. The Holy Spirit is fully God and active in convicting the human heart in ways that it needs the most. When you sense his conviction upon you through the truth of the Scripture, recognize it as something you need even if it isn't what your flesh wants.

## Questions for Reflection

1. Why do you think people have a difficult time being teachable and receiving correction?
2. List three to five sources that the Holy Spirit is regularly using in your life to bring conviction and correction to your heart. If you cannot list three to five, what does that tell you and what should you do about it?
3. Who do you look up to spiritually? What is it about their walk with the Lord that inspires you? Ask them what the keys to their growth are.
4. Many people think of an encounter with the Spirit as something more emotional, feelings based, or linked to a special event or conference. After reading this chapter, how would you define an encounter with the Spirit?
5. Why did Jesus call his departure and the Spirit's coming an advantage?

**3**

# HOW DOES THE
# SPIRIT CHANGE
# YOUR LIFE?

*But you were washed, you were sanctified, you*
*were justified in the name of the Lord Jesus*
*Christ and by the Spirit of our God.*
—1 CORINTHIANS 6:11 NIV

THE HOLY SPIRIT CHANGES PEOPLE AND CAUSES them to grow. Asking how the Holy Spirit changes your life can help you better understand your own growth. Perhaps equally as important, understanding the process of how the Spirit changes people can help you be more patient with people in your life. Couldn't we all use more of that?

Addison Leitch once wrote, "When the will of God crosses the

will of man, somebody has to die."[1] What a perfect picture of the
fork in the road that you and I stand at each and every day, and of
the way God so lovingly invites us to die spiritually so that Christ
might live through us (Gal. 2:20). But important questions still
need to be answered: If the Holy Spirit changes us, why do we still
sin? Is there a secret to having a burning hunger for God's Word?
Why do people who have encountered God sometimes still act lost?
How long until we reach sinless perfection, and what is taking so
long? How can I make sense of the Bible? It seems intimidating. If
you've ever asked those questions, you are not alone.

I remember the first couple of years after my conversion and
how desperately I wanted to change and to have a greater understanding of the Word, but how slow and agonizing the process
seemed. When the Spirit opened my eyes, I suddenly understood
the gospel, my sinful ways, my hypocrisy, and my need to submit my life to Christ. Certain sins were immediately gone, such
as deceptive beliefs, indifference toward the gospel, sordid gain,
rebellion against God's ways, pride in my family name, a lack of
submission to others, and a litany of attitudes and mindsets that
were antithetical to faithful Christianity. But other sins lingered
longer than I wanted, and there were spiritual disciplines that I
still needed to develop. Certain sins didn't just disappear, even
though I hated them. Sins like anger festered and surged almost
daily with no end in sight. I would get frustrated at so many
things, big and small. I was angry that I lost my family, angry
when things didn't go my way, angry that nobody understood
me, angry when my wife pointed out my self-pity, angry when
we couldn't pay our bills, angry when we were on food stamps,
angry when the car got towed and it was my fault, angry when I
couldn't learn something fast enough, angry when I thought about
how late a convert I was and how it would take forever to catch

---

1. Addison Leitch, quoted in Elisabeth Elliot, *Passion and Purity: Learning to Bring
Your Love Life under Christ's Control* (Old Tappan, NJ: Revell, 1984), 72.

up to others who were my age. I was an angry man. What was even more dangerous was that I had been a false convert earlier and involved in false teaching most of my life up to that point. Even when I lived a worldly and hypocritical lifestyle throughout my college years, I still held baseline beliefs attached to the prosperity gospel. Why was this dangerous? Because I knew Bible verses, had memorized Scripture growing up, and had a twisted interpretation on a lot of key doctrinal truths. When I got saved, I could still be considered to be higher on the spectrum of biblical knowledge, but it was the wrong kind. I was considered gifted in ministry aptitude, but I was low on character. Even after several months of unraveling and reinterpreting basic Bible passages that I had gotten wrong, I grew frustrated with how much longer character takes to develop than knowledge takes to acquire. At that point, I had a better grasp on doctrine, but I had little spiritual maturity. This is a recipe for disaster if you are not discipled. Many people have gifts, knowledge, talent, and influence, but bad character and a lack of discipleship undermine their lives and ministries, leading to collapse and hurt lives.

Thankfully, the Lord used godly men and women around me and my wife to provide counseling, discipleship, character tests, and training for our home, my heart, and my head. It took more than a year of biblical counseling before change became obvious and increasingly consistent. This was no work of my own. This was the Spirit working through the Word and uprooting the heart issues that led to my sin. Furthermore, I received leadership counseling and theological training, and my wife was discipled by a "Titus 2 woman" every Friday morning as well. Our entire home underwent a spiritual heart transplant, but because I was the primary problem, I got the most attention on the operating table. I frequently questioned myself throughout those first two years of being truly saved. *Will I always be this way? Why is this taking so long? How come other men are so godly and I am not? Why doesn't reading a book on*

*the Puritans suddenly fix all my problems? Is my past too messy for God
to ever use me? Why can't I be like one of those neat and tidy seminary
guys who seem to have it all together?*

Now, more than a decade later, like all genuinely saved
Christians, I have seen the Spirit's work in my hopeless life to the
degree that I cannot deny that I am his temple (1 Cor. 6:19–20).
I have agonizingly witnessed the clock of change tick slowly but
surely. I have also seen the ugliness of my heart as each day in
Christ reveals just how sinful and deceitful my heart can be (Jer.
17:9). Yet I have breathed in the new morning mercies of God that
come with each passing day. I have seen grace upon grace poured
out and have been overwhelmed by the humbling realization that I
am weak, but he is strong (2 Cor. 12:10). Why? Because he changes
us from glory to glory and shows us that we need him every single
day until heaven.

A couple of years ago, I was sitting in a morning men's Bible
study that I lead every Tuesday at 6:00 a.m. We've had men ranging
in age from twenty to eighty-two attend. One particular morning we were talking about sin and the battles we fight against it.
I asked an eighty-two-year-old man in the group to share what
he has learned after all these years of serving the Lord. He said
something profound that sent humbling shockwaves through all of
us that day. "After all these years, I have not come to find myself
more perfect, but instead, I have learned just how sinful I truly am."
The room fell silent. It was the truth we needed to hear. We have
this idea that the older we get, the more perfect we will be and that
eventually we don't ever sin. But older men who have been growing in godliness for years are much less likely to talk about their
sinless perfection. On the contrary, their increase in wisdom with
age breeds great humility. Of course, we go through much change
when we serve the Lord for decades and the Spirit is changing us
from glory to glory. Still, that morning my brother reminded us
how true Jeremiah 17:9 is and that if we have grown in holiness

and been changed at all, it is by the power of the Spirit. What a humbling reality that even though we are great sinners, our God is a greater savior.

Spiritual change is not a microwave, it's an oven. Low and slow is how the Spirit works, tenderizing our hearts until they are soft, pliable, and conforming to his hand.

So how does it work? By what divine mechanism does the Spirit change us, grow us, and keep us changing and growing? I want to equip with you a solid understanding of at least four ways in which the Holy Spirit works in our lives: his work in salvation, illumination, sanctification, and preservation.

Let's take a dive into each one, along with some related doctrines, and then apply these glorious truths to our lives, because the goal is not just information but transformation.

## THE HOLY SPIRIT'S WORK IN SALVATION

You may have heard the phrase "the agent of salvation" used to describe the role of the Spirit in carrying out specific tasks in our lives related to salvation. You could say that the Father prepared our salvation, Jesus paid for our salvation, and the Holy Spirit applies to our lives what the Father prepared and what the Son Jesus paid for. The Father sent his Son Jesus to be our savior (1 John 4:14), Jesus came in the flesh and dwelt among us (John 1:14), and the Father and Jesus are both involved with sending the Holy Spirit to be our helper (John 15:26).

To get a foundational understanding of the Spirit's work in salvation, we must understand regeneration and justification (among several other important doctrines). Understanding these will further elevate your view of God's power and the Spirit's transformational work in you.

## REGENERATION

*Regeneration* is a term that also is translated as "rebirth" or "renewal" and comes from passages like Titus 3:4–7, which says, "But when the kindness of God our Savior and His love for mankind appeared, He saved us, not on the basis of deeds which we did in righteousness, but in accordance with His mercy, *by the washing of regeneration and renewing by the Holy Spirit*, whom He richly poured out upon us through Jesus Christ our Savior, so that being justified by His grace we would be made heirs according to the hope of eternal life" (emphasis added).

The Bible clearly teaches that regeneration or rebirth is a work carried out by the Holy Spirit and emphasizes that he makes all things new in our lives. When you look up the use of the word *regeneration* in the New Testament, you will find the same Greek word used in Matthew 19:28, where Jesus refers to his new and coming kingdom in which we will see a world free of the brokenness of sin and the wiles of Satan. *Regeneration* refers to something being renewed or being made completely new. This is the same as being "born again" (John 3:7). The Holy Spirit's work in regeneration includes raising us up from being dead in sin to being made alive together with Christ (Eph. 2:1–7). The Spirit gives us new life (Rom. 8:2). In giving us new spiritual life, the Spirit changes our status from being wretched sinners to being righteous saints. This is what Titus 3:5 is saying when Paul uses the words "washing" and "renewing." We are no longer stained by the curse of sin. Yes, you will still sin at times (more on that in the section regarding sanctification), but the Spirit has made all who are in Christ a new creation. The old you is not the dominating force in your life anymore. The Spirit is in control of you now, and it's a total transformation. Second Corinthians 5:17 beautifully describes the Spirit's washing and renewing this way: "Therefore, if anyone is in Christ, the new creation has come: The old has gone, the new is here!" (NIV).

## JUSTIFICATION

The doctrine of justification means that a believer has been justified by God and is not going to be condemned of the punishment that accompanies sin, which is death (Rom. 6:23). In its theological sense, *justification* is a forensic or legal term. It describes what God declares about the believer. Justification is about your position: You will still sin, but you are justified. You may endure trials, temptation, persecution, or suffering, but you are justified. Nothing can change what God declares about you. The reason that God declares a believer justified is only because of faith in Jesus Christ. This is what is meant by "justification by faith." According to religions like Mormonism, someone is justified by works in addition to faith. In the Book of Mormon, 2 Nephi 25:23 says, "For we know that it is by grace that we are saved, after all we can do." But Christianity holds that one is justified apart from works and only by having faith in Jesus Christ. When God sees a justified sinner, he looks upon that sinner through the lens of Christ and only through Christ—not according to our works or anything we can do.

The concept of justification by faith alone is found all over the New Testament. It is at the core of the gospel. According to Romans 3:24, we are justified by God's grace and it is a gift through Christ. Paul says in Titus 3:7 that we are "justified by [God's] grace." This is so vital to understand because justification and the grace of God are closely related concepts that liberate Christians from the burden of works-based religious systems. According to Romans 3:20, no one can be justified by doing deeds or by "works of the law." Romans 5:1 tells us that because we have been justified by faith, we are able to "have peace with God." Romans 5:9 declares that we are justified by the blood of Christ and saved from the wrath of God. Finally, Romans 8:30 boldly states that if God has called you, you are justified. Nothing can stop that divine work.

First Corinthians 6:9–11 explains how the Spirit takes us

from being guilty, dirty, and condemned sinners to being justified, cleansed, and destined saints. Paul writes, "Or do you not know that wrongdoers will not inherit the kingdom of God? Do not be deceived: Neither the sexually immoral nor idolaters nor adulterers nor men who have sex with men nor thieves nor the greedy nor drunkards nor slanderers nor swindlers will inherit the kingdom of God. And that is what some of you were. But you were washed, you were sanctified, you were *justified* in the name of the Lord Jesus Christ and *by the Spirit of our God*" (NIV, emphases added).

What a list of sins, what a life we lived, what a destructive pattern we followed until the Spirit intervened and applied the Father's decree "Justified!" to us. Isn't God's grace incredible? Could there be a more humbling reality that causes us to want to praise God and devote our lives to him? In the courtroom of heaven, we stand guilty of sin and deserving of death (Rom. 6:23), but God slams down the gavel and proclaims us justified and dismisses the case because "Jesus paid it all / All to him I owe / Sin had left a crimson stain / He washed it white as snow." The Spirit stamps God's decision upon us for all of eternity: justified!

But we are not just set up for eternity through justification, we are spiritually transformed on earth through sanctification.

## THE HOLY SPIRIT'S WORK
## IN SANCTIFICATION

If you think you're going to follow Jesus and not be changed by the Holy Spirit, you've got another think coming. All believers get the joy of experiencing the sanctifying work of the Spirit because it is God's will. Obedience is our part, change is his part. First Thessalonians 4:3 says, "For this is the will of God, your sanctification." In this verse, Paul explains the church's need to steer clear of sexual immorality and to use their bodies to honor God.

He encourages them to remember that no matter what their flesh wants, as believers they ought to seek what God wants: their sanctification.

The word *sanctification* or *sanctified* in the Bible is synonymous with words like *saints* and *holy ones* and the concept of being "set apart." This is how the Bible describes followers of Jesus because we are in this world, but not of it. We may still sin, but because of Christ we are saints. We do not live according to the ways and patterns of this world, but we seek to be holy as he is holy (1 Peter 1:15–16). To be holy and set apart means to live your life in a way that seeks to honor God above anything or anyone else. To be holy as he is holy means to consider your conduct, decisions, worldview, and mindset in light of his Word, not according to the pressures or winds of this world. This is what it means to be sanctified.

God wants this for his people because we are called to be salt and light (Matt. 5:13–16). If we look like the world, sound like the world, and think like the world, how can we be salt and light in the world? If we blend in so much, then how will we ever stand out? If we tell the world they need Jesus, but our lives look no different from theirs, why should they do anything except continue on their own way? Sanctification is not merely doctrine, it's our faith in practice. It is the Spirit's work in changing us and our living out that change. It is him transforming our hearts and then our transformed hearts pouring out renewed words and actions that reflect a completely different person than who we were before.

But it's not always so clean and perfect, is it? After salvation, all believers notice that their hearts change and their desire for sin decreases, but that doesn't mean the battle against sin is over. The strongest Christian still sins, wrestles with pride, says things they wish they didn't, covets what others have, loses eternal perspective, and makes decisions they regret. Even if they've mastered being well-behaved on the outside, the mind is the last great battleground against sin. Our actions may be tamed, but our thoughts need to be taken captive daily (2 Cor. 10:5) and maybe, for some of us, hourly and by the second! Sanctification is not instant perfection but steady progress toward eternal perfection. To better understand this, I want to unpack the three types of sanctification that are clear in Scripture.

# THREE TYPES OF SANCTIFICATION

Is sanctification instant or progressive? Another way to ask this is to say, Are you immediately going to stop sinning and be perfect when you become a Christian, or are you going to progressively grow in holiness as the Spirit does a work in your life day by day? Some people teach what is called "entire sanctification," which is the idea that after salvation, Christians experience a "second blessing" that turns their hearts completely to God and makes them totally obedient and holy. This theological position leads some to teach that you can reach a state of holiness in which you stop sinning completely on this side of heaven. This is why entire sanctification is sometimes called "Christian perfection." But this position has no foundation in Scripture. Why would Paul the apostle cry out in anguish over his sin in Romans 7:18–19, saying, "For I have the desire to do what is good, but I cannot carry it out. For I do not do the good I want to do, but the evil I do not want to do—this I keep on doing" (NIV)? Then, in verses 24–25 he declares, "What a wretched man I am! Who will rescue me from this body that is subject to death? Thanks be to God, who delivers me through Jesus Christ our Lord!" Paul was a strong believer, a miracle-working apostolic leader, a world-changing missionary, and a courageous preacher who never once backed down from pro-claiming the gospel. Yet even he wrestled with sin and hated it. Even he longed for a day when he would finally be delivered from this body that is subject to death. Even he knew that his ultimate deliverance from sin was only through Jesus Christ. Yet this same Paul commanded Christians to repent and flee from sin (1 Cor. 6:18) because sanctification is not perfection. Sanctification is progression. To understand sanctification, it's best to let Scripture shape our doctrine. We see three types of sanctification (being set apart and made holy) in the Bible, and only the final one is the realization of sinless perfection: positional sanctification, progressive sanctification, and perfect sanctification.

Let me break these down for you biblically so that we can understand the Spirit's work here on earth and look forward to the perfection of heaven.

First, *positional sanctification* is your spiritual position now as a born-again believer. You were placed there the second you were converted and your position never changes. You now belong to God. Once you were far off, now you've been brought near (Eph. 2:13) and you've been set free from being a slave to sin (Rom. 6:18). You are no longer an enemy of God, and you have received not a spirit of slavery but a spirit of adoption. You are a son or daughter of God (Rom. 8:15). In Christ, you are a totally new creation. The old you is gone and the new you is here to stay (2 Cor. 5:17). You were once lost in darkness, and now you walk in light (Eph. 5:8). Positional sanctification is once and for all and is the setting apart of believers for God's special purposes and calling.

One of the best examples of positional sanctification is in 1 Corinthians 1:2, where Paul calls the Corinthian Christians "sanctified." Why is that a big deal? Because they were very sinful. I've often referred to Corinth as "Vegas on steroids" because it was such a sinful city, and the Christians in the church there had numerous issues with sexual immorality and everything else under the sun. Yet Paul still calls them sanctified in his first letter to them. This is a great picture of how even when we are sinning or need to be called out on our sin, our position in Christ is still secure. True believers will run toward conviction, not away from it. We repent just like the church at Corinth did (2 Cor. 7:9–11).

Second, *progressive sanctification* is the ongoing process of spiritual growth and holiness while still in this fallen world. The word *progressive* is helpful in describing what Paul the apostle expressed throughout his letters by saying that he had not obtained any kind of perfection yet but pressed on toward the upward call of God in Christ Jesus (Phil. 3:12). He told the church repeatedly to confess their sin (which means they still sinned!), but he still considered them to be holy and set apart by God. The truth is, we all still sin from time to time. In Philippians 1:6 there is encouragement for those who struggle with sin but hate it: "He who began a good work in you will perfect it until the day of Christ Jesus" (NASB 1995). The word *perfect* means "mature," meaning that God is going to keep doing a work in you. I'm sure you've experienced this like I have. You are not who you used to be, but you're not yet who you're going to be. I look back and see times in my saved life when specific patterns of sin were more frequent than they are now. Not to say that I am at all perfect in these ways, but specific sins and habits fade as the Holy Spirit brings conviction and the Word does a work on our hearts.

To those who preach entire sanctification (that you can achieve sinlessness in this life), I would argue that if Paul the apostle wasn't perfect, you never will be. Paul humbly confesses in Romans 7:15–20, "I do not understand what I do. For what I want to do I do not do, but what I hate I do. And if I do what I do not want to do, I agree that the law is good. As it is, it is no longer I myself who do it, but it is sin living in me. For I know that good itself does not dwell in me, that is, in my sinful nature. For I have the desire to do what is good, but I cannot carry it out. For I do not do the good I want to do, but the evil I do not want to do—this I keep on doing. Now if I do what I do not want to do, it is no longer I who do it, but it is sin living in me that does it" (NIV).

Thankfully, we are changed from glory to glory, and the work of the Spirit continues in our lives. One of the key ways that progressive sanctification works is through the washing and renewal of the Word. This is why the psalmist so often says things like, "Thy word have I hid in mine heart, that I might not sin against thee" (Ps. 119:11 KJV), and in the gospel of John, Jesus prays to the Father and says, "Sanctify them in the truth; Your word is truth" (John 17:17). We need the Word, and the Spirit uses the Word to bring about a work in us.

Now, it is sometimes asked, If two people get saved at the same time, yet a year later one person has grown more than the other, what accounts for that? Two biblical ideas are important to keep in mind:

1. *God is sovereign in salvation and sanctification.* Some people wish they had been saved earlier, but in God's timing they were not. Some people wish they were being sanctified much faster, but they are not. God works at his own sovereign pace, and we need to trust him. He was powerful enough to accomplish his saving work regardless of our weakness and spiritual deadness, and he is powerful enough to finish his sanctifying work regardless of our weaknesses. Maybe you feel like your growth is too slow. Maybe you have been reading the Word, praying, trying to grow, and you still feel weak spiritually. This won't stop God. In 2 Corinthians 12:9, God tells Paul, "My power is made perfect in weakness" (NIV). This a great example of how God will sanctify us and work through us, even in our weakness. But based on what the Bible teaches, there does seem to be an aspect of sanctification that depends on our responding in obedience to God.

2. *We are commanded to be holy and separate.* I am not talking about works-based salvation, I am talking about God using

our obedience in our sanctification. For example, God's Word commands us to gather for church (Heb. 10:24–25), and obeying that command, as opposed to disobeying it and going golfing every Sunday, benefits our growth. Some people are more obedient, and they mature more quickly than others. Some people sit under faithful teaching regularly; others do not, so naturally they are not as mature. Similar to the way salvation is a work of God, yet we are responsible to respond in faith, sanctification is a work of God, yet we are responsible to apply ourselves to growing in the faith. Both of Peter's letters call believers to be obedient. You are to "long for the pure milk of the word," like 1 Peter 2:2 says, "so that by it you may grow in respect to salvation." Second Peter 1:3–9 tells us about the resources we have in Christ. Peter says that God's "divine power has granted to us everything pertaining to life and godliness," and then he says that once we are saved, we ought to supply some things to our faith with all diligence, including moral excellence, knowledge, self-control, perseverance, godliness, kindness, and love. The bottom line is that though the two people were saved at the time same, one person is more diligent in seeking out solid teaching, discipleship, prayer, knowledge, and nurturing their growth, while the other is more lazy in their effort. Both are saved, but one is more diligent, so that person grows all the more.

God is sovereign in sanctifying us progressively, and he will not be stopped in purifying us, no matter how slow it seems to take at times. Genuine believers experience the power of the Spirit at work in their lives. Law keeping and shallow moral obedience are not the kind of obedience the Bible links to our sanctification. It is obedience driven by the power of the Spirit. First Thessalonians 4:7–8 says, "For God has not called us for impurity, but in holiness.

Therefore whoever disregards this, disregards not man but God, who gives his Holy Spirit to you" (ESV).

Third, *perfect sanctification* or what some call *ultimate sanctification* is going to happen in heaven. This is Paul's greatest desire for believers. First Thessalonians 5:23 says, "Now may the God of peace himself sanctify you completely, and may your whole spirit and soul and body be kept blameless at the coming of our Lord Jesus Christ" (ESV). When Christ returns or calls us home, then and only then will we be free of sin and 100 percent sanctified. It's a work he promises to complete and in glory. It is a now-but-not-yet promise. There is no special place in heaven you go first to finish up your sanctification. You don't spend time in purgatory or have to do any works to pay the last little bit of your sin off and get clean for glory. Revelation 21:4 describes heaven as a place with no more sin, no more pain, and no more death. The reason death came into the picture was because of sin, so in heaven there will be no sin, only perfect harmony between God and humans. Perhaps one of the greatest treasures is the end of time limitations; we get to spend infinite eternity in perfect fellowship together and with God. Perfect sanctification awaits us in heaven!

# THE HOLY SPIRIT'S WORK IN ILLUMINATION

Part of the Spirit's transforming work in our lives includes illumination, which I like to describe as the lightbulb moment either related to your salvation (like getting saved when reading the Bible) or when the Bible and its teaching becomes a lifeline for you to hear God's voice. Illumination is the Holy Spirit invading our darkened minds with understanding, and it is what causes us to embrace Scripture as God's sufficient and authoritative word to us.

The Spirit's work of illumination in our lives reaches all the way back to his work of special revelation through the disciples' lives. Prior to the birth of the church, Jesus told his disciples that the Spirit would give them revelation, telling them in John 14:26, "But the Helper, the Holy Spirit whom the Father will send in My name, He will teach you all things, and remind you of all that I said to you." This passage specifically refers to the disciples' writing the special revelation of Scripture after Jesus left them. The Spirit recalled to them with perfect accuracy the events, sayings, and truths centering on Christ. Remember, the disciples weren't walking around with pens and parchment saying, "Hold on, Jesus! Can you say that one more time so Luke can write it down?" "Hey, Mark! Did you get that one bit about paying taxes to Caesar? No? Can someone ask the Pharisees to ask that question again?" They had been left to be witnesses for Christ (Acts 1:8) and the Holy Spirit was going to be their personal teacher and help them remember everything they needed to write Scripture. The disciples were so confident that they were receiving direct revelation from the Spirit of God that John writes, "We are from God, and whoever knows God listens to us; but whoever is not from God does not listen to us. This is how we recognize the Spirit of truth and the spirit of falsehood" (1 John 4:6 NIV).

Today, while we are not apostles receiving direct revelation to write down Holy Scripture, the Spirit is our teacher and he uses the Word implanted in our lives to bring about spiritual fruit. He uses the revelation given to the apostles to trigger illumination in our lives as modern-day disciples. We are not the direct audience in John 14:26, but we are the direct beneficiaries of it. What a beautiful promise! The Spirit gave special revelation to the apostles to write Holy Scripture, and now the Spirit gives us illumination to help us embrace and understand it. How desperate we ought to be for his supernatural work through the Word.

A number of passages in the Old and New Testaments describe our need for illumination and the Spirit's work in illumination, including:

- Psalm 119:18: The psalmist asks for open eyes to see wondrous truths from God.
- Psalm 119:105: God's Word is a lamp to our feet and a light to our paths.
- Psalm 119:144: We need God's understanding to live for him.
- 1 Corinthians 2:13: The Holy Spirit imparts and teaches the truth.
- Ephesians 1:17–18: Paul prays that the eyes of the Ephesians' hearts would be enlightened.

My favorite chapter for understanding the power of God's Word and our need for understanding is Psalm 119. Time and time again the psalmist cries out to God for understanding and to be taught his ways. Psalm 119:73 is one of nearly ten passages calling for understanding; it says, "Thy hands have made me and fashioned me: give me understanding that I may learn thy commandments" (KJV). The psalmist knew what was needed to thrive in faith and godliness. Paul the apostle knew what the church needed to know their God and endure to the end.

The Spirit works through the Word, helps us embrace the Word, and helps us understand the Word. Without the Spirit, we are merely engaged in academic exercise, reading the Bible as though it were a rule book or history book. Many scholars and even pagans have engaged the Scriptures, only to end at reading them for academic or religious critique. If all anyone needed was to be able to read to understand the Bible, there would be no need for the Spirit's work. One person can read the Bible and nothing supernatural will occur, while another reads the Bible and the heavens seem to open up and pour out grace, wisdom, understanding, and salvation upon their soul. What happened? The Spirit illuminated the latter. First Corinthians 2:14 says, "The person without the Spirit does not accept the things that come from the Spirit of God but considers them foolishness, and cannot understand them because they are discerned only through the Spirit" (NIV).

Many people in the church today think that merely reading the Bible is going to change them. But merely reading words isn't the power, the Spirit working through the Word is the power. This is why some people check off all of the boxes in their annual Bible reading plan but get frustrated that they experience no transformation and acquire no greater understanding of God. They are disciplined in their reading but neglect to ask the Spirit to illuminate the Word. How slippery is the slope of morally good works without the power of the Spirit opening our eyes and changing our hearts. This is empty religion at its peak. Nothing happens outside of the Spirit's power. I read somewhere once that Pastor John MacArthur illustrates it this way: "God must open the eyes of our understanding before we can truly know and rightly interpret His truth. . . . Only the Spirit can illumine Scripture. Just as the physically blind cannot see the sun, the spiritually blind cannot see the Son. Both lack proper illumination." Martin Luther once said, "Nobody who has not the Spirit of God sees a jot of what is in the Scriptures. The Spirit is needed for the understanding of all Scripture and every part of Scripture."[2] Today we daily need the Spirit's illuminating work.

There are three questions that you might be asking at this point, and I want to address them.

*Question 1: If the Spirit opens our eyes and helps us embrace and understand Scripture through illumination, then why do so many Christians disagree on certain teachings?* This is because illumination from the Spirit does not negate interpretation by humans. Two Spirit-filled Christians may both see a teaching of Scripture differently. As Wayne Grudem says, "The existence of many disagreements

---

2. Martin Luther, *Bondage of the Will.*

about the meaning of Scripture reminds us that the doctrine of the clarity of Scripture does not imply or suggest that all believers will agree on all the teachings of Scripture. Nevertheless, it does tell us something very important—that the problem always lies not with Scripture but with ourselves."[3] We do well to remember that even the best of men disagree on interpretations at times. Even Paul and Peter had a sharp disagreement because they saw things differently (Gal. 2:11–15). While the Spirit had supernaturally worked in their lives through both revelation and illumination, they still had come to different conclusions.

*Question 2: If the Spirit works through illumination, why do I need to study the Bible?* Illumination is a supernatural work, but it does not negate our spiritual diligence. If anyone could have been given permission to avoid hard study, it would have been Paul's protégé in the faith, Timothy. But instead of giving Timothy a free pass on Bible study, Paul says, "Be diligent to present yourself approved to God as a worker who does not need to be ashamed, accurately handling the word of truth" (2 Tim. 2:15). Even apostles advocated for the faithful study of God's Word.

*Question 3: If the Spirit works through illumination, why do people live out the Scriptures in different ways?* This question centers not on illumination or interpretation but on application. Two people can experience illumination and come to the same interpretation, but then engage in different application. For example, a married person and a single person would apply passages on marriage in different ways because they are in different life stages, or two deacons who attend two different churches might care for orphans and widows in different ways, while both agreeing that they should be cared for. And a passage on sin might be applied by one person who is struggling with a particular sin, while another person feels convicted about a different sin in their life.

---

3. Wayne Grudem, *Systematic Theology* (Grand Rapids: Zondervan, 1994), 109.

One of the most helpful books I have ever read on the subject of studying God's Word is by my friend Nate Pickowicz, titled *How to Eat Your Bible*. In this short book, Nate explains a simple approach to studying the Bible that gives you the tools needed to understand and apply God's Word. He teaches that application can be done right only if we find the timeless principle from the text first. He couldn't be more right, since many Christians (even with the best of intentions) study the Bible by jumping to conclusions and making God say things to them that were never meant for them. He boils application down to "things to know" and "things to do."[4] We need to first understand what the Bible is saying to the original audience, faithfully interpret it, then apply it to our lives in the modern era.

Another helpful approach I have heard of is an acronym for application in Bible study called SPECK. After reading the passage and making observations, one can ask the following questions and apply the passage faithfully, being careful to remember that not all of these questions will be answered in every Bible passage:

- **Sin:** Is there sin to confess or avoid?
- **Promise:** Is there a promise God is making that is specifically for me?
- **Example:** Is there an example in the passage that I should follow?
- **Command:** Is there a command I should obey?
- **Knowledge:** Is there knowledge about God that deepens worship and my relationship with him?

In summary, illumination is a supernatural starting point for all believers, while the ongoing study of God's Word is the journey of a

---

4. Nate Pickowicz, *How to Eat Your Bible: A Simple Approach to Learning and Loving the Word of God* (Chicago: Moody, 2021), 97–117.

lifetime. I recommend getting a book like *How to Eat Your Bible* by Nate Pickowicz or *The Hermeneutics of the Biblical Writers: Learning to Interpret Scripture from the Prophets and Apostles* by Abner Chou.[5] Both of these books have been paramount for me in my personal study and for many people in my congregation.

## THE HOLY SPIRIT'S WORK IN PRESERVATION

One of the names for the Holy Spirit is the "Spirit of Promise," because the Bible teaches that he is the one who keeps us sealed in the promise of salvation.

Ephesians 1:13–14 says, "In Him, you also, after listening to the message of truth, the gospel of your salvation—having also believed, you were sealed in Him with the Holy Spirit of promise, who is given as a pledge of our inheritance, with a view to the redemption of God's own possession, to the praise of His glory" (NASB 1995). In biblical times, a seal was a mark or a way to identify something as belonging to someone. It also carried the idea of authority and authenticity, just like an official government letter would have a seal on it from the emperor or a king. Seals could also be found on deeds to symbolize ownership. In the same way, spiritually speaking, you are marked by the Holy Spirit as belonging to God. You may not be immune to troubles in this world, but you are spiritually protected or preserved because you bear his mark.

Scriptural truths like this are linked to eternal security, which means that nothing can steal your salvation once you are truly saved. All genuine believers are eternally secure. Some call this "perseverance of the saints" or "preservation of the saints," because

---

5. Abner Chou, *The Hermeneutics of the Biblical Writers: Learning to Interpret Scripture from the Prophets and Apostles* (Grand Rapids: Kregel, 2018).

truly saved people will persevere until the end. When Paul says that the Holy Spirit is a pledge, he uses the Greek word *arrabon*, which often refers to a down payment or first installment with a guarantee that the rest will follow. Saying that the Holy Spirit is a pledge represents his being your down payment and guarantee. You have the promise of his sealing you, dwelling in you, and growing you until you reach heaven.

But what about all those people who make professions of faith and appear to be saved for a little while or seem to be on fire, then they appear to backslide or lose their salvation? The Bible gives us clear answers to consider. First John 2:19 speaks of false teachers and false converts who "went out from us, but they were not really of us." Many people look the part but in the end prove to be false. John 10:28 records Jesus saying that none will be snatched out of his hand to whom he gives eternal life. Matthew 7:21–23 is one of the best and perhaps most frightening answers to what is happening when someone appears to be saved and sealed but doesn't continue in the faith long-term. Jesus says, "Not everyone who says to Me, 'Lord, Lord,' will enter the kingdom of heaven, but the one who does the will of My Father who is in heaven will enter. Many will say to Me on that day, 'Lord, Lord, did we not prophesy in Your name, and in Your name cast out demons, and in Your name perform many miracles?' And then I will declare to them, 'I never knew you; leave Me, you who practice lawlessness.'"

Jesus doesn't say they were saved and then lost their salvation. He makes it clear that he never knew them. This doctrine challenges us because we all can think of people who seemed to be all in but now they're not. If you've felt grief over people like this, it's a good sign of your own salvation, because a deep love for others is the mark of a genuine believer (John 13:35). The heartbreaking reality is that there are false followers, and that's why Jesus and the apostles addressed it. You might invite someone to church and they seem interested. Next thing you know, they seem to be changed or at least want to be more purposeful in life. They get baptized. They serve. They sing. They read the Bible. Then some aspect of the teaching offends them or they get busy or they don't want to accept, believe, or submit to the truth of Scripture anymore. What happened? They were never really saved. Some other reason kept them hanging around. It could have been something good the church did, like community service or fun events, but it wasn't the ultimate thing.

When you are sealed by the Holy Spirit—a genuine believer— you're not going anywhere for long. Will you struggle with sin? Yes. Will you go through hard times? Yes. Will you have conflict with others? Yes. Will you grow weary of failures in life and long for the perfection of heaven? Yes. But the truly saved are saved by the promise and power of the Spirit, even if things get choppy in some seasons of life. We must always be wise and Word driven in how we judge, remembering that Paul the apostle struggled with sin that he despised (Rom. 7:15–10) and that Peter was often in need of the Lord's correction (Mark 8:33). Sometimes we are much too quick to judge someone's salvation in their moment of sinful weakness, rather than walking with them through repentance and restoration. Paul's relationship with the Corinthians is a humbling reminder that strong rebuke for sin can also be accompanied by loving patience, rather than making premature judgments that someone is a false believer for needing to be confronted.

I think of a situation I observed with a pastor who was very new to the ministry. He was counseling a husband and wife. In the first counseling meeting, the husband confessed that a particular sin would reoccur from time to time, and the wife explained that she had confronted her husband regarding that sin over the course of the previous two years. The inexperienced pastor immediately said that the man was a false convert, claiming that no true believer would experience such reoccurring moments with this sin for two years. The man wept, pleading with the pastor for help and wanting to be right with the Lord, but the pastor continued to call him a false convert. This pastor never slowed down to ask whether this was the first time the man had confessed to someone other than his wife and sought counsel (it was), or if he had made any progress during the two years (he had). Even when the husband pointed out his obedience in other areas, the pastor still insisted that no true believer would continue to wrestle with this sin. Examples like this are too plentiful in the church today, so we would do well to slow down, ask questions, be patient, and consistently speak the truth. Some people are false converts. I believe the Lord will make that clear. Many are unsanctified believers who are slowly but surely growing, albeit at a pace that bothers self-righteous types. Let us be more careful, caring, and hopeful, knowing that the Spirit is active in our lives from salvation to final glorification, changing us and growing us day by day.

# LEARNING TO LIVE

### 1. Ask the Spirit to Give You Confidence in Your Salvation

You may or may not struggle with assurance regarding your salvation, but no matter what, asking the Spirit to give you confidence in your salvation will do one of two things. You will either receive new and great confidence as he bears witness within your spirit that you are a child of God (Rom. 8:16), or, with your confidence strengthened, the Spirit will embolden you to not just be satisfied with your salvation but to proclaim the gospel to see others saved as well.

### 2. Ask the Spirit to Open Your Eyes through Illumination

Are you struggling with a hunger for the Word? Do you doubt whether the Bible is sufficient as God's Word to you? Do you have good discipline but feel your time with the Lord is mostly just a religious routine? Instead of checking the box on your daily reading plan and going through the motions, spend more time in prayer today or tomorrow, asking the Spirit to open your eyes, to ignite your heart with a never-ending hunger for the Word, and to give you greater understanding of and appreciation for who your God is and how you ought to live (Eph. 1:17–18).

### 3. Make a Bigger Deal about Your Sanctification

Yes, God is sovereign over your sanctification *and* he provides opportunities for spiritual growth that you can take advantage of. Do you want to be more mature? Do you want to deal with sin and get the help you need to fight your battles against it? Are you tired of a marriage that goes through the motions? Is your parenting approach little more than a long fuse of passive tolerance followed by an angry outburst of, "That's it! I've had enough!"? Have you relegated church gatherings to the back burner, considering small groups or equipping classes to be mostly for other people? Are morning devotions or evening prayer getting in the way of your fitness routine or scrolling through social media?

It doesn't matter whether we're pastors or new Christians, you and I need to make a bigger deal about our sanctification. Let's admit our weakness, embrace the Spirit's strength, and prioritize the things that progressively grow us, not the things that prohibit our growth. This is not a fear tactic, it's just the honest to God truth: one day you will either look back with gratitude on the hard decisions you made to prioritize your sanctification, or you'll look back with excuses and regrets. Which is it going to be?

## Questions for Reflection

1. In what ways can progressive sanctification relieve the burden and shame of never being perfect enough for God and others?

2. The Father prepared our salvation, the Son paid for our salvation, and the Spirit preserves our salvation. How should this reality impact the way you pray and praise God?

3. Using Scripture and your own words, how would you respond to someone who told you that you could lose your salvation?

4. What are some practical ways that you are going to take holiness more seriously?

## 4

# WHAT DOES IT
# MEAN TO WALK
# BY THE SPIRIT?

*But I say, walk by the Spirit, and you will
not carry out the desire of the flesh.*

—GALATIANS 5:16

TAKEO YOSHIKAWA WAS A GRADUATE OF THE
Imperial Japanese Naval Academy and eventually became a Japanese
spy who embarked on a secret mission in Hawaii. Yoshikawa did
not know the specifics regarding Japan's pending attack on Pearl
Harbor, but he knew his work was contributing to Japanese interests at home and abroad, and bringing down the United States was
not far from his mind. He blended in well because of the many
Japanese Americans who lived on the Hawaiian islands. One might
think the Japanese populace in Hawaii would have helped his effort,

but many Japanese Americans were extremely loyal to the US and would not assist him. This only stirred Yoshikawa's zeal to do an excellent job with his spy work.

The intelligence Yoshikawa gathered covered myriad details, including the number of US warships in the harbor, the depth of the harbor at various locations, and even the width of the runways at Wheeler Airbase. He did all of this under cleverly disguised circumstances. During two different intelligence-gathering efforts, he took tourist flights over Oahu, appearing to be nothing more than a Japanese tourist enjoying the sights, but during the first flight, he counted the number of aircraft and hangars on Wheeler Airbase, and during the second, he confirmed that the Americans kept their aircraft in one location and did not spread them around as the Japanese had speculated.[1]

Yoshikawa's intelligence provided the Japanese with valuable insights and was instrumental in their ability to inflict maximum damage during their attack on Pearl Harbor. More than 2,400 lives were lost in one of the most horrific attacks on US soil in history. This event triggered the United States' involvement in World War II, which, near the end of the war, culminated in President Harry S. Truman's order to drop atomic bombs on the Japanese cities of Hiroshima and Nagasaki.

In Hiroshima, an estimated 90,000 to 150,000 people died. In Nagasaki, an estimated 40,000 to 80,000 more were killed. The numbers are staggering, and the destruction was unimaginable.

Spiritually speaking, what Yoshikawa and the Japanese accomplished at Pearl Harbor to bring about chaos and destruction is a good picture of what sin and the flesh can do to your life. The flesh (your carnality and old nature) is the enemy's favorite mole behind the lines of your life. The mission is to bring you down.

---

1. Nicholas Best, "Takeo Yoshikawa: The Japanese Spy at Pearl Harbor," History Reader, December 2, 2016, www.thehistoryreader.com/military-history/takeo-yoshikawa/.

The devil and his demonic minions work overtime to calculate your weaknesses, take inventory of your vices, and lure you into sinful actions under the guise of pleasure and enjoying your life.

If we're going to talk about what it means to walk by the Spirit, we have to start with understanding that the enemy doesn't sleep. He wants you to walk by the flesh and to carry out the deeds of the old nature. A war is going on inside of you between the Spirit and the flesh.

## WALKING BY THE FLESH

In Galatians 5:16–17, the apostle Paul issues a strong command under the guidance of the Holy Spirit. He says, "But I say, walk by the Spirit, and you will not carry out the desire of the flesh. For the desire of the flesh is against the Spirit, and the Spirit against the flesh; for these are in opposition to one another." The word Paul uses for "walk" is the Greek word *peripateo*, and it means "to go here and there." It's a present-active verb that describes someone being preoccupied with a direction and a purpose. Imagine those shoppers in the grocery store who bolt here, there, and everywhere with their carts like they are on a mission—or maybe that's you! This is how many of us live. We either live purposefully according to the flesh, or we live purposefully according to the Spirit. If you preoccupy yourself with worldly pursuits, the deeds of the flesh are going to dominate you. If you preoccupy yourself with Spirit-focused pursuits, the deeds of the Spirit will direct and rule you.

Walking by the flesh can lead us to three pitfalls: an over-dependence on man-made rules (a legalistic spirit), an overemphasis on enjoying our freedoms (using grace as a license), and an outright indulgence in the deeds of the flesh (a lifestyle of sin). Let's take a deeper look at these three pitfalls first, then look at the fruit of walking by the Spirit.

# PITFALL 1: A LEGALISTIC SPIRIT

Legalism loves to parade around like it's genuine Spirit-borne fruit, but it's not. We can all be tempted to this sort of moralistic mentality, hanging fake fruit on trees instead of growing it. When we boast about how many days in a row we've read the Bible without ever missing or about how we don't dress a certain way or about how we don't waste time on such earthly things as sports and recreation, we're essentially saying, "I am really earning God's favor because I do really spiritual things." We're wearing a mask of morality to hide what is really happening on the inside. Such pride guarantees that the origin of that fruit is not the Holy Spirit but a legalistic spirit.

The background and context of Paul's command is a situation in the church in Galatia. The believers there had experienced the gospel of grace and had been set free from a works-based religiosity like that of the Jews who believed that keeping the Law would lead to salvation. Paul had spent a significant amount of time investing in the church there and had preached the grace of God through the gospel to them, and they believed it. Yet in just a short time, the Galatians reverted to their old ways of thinking. In chapter 1 Paul makes a strong statement about their going back to the legalistic ways of works-based religion, calling it "a different gospel" (Gal. 1:6), and then says that anyone preaching another gospel should be "accursed" (v. 9). Paul is utterly perplexed at their decision (4:20) because they had been set free from such things. In their spiritual immaturity, they traded a treasure of grace for a yoke of slavery, so Paul calls them to get back to the basics of God's grace and live out the freedom they received from legalistic rule-keeping. In Galatians 5:1, he declares, "It was for freedom that Christ set us free." He reminds them what they already know to be true. Jesus gives us new life and the Spirit empowers our new life. We have no need to go back to the works of the Law to earn our salvation. The grace of God fuels us to obey, serve, give, love, and honor God. "Therefore, keep standing firm and do not be subject to a yoke of slavery" (5:1).

Legalism stands in direct contradiction to walking by the Spirit. Legalism depends on its own merits and works rather than on walking by the Spirit. Chuck Swindoll offers a sobering definition of legalism that we can all be guilty of buying into at times:

> Legalism is an attitude, a mentality based on pride. It is an obsessive conformity to an artificial standard for the purpose of exalting oneself. A legalist assumes the place of authority and pushes it to unwarranted extremes. In so many words, legalism says, "I do this or I don't do that, and therefore I am pleasing God." Or, "If only I could do this or not do that, I would be pleasing to God." Or perhaps, "These things that I'm doing or not doing are the things I perform to win God's favor." They aren't spelled out in Scripture, you understand. They've been passed down or they have been dictated to the legalist and have become an obsession to him or her. Legalism is rigid, grim, exacting, and lawlike in nature. Pride, which is at the heart of legalism, works in sync with other motivating factors. Like guilt. And fear. And shame. It leads to an emphasis on what one should *not* be and what one should *not* do.[2]

Legalism is attractive because it offers us a sense of control. And if we're honest, we're really into control. It's easy to lean into legalism because most things in life have some sort of effort attached to them. If you want to raise your income, you work longer and harder than others. If you want to have a high level of fitness, you work out more than others. If you want to run faster, hit harder, throw

---

2. Chuck Swindoll, "Defining Legalism," Insight for Today: A Daily Devotional by Pastor Chuck Swindoll, Insight for Living Ministries, January 13, 2016, insight.org /resources/daily-devotional/individual/defining-legalism.

farther, jump higher, or last longer than others, you work to earn
that advantage. Effort in equals results out, right? Not necessarily.
When it comes to earning God's favor and the benefits of salvation,
you can't work hard enough to earn them. You can only trust Christ
and his merits. You can only depend on the grace of God. You can
only fix your gaze on him and him alone. If you want to work hard
at something, work hard at resisting legalism. Work hard at cutting
out anything that tempts you to think you can earn God's favor by
man-made rules. Work hard at fixing your eyes on Jesus.

Legalism is a pitfall the enemy would love for you to stumble
into, but there is another one, which swings to the other extreme.

## PITFALL 2: A LICENSE TO SIN

On the flip side of legalism, Paul warns the Galatians against
abusing their freedoms as a license to sin. In Galatians 5:13, he
says, "For you were called to freedom, brothers and sisters; only
do not turn your freedom into an opportunity for the flesh, but
serve one another through love." Paul knew well what the church
would struggle with and what our struggle still is today. We tend
to swing to the extreme of legalism or the extreme of license. We
either make up rules to control people in an effort to keep them
from sinning or we throw out all rules and use the grace of God
as a reason to expand our Christian liberties and sin however we
want. Using grace as a license to sin is antithetical to walking by the
Spirit because abusing grace and downplaying sin is antithetical to
God. Christ shed his blood in death. He became a curse for us, then
sent the Holy Spirit to be our helper. We ought to take care never
to treat grace with indifference. Holiness matters, and Christian
freedom is to be used not to push the limits of sin but to serve and
love others.

# PITFALL 3: A LIFESTYLE OF SIN

The list of the "deeds of the flesh" in Galatians 5:19–21 is extensive, and Paul follows it up by saying, "As I have forewarned you, that those who practice such things will not inherit the kingdom of God" (v. 21b). The word "practice" means to habitually engage in this type of behavior again and again as a part of your lifestyle. Though his list is not meant to be exhaustive, the fifteen sins he specifies cover basically every category that any sin could fall under. Here is a description of each one. If you want to follow along with this list, grab your Bible and turn to Galatians 5:19–21:[3]

1. *Immorality* is the Greek word *porneia*, from which we get the word *pornography*. Paul is using it here to express a wide range of sexual activities, including irregular ones. Some of the New Testament churches were so exposed to pagan practices that included sexual sin that they were used to them and tolerant of them.

2. *Impurity* describes sexual sin but also extends to moral evil in general, as well as impure motives toward others.

3. *Sensuality*, also translated "wantonness," is the casting aside of all restraints and living out pleasures unashamed. This sinful behavior does not care what others think or how personal sin makes others feel. It flaunts the attitude, "If it makes me feel good, I do it."

4. *Idolatry* applies to graven images and the worship of and obsession over anything besides the one true God. F. F. Bruce writes, "In Col. 3:5 covetousness is described

---

3. F. F. Bruce, *The Epistle to the Galatians: A Commentary on the Greek Text*, New International Greek Testament Commentary, ed. I. Marshall Howard and W. Ward Gasque (Grand Rapids: Eerdmans, 1982), 247–49. The specific words in the following list are from the 1995 edition of the NASB.

as a form of idolatry, because the thing coveted becomes an object of worship. In 1 Cor. 10:14 participation in a feast in a pagan temple is participation in idolatry."[4]

5. *Sorcery* is a Greek word used by Paul from which we get the word *pharmaceuticals*. It originally carried no negative connotations and simply referred to giving medicine to someone. Eventually, it became synonymous with drugs that altered the state of mind or poisoned people. In ancient times, just like now, cults used drugs in their practices of worship, and drugs destroyed people's lives and sanity. They were also used in witchcraft and dark arts.

6. *Enmities*, also translated "hostilities," between individuals or between communities on political, racial, or religious grounds. This word refers not only to hostile acts but also to underlying hostile sentiments and intentions. Someone guilty of this sin is one who cherishes the hostile thought and performs the hostile act.[5]

7. *Strife*, a quarrelsome spirit that is antithetical to peace and unity for believers in the church. Where there is constant strife, one should rightly question whether the deeds of the flesh are dominating that environment.

8. *Jealousy* is the Greek word *zelos*, from which we get the English word *zeal*, and isn't necessarily always a bad thing. (For example, God's being rightfully jealous for his glory or for our love, or our being zealous for people to live righteous lives.) But when jealousy is sinful and when zeal goes too far, the intensity level rises, and soon one's attitude stirs with envy and a competitive spirit against those whom we should be unified with. Once again, Bruce is helpful here: "Another's success may move a man to [zeal] in the sense of

4. Ibid., 247.
5. Ibid., 248.

noble emulation, which is a good thing, or it may stir him to [zeal] in the sense of resentment that another has enjoyed success or distinction (thus far) denied to him, and that is a bad thing, a work of the flesh."[6]

9. *Outbursts of anger* is exactly what it says. Some translate it as "wrath" or "rage," as in someone making people "feel their wrath" in frustration and angry outbursts. A lifestyle of explosive anger is the mark of someone who lives out the deeds of the flesh and is not walking by the Spirit.

10. *Disputes*, which is translated as "rivalries" in the English Standard Version and as "selfish ambition" in James 3:14. This is the mark of people who constantly engage in rivalry and contention with others. This sin destroys relationships and even connects to demonic wisdom rather than divine wisdom. James 3:14–16 says, "But if you have bitter jealousy and selfish ambition in your hearts, do not boast and be false to the truth. This is not the wisdom that comes down from above, but is earthly, unspiritual, demonic. For where jealousy and selfish ambition exist, there will be disorder and every vile practice" (ESV).

11. *Dissensions* refers to divisions between people, and Paul is linking it to the way legalism and false teaching wreak havoc in the church and divide people from the truth and one another. Refraining from this sin leads not to false unity but rather to unity in truth and to unified resistance to false teachers who try to divide and conquer the flock.

12. *Factions*: Once again Paul refers to sins of division. The word he uses is *hairesis*, which when pronounced sounds a lot like our English word *heresies*, because that's where we get it from. In Acts it is used of parties within Judaism— the Sadducees (5:17), the Pharisees (15:5; 26:5), and the

---

6. Ibid.

Nazarenes (24:5, 14; 28:22).[7] Think of when some in the church at Corinth were saying, "I am with Paul!" while others claimed, "I am with Apollos!" and still others announced, "I am with Cephas [Peter]!" (1 Cor. 1:12). Bruce calls this a "party spirit,"[8] in which people who should not be divided choose sides. To this Paul says, "Is Christ divided?" (1 Cor. 1:13 NIV).

13. *Envying* is a begrudging spirit that cannot stand the success or prosperity of others. A form of this word is used in the parable of the vineyard workers that Jesus' tells in Matthew 20:15. It's described as a kind of evil eye that perceives with the blurry vision of envy.

14. *Drunkenness*: In the context of the Galatian letter, this word carried the disturbing idea of the drunken orgies that accompanied pagan worship practices. In their past, the Galatians (and others in Corinth) likely would have participated in these experiences or were certainly familiar with them. Drunkenness was the same then as it is now, complete with the removal of inhibition, filled with abuses, including verbal, sexual, and physical, and rife with bad decisions and consequences.

15. *Carousing*, also translated "revelry," is used three times in the New Testament. Each time it is closely related to drunkenness. Think of this sinful behavior as relishing the lifestyle of drinking, partying, and vulgar activities. It's the "what happens in Vegas stays in Vegas" attitude that marks much of our society. Carousers love their sin and love to indulge in the flesh.

---

7. Ibid., 249.
8. Ibid.

What a list of sins and what a picture of how all Christians lived according to the flesh before the Spirit raised their spiritually dead hearts to new life. In our broken world, sin continues to wage war against us. All believers may struggle at various times with some aspect of these fifteen deeds listed by Paul, but unbelievers are marked by these "evidences" in their lifestyles. They live out the deeds of the flesh as a way of life, and the devil is cheering them on. More than that, he would love it if immature Christians were tempted to think that the wicked are having all the fun and then get sucked back into sins that cause ripples of destruction in their lives and in the lives of others. That is why Proverbs 24:1 offers a warning of wisdom saying, "Do not envy the wicked, do not desire their company" (NIV).

Jesus frequently issued warnings to the legalistic Pharisees and those living a lifestyle of sin. In Mark 7:20–23, Jesus explains that "what comes out of a person is what defiles them. For it is from within, out of a person's heart, that evil thoughts come—sexual immorality, theft, murder, adultery, greed, malice, deceit, lewdness, envy, slander, arrogance and folly. All these evils come from inside and defile a person" (NIV). Don't miss that last statement. Where do all of these evils come from? The inside. The heart of a person is what defiles, and when the heart is set on sin, it cannot help but continue in a lifestyle of sin. Someone who is living in habitual sin and according to the deeds of the flesh is not a believer, according to Scripture (1 John 3:5–6). Jesus says, "A good tree cannot bear bad fruit, and a bad tree cannot bear good fruit" (Matt. 7:18 NIV). Nothing is more antithetical to walking by the Spirit than walking according to the deeds of the flesh.

So how do we avoid the pitfalls of legalism, using freedom as a license to sin, and a lifestyle of licentiousness? I believe the answer is found in getting our eyes off the "do's and don'ts" and the selfish desire to live for ourselves, and instead to become preoccupied with the things of the Spirit. Let's talk about how to do just that.

# WALKING BY THE SPIRIT

In agriculture, in biology, and in most every facet of life, what you feed will grow. Spiritually speaking, if you feed the flesh, it will grow stronger and stronger. If you feed your spirit by walking with the Spirit, then it will grow stronger and stronger. Picture the person described in Psalm 1 (NIV) as the kind of person whose spiritual life is growing healthy, strong roots.

> Blessed is the one
>   who does not walk in step with the wicked
> or stand in the way that sinners take
>   or sit in the company of mockers,
> but whose delight is in the law of the LORD,
>   and who meditates on his law day and night.
> That person is like a tree planted by streams of water,
>   which yields its fruit in season
> and whose leaf does not wither—
>   whatever they do prospers.
>
> Not so the wicked!
>   They are like chaff
>   that the wind blows away.
> Therefore the wicked will not stand in the judgment,
>   nor sinners in the assembly of the righteous.
>
> For the LORD watches over the way of the righteous,
>   but the way of the wicked leads to destruction.

The psalmist says that the wicked do not prosper in all the ways that matter, while the righteous delight in God's Word. The wicked are fueled by the flesh. The righteous are fueled by the Spirit. The wicked feed on pleasures and relish their sin. The righteous feed on God's Word and relish his ways. The results are not surprising, are they? One road leads to being like "a tree planted by streams of water," bearing fruit and prospering in the Lord. The other leads to a desolate life that ends in destruction.

This psalm illustrates what Paul presents to the Galatians when he contrasts walking by the flesh with walking by the Spirit, and when he contrasts the deeds of the flesh with the fruit of the Spirit. Walking by the flesh produces the sinful behaviors we covered earlier. Walking by the Spirit produces a different result. The Scriptures call this result the fruit of the Spirit (Gal. 5:22–23). It's not "fruits," plural, for a reason, by the way, because unlike the deeds of the flesh, which you can pick and choose from, the fruit of the Spirit is an all-inclusive result of walking by the Spirit. When you read the following list of the fruit of the Spirit, you should think of it as singular evidence for the Spirit's work in a believer's life. Only believers will exhibit it, and only the Spirit of God can consistently make it happen.

You might wonder, *Can't unbelievers exhibit these qualities too? We see this all the time.* Yes, you could even say that qualities like love, patience, and even joy are common in today's world. People love their dogs, families, and strangers. People are filled with exuberant joy when they have a baby or get married, even as atheists. So what is the difference maker? The difference is not a *what* but a *who*. The Holy Spirit does something supernatural with these qualities. The object of these qualities shifts in a believer. New motives replace old ones. New desires replace old ones. New recipients replace old ones. The Spirit bears love, and we begin to love God, love others, and love what is righteous. The Spirit bears peace, and we begin to have peace with God and find peace in God. The Spirit bears joy, and we begin to take joy in obedience, in being a part of the church, and our hearts become full of excitement for eternity while this earth passes away. The Spirit bears self-control, and we begin to yield to his leading with the kind of submission that nothing in this world could ever put in our hearts. I could go on with each one, but you get the point. The Spirit causes all of these qualities, which are civil or moral virtues common to humanity, to burst forth with his glory in mind. The Spirit aims to use our lives to bring glory to Jesus (John 16:14).

1. *Love*: The love that the Spirit pours out through believers is unlike any other kind of love because it's an unconditional love that does not decide to act based on a response to it but loves simply because one loves. Spirit-filled love is not transactional, it's unconditional. Romans 5:5 says, "The love of God has been poured out within our hearts through the Holy Spirit who was given to us." There is no evidence of the Spirit's work in your life if you are without love. God's divine love is obviously the greatest love of all, but since we have been loved by God, we are also called to love like God. Love fueled the apostle Paul's ministry and life. He says in 2 Corinthians 5:14–15, "For Christ's love compels us, because we are convinced that one died for all, and therefore all died. And he died for all, that those who live should no longer live for themselves but for him who died for them and was raised again" (NIV). Love is how you know you are walking by the Spirit.

2. *Joy*: Genuine joy and happiness are based not on earthly realities but on heavenly ones. The Holy Spirit enables us to focus on our spiritual blessings in the midst of challenging situations. A person who is walking by the Spirit exudes a joy that you cannot explain by natural means because it has a supernatural origin. The book of Philippians has often been considered a letter about joy, yet some troubling events were taking place around the time it was written and received. Paul was in prison while writing it, and the people there were enduring persecution for being Roman citizens who

converted to Christianity. (See Acts 16.) Only someone who is preoccupied with the things of the Spirit can have unimaginable joy while being crushed by persecution and imprisonment for preaching the gospel.

3. *Peace*: Peace is linked primarily to salvation since walking by the Spirit is possible only for those who have faith in Jesus Christ. The Spirit produces ongoing, habitual, supernatural peace in believers because they are at peace with God. I love to remind people who are looking for peace that you cannot have peace from God until you are at peace *with* God. Philippians 4:7 describes the peace that comes from walking by the Spirit rather than walking by the flesh in anxiety, worry, and ungratefulness, saying, "And the peace of God, which transcends all understanding, will guard your hearts and your minds in Christ Jesus."

4. *Patience*: The word Paul uses for patience describes the ability to be steadfast. The Hebrew form of this word literally translates as "long nostrils," which is the idea of being "long tempered" or slow to anger instead of short-tempered and quick to breathe out wrath. God is this way with us, and the Spirit of God enables us to be like him. When we are preoccupied with the Spirit and filter all thoughts and emotions through the Word of God, then we will live out Paul's words to the Colossians. He writes, "Put on a heart of compassion, kindness, humility, gentleness, and patience; bearing with one another, and forgiving each other, whoever has a complaint against anyone; just as the Lord forgave you, so must you do also. In addition to all these things put on love, which is the perfect bond of unity. Let the peace of Christ, to which you were indeed called in one body, rule in your hearts; and be thankful" (Col. 3:12–15). On top of all that, God's patience is an example to us. It will be difficult and nearly impossible for someone who is walking by the flesh

to produce the habit of patience, but a believer who is walking by the Spirit can, by his power, be marked by patience in life.

5. *Kindness*: I can't remember where I heard the quote, but someone once said, "If you want to win people, melt them, don't hammer them." I am convicted every time I am reminded of that quote. Kindness always goes farther than hammering, and that's God's approach too, until the day of judgment we know is to come. Romans 2:4 says, "Or do you show contempt for the riches of his kindness, forbearance and patience, not realizing that God's kindness is intended to lead you to repentance?" (NIV). What a powerful reminder! Kindness is what the Spirit produces when we walk his way. Does this mean we don't speak hard truth? Of course not. Ephesians 5:11 tells us to expose evil deeds. Does this mean everyone should just overlook dangerous false teachers? No. Paul the apostle loved the flock and was kind to countless people but still did his job in calling out dangers, which is a form of kindness. *Kindness* is from a Greek word that refers to a gentle and caring concern for others. Kindness serves others. Kindness seeks the betterment of others and considers the needs of others and not merely your own (Phil. 2:3–7). Therefore, one can be both kind to people and clear with truth.

6. *Goodness*: *Goodness* is from the Greek word *agathosune* and means to be generous in your good works toward others. The word could apply to every kind of good act, including giving to the poor, serving an enemy, correcting someone in love, adopting orphans, helping widows, and caring for one's family. Any human being can do something morally good for someone else, but only the Spirit can produce the consistent fruit of goodness in the life of a believer, so our goodness is not just civil virtue but righteous acts motivated

by a love for God. Believers don't want recognition for their goodness. We know that every good and perfect gift comes from God (James 1:17). Therefore, when we do good deeds, we point to our God, who enables us to do them.

7. *Faithfulness*: In this context, Paul is referring not to faith in God but to an ethical faithfulness to others in our lives. Without the Spirit, we will be unfaithful friends, spouses, and gospel partners. The Spirit causes us to be dependable, so when we walk by the Spirit, we will be marked by this quality. Faithfulness is the quality of keeping commitments in relationships. The Galatians had proved to be fickle in their attitude toward Paul (Gal. 4:13–16). Only the Spirit can produce the quality of loyalty no matter the cost.[9]

8. *Gentleness*: Walter Hansen describes gentleness so well when he writes, "Gentleness is the opposite of 'selfish ambition.' Gentle people are not 'conceited, provoking and envying each other' [Gal. 5:26]. Gentleness is an expression of humility, considering the needs and hurts of others before one's personal goals."[10] Gentleness reflects a meekness and humility that can be a habit in our lives only if we walk by the Spirit and not according to the flesh. *Meekness* is an important word to use when understanding gentleness because they are synonymous. Gentleness always uses its resources appropriately, unlike the out-of-control emotions that so often are destructive and have no place in your life as a believer. People who are gentle can have steel spines and soft hearts. Gentle people are teachable and submit to God's Word. As the writer of Proverbs says, "One who is slow to anger is better than the mighty, and one who rules his spirit, than one who captures a city" (Prov. 16:32). In contrast, the

---

9. G. Walter Hansen, *Galatians*, IVP New Testament Commentary Series, ed. Grant R. Osborne (Downers Grove, IL: InterVarsity Press, 1994), Gal. 5:22–26.

10. Ibid.

individual who is not gentle is likened to "a city that is broken into and without walls" (Prov. 25:28).

9. *Self-Control*: Self-control is surrendering to the Spirit's leading and not to our feelings and passions of the flesh. For many of us, self-control is one of the hardest character qualities to form as a habit. But as impossible as it may seem, the Spirit will sanctify believers and continue to conform us to the image of Christ day by day. Self-control is restraining oneself from certain passions and was a theme of Paul's encouragement to Christians in every stage of their maturity. He required elders to be self-controlled (1 Tim. 3:2; Titus 1:8), he expected self-control of himself (1 Cor. 9:27), and he called believers to use their bodies in a way that honors the Holy Spirit (1 Cor. 6:19–20).

At the culmination of this remarkable list Paul says, "Against such things there is no law" (Gal. 5:23). I always imagine this as believers being told, "Feel free to be as excessive and over the top with these actions as you'd like. Go crazy!" Instead of viewing walking by the Spirit as a negative prohibition against doing bad things, Paul provides a positive focus on Spirit-focused things. Our spiritual immaturity will sometimes cause us to focus on what we can't do, rather than focus on what we can do. The Spirit liberates us from all of that and unleashes his fruit in our lives when we are preoccupied with living in surrender to him.

If you want to walk by the Spirit and bear the fruit of the Spirit, then you must be baptized and filled with the Spirit. The next chapter will be pivotal to your understanding the Spirit's work. Let's learn to live, then keep learning.

# LEARNING TO LIVE

## 1. Live like You Are at War

Sin is a big deal, and we should resist the temptation to down-play it. To walk by the Spirit consistently, we need to remember that the flesh will not go down without a fight. The flesh is not neutral. It sets its desire against the Spirit (Gal. 5:17). Living like you are at war with sin will keep you on high alert. You don't need to fear sin, but you need to be ready to fight it. Your emotions, temptations, old vices, new vices, and even pride in thinking you've conquered all the toughest sins and can hit cruise control must be treated with the utmost seriousness. First Corinthians 10:12 says, "Let him who thinks he stands take heed lest he fall" (NKJV). I know it can feel exhausting at times, but the Spirit will empower you to endure in the fight of your life against the flesh. Ask him for help.

## 2. Take Inventory of Your Spiritual Orchard

Florida oranges are so important to the juice economy that the harvest is closely watched every year. On average, some 11 million tons of oranges are produced in Florida, accounting for 70 percent of all orange production. Florida orange producers go to great lengths to prepare and protect their harvests because their livelihoods are dependent on their inventory. In the same way, your spiritual livelihood is linked to the fruit of the Spirit. If it is not being produced in your life in a healthy and regular way, your next step is the most crucial. If you've never taken inventory of your spiritual orchard, you ought to because it's a great opportunity to be assured of the Spirit's work in your life or to be convicted that you are walking according to the flesh. Are you seeing the fruit of the Spirit in your life? Be encouraged. The Spirit is working in you. Are you not seeing the fruit of the Spirit in your life? Be repentant and ask the Holy Spirit to produce his fruit in you as you humble yourself. God always responds favorably to the broken and contrite heart (Ps. 51:17).

### 3. Reject the Extremes

Do you lean more toward loose boundaries and overusing your Christian liberty, or do you tend to lean more toward legalism? Reject both extremes. Christian liberty is good, but we must take care how we use it. Walking by the Spirit means that even when we *can* do something, we are still sensitive to how it can impact others or how it could tempt us to go too far (Rom. 14:13; Gal. 5:13). Furthermore, walking by the Spirit also means we are reliant on the Spirit, and not on our man-made rules and regulations, as we live, practice morality, and seek to walk in righteousness. Reject extremes. Embrace biblical balance.

### 4. Get Biblically Busy

We now understand that walking by the Spirit means to be preoccupied with the Spirit and to go everywhere focused on what the Spirit would have us do. The best strategy against the flesh is not to be passive or reactive but to be aggressive and proactive. You don't have to do all of the following suggestions, but consider getting busy with some of these: Get involved in your church if you're not already, serve your community, give generously, put your hands to work in spiritual ways, get counseling, dig in with a small group, go on a short-term missions trip, be a long-term missionary, take an equipping class at your church, go on a marriage retreat, or invest in your kids' spiritual growth and not just their athletic or artistic growth. In all of your busyness to succeed in many facets of life, are you biblically busy? Walking by the Spirit means that wherever life takes you, you look at every situation through the lens of what God wants for you, not just what you want.

## Questions for Reflection

1. Do some deeds of the flesh tempt you more than others? Name them and identify why they tempt you.

2. List four or five things that keep you busy every week. After that, list four or five spiritual things that keep you busy every week. Is there an area the Spirit has been convicting you in to bring balance? Is there something you believe you should focus on more or shouldn't be focusing on as much?

3. Do you struggle with legalism or overusing your liberty? What steps can you take this week to shift into more balance?

4. Why do you think people don't take sin as seriously as they should? Why should we live like we are at war with the flesh?

# 5

# WHAT ARE THE BAPTISM AND FILLING OF THE HOLY SPIRIT?

*For we were all baptized by one Spirit so as to form*
*one body—whether Jews or Gentiles, slave or free—*
*and we were all given the one Spirit to drink.*
—1 CORINTHIANS 12:13 NIV

WE NOW BEGIN WHAT MIGHT BE, FOR THOSE WHO come from more charismatic or Pentecostal theological frameworks, the most helpful or the most debated three chapters of the book. Regardless of your background, I hope you will find these chapters to be gracious, biblically based, and encouraging. If you've come to this book with your views already established, I encourage you to weigh my arguments using Scripture alone, even if you do not agree experientially. If you've come to this book without your views established, I hope you will find my arguments to be convincing and biblical, rather than a debate with "the other guys." If you've come to this book confused by the abuses of some people who take things too far, I strongly believe you will be blessed by these next chapters.

There is widespread need for respectful dialogue on the subject of the baptism and filling of the Holy Spirit, and perhaps even a need to disagree agreeably because not every issue is a primary issue and believers have differed on these doctrinal matters for hundreds of years. The goal of these chapters is to edify and to provide a good foundation for your own position as you wrestle with God's Word, and to trigger discussions with others who hold different views or feel confused.

My belief is that in this first chapter there shouldn't be much disagreement across denominational lines, because primarily I will lay out what the Bible says about the baptism and the filling of the Holy Spirit. You might not agree 100 percent with my conclusions, but I hope we will find ourselves generally unified regarding the distinctions Scripture makes between the baptism and the filling.

Let's begin by looking at the baptism of the Holy Spirit in the New Testament, then use what the Bible says to make some helpful observations and applications for today.

## THE BAPTISM OF THE HOLY SPIRIT

The New Testament uses the phrase "baptism in the Holy Spirit" seven times. In addition, the description of the historical moment of Pentecost in Acts 2:4 references only a "filling," but even this is a fulfillment of Acts 1:3–9, where Jesus says that the disciples will be "baptized with the Holy Spirit." If we seek to understand each use of the phrase and the experiences of the early church at Pentecost, I believe we can come to the most accurate conclusions possible about the baptism and filling of the Holy Spirit.

1. *John the Baptist predicts the baptism of the Holy Spirit (Matt. 3:11; Mark 1:8; Luke 3:16).* All three Synoptic Gospels record John the Baptist predicting the coming of one who would baptize with the Holy Spirit and with fire. Each reference contains the word "baptize" and "with the Holy Spirit." The Greek word *en* is translated "with" but can be translated as "in" or "by," which is why you might hear this phrase said in any of those ways. John the Baptist's ministry was to call Jews to repent and be baptized with water, and to prepare for one who would come to baptize the repentant sinner in the Holy Spirit, and the unrepentant sinner in fire (which represented judgment). In John's ministry, we see three baptisms that are all exactly what they appear to be: baptism in water signifies repentance of sin, baptism in the Holy Spirit marks being a part of the church (his listeners didn't fully understand this, but soon they would at Pentecost), and baptism by fire represents judgment of those who do not repent. All of these baptisms harmonize with passages in the rest of the New Testament: after the cross, believers were baptized in water as a symbol of their repentance and faith in Christ (Matt. 28:16–20), believers were baptized by the Holy Spirit into the body of Christ (1 Cor. 12:13), and eventually unbelievers will be baptized by fire in judgment (Rev. 20:14–15).

2. *Jesus prepares the disciples for the baptism of the Holy Spirit (Acts 1:3–10).* Throughout Jesus' time on earth, he preached, cast out demons, saved repentant sinners, rebuked the Pharisees, healed the sick, and made disciples. In all he did, never once did he baptize anyone in the Holy Spirit, because it was not time for that. The work of the cross had not yet been accomplished, the church had not yet been established, and the Holy Spirit had not yet been sent to baptize and fill believers with power. Jesus did, however, prepare

his disciples *for* the baptism of the Holy Spirit. The book of Acts records a historic moment when Jesus instructs his disciples about the baptism of the Holy Spirit and where to go and wait for it to happen:

> After his suffering, he presented himself to them and gave many convincing proofs that he was alive. He appeared to them over a period of forty days and spoke about the kingdom of God. On one occasion, while he was eating with them, he gave them this command: "Do not leave Jerusalem, but wait for the gift my Father promised, which you have heard me speak about. For John baptized with water, but in a few days you will be baptized with the Holy Spirit."
>
> Then they gathered around him and asked him, "Lord, are you at this time going to restore the kingdom to Israel?"
>
> He said to them: "It is not for you to know the times or dates the Father has set by his own authority. But you will receive power when the Holy Spirit comes on you; and you will be my witnesses in Jerusalem, and in all Judea and Samaria, and to the ends of the earth."
>
> After he said this, he was taken up before their very eyes, and a cloud hid him from their sight.
>
> —ACTS 1:3–9 NIV

This is one of the most important passages for understanding the unique way the Holy Spirit was going to announce his arrival. If you recall John 16:7, where Jesus says that it was to the disciples' advantage that he go away so that the Helper could come, this was when they saw exactly what he meant. Jesus was preparing the disciples for the baptism of the Holy Spirit, which would mark the birth of the church. This birth was a special event that would never be repeated again. The church would not start, then die, then restart, and so on. It would begin and the body of Christ would be alive and well. The Holy Spirit was going to come, and Jerusalem was the place where Jesus said this would take place. Even in that moment when Jesus tells them "do not leave Jerusalem, but wait for the gift my Father promised," the disciples did not fully understand what was going to happen. They thought Jesus was going to establish his kingdom right then and there. Jesus redirects them one final time to the expectation of the Spirit, who will fill them with power to be his witnesses. Why? Because according to God's divine plan, the church was to be born and gather the rest of his sheep, who were not just Jews but also gentiles (John 10:16). His kingdom would eventually come, but first he would extend his gift of salvation to the ends of earth. The baptism of the Holy Spirit at Pentecost came next.

3. *Pentecost is the experienced promise of both the baptism of the Holy Spirit and the filling of the Holy Spirit (Acts 2:1–11).* Ten days after Jesus gave the disciples their final instructions and ascended to heaven, the explosive power of the Spirit birthing the church took the upper room by storm. How do we know it was ten days after Jesus ascended? Because Jesus arose from the dead on the Sunday after Passover. The Feast of Weeks, which is also called Pentecost, was fifty days after the Passover. The Greek word *pentekoste* literally means "fiftieth." And as we know from Acts 1:1–9, he ascended forty days after Passover, and so ten days before Pentecost.

Now for the incredible foreshadowing of what was about to take place: the Passover the world had just witnessed would be the last and most supernatural Passover because Jesus was the final Lamb, fulfilling prophecy foretold long before. Fifty days later, Pentecost would be the last and most supernatural Pentecost because Jesus had fulfilled his mission on earth, he had ascended to heaven, and the long-awaited prophecy would begin to unfold and be fulfilled in the last days leading up to Christ's return (Joel 2:28–32).

Acts describes the scene in the upper room when the disciples experienced the promised Holy Spirit:

When the day of Pentecost came, they were all together in one place. Suddenly a sound like the blowing of a violent wind came from heaven and filled the whole house where they were sitting. They saw what seemed to be tongues of fire that separated and came to rest on each of them. All of them were filled with the Holy Spirit and began to speak in other tongues as the Spirit enabled them.

Now there were staying in Jerusalem God-fearing Jews from every nation under heaven. When they heard this sound, a crowd came together in bewilderment, because each one heard their own language being spoken. Utterly amazed, they asked: "Aren't all these who are speaking Galileans? Then how is it that each of us hears them in our native language? Parthians, Medes and Elamites; residents of Mesopotamia, Judea and Cappadocia, Pontus and Asia, Phrygia and Pamphylia, Egypt and the parts of Libya near Cyrene; visitors from Rome (both Jews and converts to Judaism); Cretans and Arabs—we hear them declaring the wonders of God in our own tongues!"

—ACTS 2:1–11 NIV

According to Acts 1:15, 120 people were in the upper room during this historic moment. Some people believe that all 120 were speaking in tongues, while others believe it was only the apostles who were given the extraordinary experience of tongues of fire resting above their heads.[1] Both views have valid arguments, but in any case, there was both a baptism and a filling of the Spirit happening in that upper room, and they were supernaturally unique moments in history. First, the baptism of the Spirit that took place that day was the same baptism Jesus predicted in Acts 1:5. It was a baptism of those believers into the body of Christ, because the church was

---

1. Robert Gromacki holds this view and makes a rather convincing argument in his book *The Holy Spirit: Who He Is, What He Does*, Swindoll Leadership Library (Nashville: Word, 1999), 147–48.

being birthed in that moment. Second, when Luke writes, "All of them were filled with the Holy Spirit and began to speak in other tongues as the Spirit enabled them," this is to be distinguished from the baptism of the Holy Spirit. The baptism of the Holy Spirit made the disciples into the body of Christ spiritually, and the filling of the Holy Spirit manifested audibly through speaking in tongues. These tongues were known languages, as listed in verses 8–11.

It is important to note that not everyone who was baptized into the body of Christ experienced tongues the way that Acts describes of Pentecost. While some did (see the next point), the three thousand souls who were added to the church and baptized with water in Acts 2:41 were never said to have spoken in tongues as part of their being baptized in the Holy Spirit. In Acts 16, we see Lydia and the jailor both saved in Philippi, but tongues are not part of their conversion when they are baptized into the body of Christ. In Philippians, tongues are not mentioned, nor are they mentioned in any other New Testament letter except 1 Corinthians as a gift, but not as dogmatic evidence of being baptized into the body of Christ. Pentecost was part of a unique fulfillment of prophecy and something that Jesus prepared his disciples for. He was getting them ready to see the reality of his building the church (Matt. 16:18) and the power of the Holy Spirit at work in them as they went out to proclaim the gospel. There is one other moment in the book of Acts that is similar to Pentecost, at the hands of Peter. What happened in that moment teaches us something special about what God was doing during the birth of the church.

4. *Peter reports that the Spirit was baptizing gentiles without distinction (Acts 11:15–16).* Acts 10:44–48 describes a powerful moment when Peter is preaching and a gentile centurion named Cornelius and his household are baptized with the Holy Spirit and speak in other tongues. "While Peter was still speaking these words, the Holy Spirit fell upon all those who were listening to the message. And all the circumcised believers who came with Peter

were amazed, because the gift of the Holy Spirit had been poured out upon the Gentiles also. For they were hearing them speaking with tongues and exalting God. Then Peter answered, 'Surely no one can refuse the water for these to be baptized, who have received the Holy Spirit just as we did, can he?' And he ordered them to be baptized in the name of Jesus Christ. Then they asked him to stay on for a few days" (NASB 1995).

Did you notice that the Jews ("circumcised believers") were shocked by how the Spirit fell upon the gentiles too? Don't miss that detail. It's the key to unlocking the full understanding of this incredible moment.

In Acts 11:1–18 a tense scene unfolds as Peter is forced to defend that experience with Cornelius, explaining why in the world he was fellowshiping with gentiles.

The apostle Peter was put on the hot seat! The other apostles and brothers in the faith had heard that gentiles were receiving the word of God, and they "took issue" with Peter eating with these non-Jews, who ate unclean things and did not hold to Jewish traditions (vv. 1–2). Peter then explains what had taken place in Caesarea when Cornelius was converted along with his entire household. This was something entirely new for the Jewish converts because many still had the mentality that only *they* were receiving the Holy Spirit in the same way that the disciples had at Pentecost. This extraordinary outpouring on a gentile like Cornelius was a sign that there was now no distinction between Jews and gentiles in God's eyes. They were all going to be a part of the body of Christ.

One more unique aspect of Cornelius and his household's experience was that they were baptized with the Holy Spirit immediately upon repenting and believing (Acts 10:43–44; 11:18), signifying that God was doing something new with the gentiles and would pour out his Spirit on people and baptize them into the body of Christ immediately upon their believing in faith. Just as Pentecost was the unique sign of God's doing something new, though the three thousand souls who were subsequently saved in Acts 2:41 did not necessarily speak in tongues, Cornelius' experience was the unique sign of God's doing something new in adding gentiles to the church, though those who were subsequently converted in Acts did not all necessarily speak in tongues.

5. *Paul explains that we all have been baptized by one Spirit (1 Cor. 12:13).* Theologians refer to John the Baptist's and Jesus' words about the baptism of the Holy Spirit as *expectation*, then Pentecost as the *experience*, and finally Paul's words in 1 Corinthians 12:13 as *explanation*.[2] Paul explains the doctrine of Spirit baptism in 1 Corinthians 12:13, saying, "For by one Spirit we were all baptized into one body, whether Jews or Greeks, whether slaves or free, and we were all made to drink of one Spirit." We are all baptized into one body by one Spirit no matter who we are or where we're from. After the church was established at Pentecost and God moved powerfully to signify the salvation of not only Jews but also Samaritans and gentiles, the baptism of the Holy Spirit continued to be a sovereignly initiated experience in which every believer is spiritually added to the body of Christ. Like a living organism, we are many parts, but one body (Rom. 12:4). We are brought together as one people, growing as a holy temple of God, who now dwells inside of us (Eph. 2:21–22). If anyone tries to make a distinction within the body of Christ that creates two classes of Christians, that must be rejected. Some will propose that there can be believers who *are* baptized in the Holy Spirit and those who *are not* baptized in the Holy Spirit but need to be. This creates division where the Bible does not. This fosters disunity between people, spiritual elitism in those who think they are "upperclassmen" in God's family, and insecurity for those who feel they are second-class citizens.

---

2. John MacArthur and Richard Mayhue, gen. eds., *Biblical Doctrine: A Systematic Summary of Bible Truth* (Wheaton, IL: Crossway, 2017), 353–54.

# SUMMARY: WHAT SHOULD WE BELIEVE?

*1. The book of Acts presents a unique and foundational picture of the church's birth.* In all of the New Testament, only the book of Acts records the baptism of the Holy Spirit accompanied by supernatural, outward manifestations like a rushing wind (Acts 2:2), tongues of fire resting on people's heads (Acts 2:3), and an explosion of speaking in tongues by those who had never done it before (Acts 2:6–11). Beyond all of that, the church was never "birthed" again. Once it started and the Spirit came, he was here to stay and the church would be built up as Jesus promised (Matt. 16:18).

*2. No one was ever commanded to seek the baptism of the Holy Spirit or to pray for it.* Unlike some of the practices of charismatics or Pentecostals today, no one in the book of Acts, or in the whole Bible for that matter, was ever commanded to be baptized in the Holy Spirit or to seek the baptism of the Holy Spirit. It was never presented as something one must seek. Not one instance in the Scriptures even slightly mirrors today's charismatic practice of inviting people to the altar to be baptized in the Holy Spirit and receive the gift of tongues. The Spirit always came upon people according to his sovereign power and for the purpose of bringing believers into the church.

*3. The baptism of the Holy Spirit was accompanied by tongues and extraordinary events* primarily *as a sign that God was doing something new.* Many people seek the tongues experience of Pentecost, but even with the best of intentions, this seeking overlooks the purpose of these special events. Take a look at table 5.1 to see the four special cases of conversion in Acts and the specific purposes of God in fulfilling Acts 1:8. Notice the locations and the people groups. It's as though God was targeting those groups exactly as Jesus predicted.

## Table 5.1: Four Special Cases of Conversion

| Location | Jerusalem/Judea | Samaria |
|---|---|---|
| Text | Acts 2:1–21 | Acts 8:14–24 |
| Time | Day of Pentecost, ca. AD 30 | ca. AD 31–32 |
| People | Jews | Samaritans |
| Holy Spirit | Baptized and filled with the Holy Spirit | Received the Holy Spirit |
| Sign | Spoke in tongues as a sign to the Jews | None recorded |
| Circumstances | Tarrying together | Laying on of hands |

Source: John MacArthur and Richard Mayhue, Biblical Doctrine (Wheaton, IL: Crossway, 2017), 356.

This table provides a clear view of what was happening, why it was happening, and the people it was happening to. Jews experienced it in Jerusalem and Judea, Samaritans in Samaria, gentiles in Caesarea, and even the former disciples of John the Baptist were brought up to speed. These moments do not represent a normal pattern that means everyone today is supposed to speak in tongues when baptized by the Holy Spirit. Rather they are supernatural signs that what Christ said would happen during the birth of the church was being fulfilled. It is incredible to think that the extraordinary experiences in Jerusalem, Judea, Samaria, Caesarea, and Ephesus were all part of what Jesus told his disciples in Acts 1:8, saying, "But you will receive power when the Holy Spirit has come upon you; and you shall be My witnesses both in Jerusalem and in all Judea, and

| Caesarea | Ephesus |
|---|---|
| Acts 10:1–11:18 | Acts 19:1–7 |
| ca. AD 36 | ca. AD 52 |
| Gentiles | Disciples of John the Baptist |
| Received the Holy Spirit | Received the Holy Spirit |
| Spoke in tongues as a sign to the Jews | Spoke in tongues and prophesied as a sign to the Jews |
| Peter preaching | Laying on of hands |

Samaria, and as far as the remotest part of the earth." The special tongues were given to exalt God and proclaim the gospel to every nation, tribe, and tongue (Acts 2:8–11; 10:46; Matt. 28:16–20). What an amazing God we serve, whose perfect plan always comes to pass, whose prophetic power never fails, and whose mighty hand is drawing in people from every nation, tribe, and tongue.

4. *After the foundational moments in Acts, Paul references the baptism of the Holy Spirit only as being associated with believers who were being added to the body of Christ.* Based on 1 Corinthians 12:13, it's clear that all believers experience the baptism of the Holy Spirit into the body of Christ upon conversion. Paul explains the normative pattern for the baptism of the Holy Spirit after the foundational experience of Pentecost and the transitional period in Acts when

the church was founded. You can call the baptism of the Spirit a "positional experience" in which we are brought into the body of Christ. It happens at conversion, makes us all one in Christ, and represents our being immersed in Christ by the power of the Spirit (Rom. 6:3–4). According to Galatians 3:27, there are now no more distinctions that create class systems in Christ. There are not two kinds of saved people: the ones who have the baptism of the Spirit and the ones who don't. We are all one in Christ.

5. *The baptism of the Holy Spirit did not always result in speaking in tongues.* Acts 8:14–24 records a moment when those in Samaria who had been baptized in water had not yet received the gift of the Holy Spirit. Signifying that God would be giving the Spirit even to Samaritans (a group the Jews hated), the Spirit came upon those in Samaria through the laying on of hands. Nowhere in this entire section of Acts 8 does Luke mention them speaking in tongues. They simply were "receiving the Holy Spirit" through the laying on of hands by the apostles (vv. 17–18).

6. *The baptism of the Holy Spirit is a free, God-given experience that is always linked to conversion or being added to the body of Christ, according to God's sovereign power, not man's.* At no time in the book of Acts or anywhere in the New Testament was the baptism of the Holy Spirit an experience separate from being added into the body of Christ, and nowhere is someone required to ask for the baptism of the Holy Spirit, give money to receive the Spirit, or do specific good works to be baptized by the Holy Spirit. When Simon dares to ask Peter if he can buy the ability to give people the Holy Spirit through the laying on of hands, he is sharply rebuked. Peter tells him, "May your silver perish with you, because you thought you could acquire the gift of God with money! You have no part or share in this matter, for your heart is not right before God" (Acts 8:20–21).

7. *The baptism of the Holy Spirit is not a normative "second blessing," as some would teach it to be.* There were some in the Scriptures who received the Holy Spirit as a "second blessing" evidenced by

tongues, including the disciples, who were already believers when they had the experience at Pentecost and the Holy Spirit baptized them, and the disciples of John the Baptist in Acts 19:1–7, but the Bible does not describe the subsequent baptism of the Holy Spirit through tongues as a normative experience for Christians. These specific moments of extraordinary experiences happened when God was signifying his doing of something new. It did not happen in every new church or even with every new convert.

8. *The baptism of the Holy Spirit is distinct from the filling of the Holy Spirit and does not guarantee tongues.* At Pentecost, the disciples received both the baptism and the filling of the Holy Spirit. The baptism of the Holy Spirit was their being made into (or brought into) the brand-new body of Christ—the church. In Acts 1:5 Jesus said this would happen. Luke, in Acts 2:4, calls the explosion of tongues in the Pentecost experience the "filling" of the Holy Spirit. After Pentecost, others were added to the body of Christ with or without tongues. The filling of the Holy Spirit also occurred to believers after Pentecost with or without tongues. Later on Ephesians 5:18 commands all believers to "be filled with the Spirit," though Paul says in 1 Corinthians 12:30 that not all will have the gift of speaking in tongues or of interpreting tongues. Therefore, we can rightly conclude that the baptism of the Holy Spirit is for all believers to be added into the body of Christ, is distinct from the filling of the Holy Spirit, and does not necessarily include tongues. Not all will speak in tongues, but all will be baptized into the body of Christ (1 Cor. 12:13), and all are commanded to be filled with the Spirit, but that doesn't mean all will experience tongues. (We'll study this next.)

Now that we understand more about the baptism of the Holy Spirit, let's dig deeper to understand what the Bible teaches about the filling of the Spirit and its distinction from the baptism of the Holy Spirit.

# THE FILLING OF THE HOLY SPIRIT

Well-known evangelist D. L. Moody was to have a big service in England. A pastor protested, "Why do we need this 'Mr. Moody'? He's uneducated and inexperienced! Who does he think he is anyway? Does he think he has a monopoly on the Holy Spirit?"

A wiser pastor rose and responded, "No, but the Holy Spirit has a monopoly on Mr. Moody."[3]

To be filled with the Holy Spirit is to be monopolized by him because your thoughts, desires, and actions are all yielded to him. To be filled with the Spirit is to be energized and controlled by the third person of the Godhead in such a way that under the acknowledged lordship of Jesus Christ, you experience the presence and power of God. Spirit-filling leads to renewal, obedience, boldness in testimony, and an arresting quality in believers' lives.[4] In the next section, I'll unpack what being filled with the Spirit looked like in the Old and New Testaments and how it is related to the Christian life. The filling of the Holy Spirit occurred in both Old and New Testaments and always represented an empowerment by God for service to God, but it's wise to understand each in their own context.

## THE FILLING OF THE HOLY SPIRIT IN THE OLD TESTAMENT

In the Old Testament only certain people were filled with or "indwelt" by the Spirit. There were many instances when he came "upon" individuals such as Moses (Num. 11:17), Othniel (Judg. 3:10), Gideon (Judg. 6:34), Samson (Judg. 14:6), David (1 Sam. 16:13), and Isaiah (Isa. 61:1). There are several more, but in all

---

3. Quoted in H. B. Charles, "Be Filled with the Spirit," sermon, https://hbcharlesjr.com/wp-content/uploads/2014/06/Be-Filled-with-the-Spirit-.pdf.

4. Martin H. Manser, *Dictionary of Bible Themes: The Accessible and Comprehensive Tool for Topical Studies* (London: Martin Manser, 2009), theme 3251.

instances people were given assignments from God to accomplish specific tasks and proclaim truth. Several direct references to "filling" include:

- Bezalel was filled with the Spirit of God to construct the tabernacle (Exod. 31:3).
- Joshua was filled with the Spirit to lead God's people after Moses (Deut. 34:9).
- Ezekiel was filled with the Spirit to speak God's truth (Ezek. 2:2; 3:24).

These examples all represent a non-normative empowerment for God's purposes within the people of Israel and the prophetic ministry of certain leaders.

## THE FILLING OF THE HOLY SPIRIT IN THE NEW TESTAMENT

In the Old Testament there is no command to be filled with the Spirit. God supernaturally works in the coming upon or filling of specific people for his purposes. In the New Testament we see a distinct change in which all believers are commanded to be filled with the Spirit. Paul the apostle writes, "And do not get drunk with wine, in which there is debauchery, but be filled with the Spirit" (Eph. 5:18). The Ephesians, in contrast to the worldly influences and pagan worship practices of the surrounding culture, were told to be immersed in the Spirit and under his influence. Unlike the baptism of the Holy Spirit, which is never sought for or commanded, the filling of the Spirit is something believers are expected to seek, want, and pray for. Ultimately, we are filled with the Spirit by yielding to God in total surrender, which unleashes the powerful work of the Spirit in our lives in several ways. Let's walk through eight truths about the filling of the Spirit and understand each one from Scripture:

1. *The filling of the Spirit is an apostolic command.* Ephesians
   5:18 is a command to "be filled with the Spirit." Christians
   are to obey this instruction and be filled.
2. *The filling of the Spirit is an ongoing experience that can happen time and time again.* The verb "be filled" in Ephesians
   5:18 is a present-tense verb, and you can translate this verse
   literally as "be being filled" to imply that we are to continue
   being filled again and again. This is what is meant when
   theologians say that there is one baptism, but there can be
   many fillings.
3. *The filling of the Spirit is yielding yourself and coming under the
   control and influence of the Spirit.* In contrast to drunkenness
   in Ephesians 5:18, Paul says to instead be under the influence of the Spirit. This would imply that some Christians
   were under the influence of the wrong things and were not
   filled with the Spirit the way they should have been. John
   MacArthur explains, "The best analogy of moment-by-
   moment yielding to the Holy Spirit's control is the figure
   of walking, the figure Paul introduced in Ephesians 4:1.
   Walking involves moving one step at a time, and can be
   done in no other way. Being filled with the Spirit is walking
   thought by thought, decision by decision, act by act under
   the Spirit's control. The Spirit-filled life yields to every step
   of the Spirit of God."[5]
4. *The filling of the Spirit can be hindered by ongoing sin.* We have
   all been baptized in the Spirit, but the filling of the Spirit is
   dependent on our surrender to God's way and rejecting our
   own flesh. You cannot experience the ongoing filling of the
   Spirit and the benefits of that if you walk in the flesh. This
   is why Paul says to lay aside sins like drunkenness and be

5. John F. MacArthur, *Ephesians*, MacArthur New Testament Commentary (Chicago: Moody Bible Institute, 1986), 253.

filled with the Spirit (Eph. 5:18) and tells the Corinthians to flee immorality and that they are the temple of the Holy Spirit (1 Cor. 6:19–20).

5. *The filling of the Spirit produces Christlike character and fruit in our lives.* Having been filled with the Spirit has results that can be linked only to a genuine work of the Spirit. Walking by the Spirit (as we studied in the previous chapter) is possible only if one is filled with the Spirit. The fruit of the Spirit (Gal. 5:22–23) is also the result of being filled. When the Holy Spirit is the dominating influence over a person's life, that person will produce fruit from the Spirit.

6. *The filling of the Spirit stirs us to boldly proclaim the gospel.* In the passages we looked at from the book of Acts, something always happens when people are filled with the Holy Spirit: they proclaim the gospel. In Acts 2:4 the gospel explodes out from Pentecost and eventually three thousand souls are saved (Acts 2:41), and in Acts 7:55 Stephen courageously continues to preach the gospel and keep his eyes on heaven while he is being martyred, because he is a man "full of the Holy Spirit." If you have a difficult time sharing the gospel or being bold about your faith, it is perfectly biblical to seek the Spirit's filling for the purpose of declaring the gospel.

7. *The filling of the Spirit produces singing, thanksgiving, and submission.* In Ephesians 5, Paul answers the question that might enter readers' minds when they see "be filled with the Spirit." *But what will that look like Paul?* He says, "Be filled with the Spirit, speaking to one another in psalms and hymns and spiritual songs, singing and making melody with your hearts to the Lord; always giving thanks for all things in the name of our Lord Jesus Christ to God our Father; and subject yourselves to one another in the fear of Christ" (Eph. 5:18–21). This passage showcases the results emanating from the Spirit-filled life. We will sing praises to

God, be thankful for all things in Christ, and be mutually submissive to one another in the fear of Christ—meaning we will consider how Jesus wants us to live and be teachable, loving, and mature in our relationships with other believers. In the verses that follow, Paul gets into marriage, parenting, and employer-employee relationships, which certainly require copious amounts of grace and submissiveness in our hearts.

8. *The filling of the Spirit does not guarantee you will speak in tongues but rather provides the empowerment of the Spirit to live a faithful and godly life each day.* Remember the unique way the Spirit came upon people and filled them in the book of Acts. These signs were supernatural authentications that God was filling people from all different ethnicities and religious backgrounds, making them a part of the body of Christ. But we still must harmonize Ephesians 5:18, when Paul commands the church to be filled with the Spirit, with 1 Corinthians 12:30, in which he says that not all people will speak in tongues. You will hear some people teach that the filling of the Spirit is a euphoric or miraculous experience. Perhaps someone you know says they spoke in tongues, or someone else says they had a vision, or an influential pastor says that he can fill you with the Spirit if you'll attend a special service and receive the laying on of hands. Based on what Scripture teaches, the filling of the Spirit may accompany a special zeal or a feeling of exuberance and joy or a deep conviction that erupts into godly action, but much of it will focus on obedience to Christ and bearing fruit in everyday life.

Table 5.2 compares the baptism of the Holy Spirit and the filling of the Holy Spirit. Notice the differences between each and the impact it will have on a believer.

## Table 5.2: The Baptism of the Holy Spirit versus the Filling of the Holy Spirit

| Baptism of the Spirit | Filling of the Spirit |
| --- | --- |
| Occurs only once in each believer's life | Is a repeated experience |
| Never happened before the day of Pentecost | Occurred in the Old Testament |
| True of all believers | Not necessarily experienced by all |
| Cannot be undone | Can be lost |
| Results in a position | Results in power |
| Occurs when we believe in Christ | Occurs throughout the Christian life |
| No prerequisite (except faith in Christ) | Depends on yieldedness |

*Source: Charles Ryrie, Basic Theology (Wheaton, IL: Victor, 1986), 379.*

# LEARNING TO LIVE

How might we live in light of the truths we've walked through in this chapter? Let me offer you three simple steps you can take today.

## 1. Filter All Experiences through Scripture

No matter where you are on the theological spectrum, a wise Christian will filter all experiences through the Scriptures and "test the spirits" (1 John 4:1). There are many healthy debates regarding the baptism of the Holy Spirit that can take place across denominational lines, but there are also many outlandish claims and many dangerous teachers who put words into God's mouth and teach a twisted version of the passages we've unpacked here. Charismatics, Pentecostals, Reformed Baptists, Lutherans, and everyone in between will not agree on every aspect of this subject, but if we all submit to the Word, we can have more unity than we've often experienced.

## 2. Seek the Filling of the Holy Spirit through Prayer and Reading Scripture

Since being filled with the Spirit is being yielded and submissive to him and being preoccupied with what he desires over our fleshly desires, ask him to fill you each and every day and to fill your mind with the Word (Col. 3:16). There is no need to look for fillings anywhere other than your prayer life and the Word. These are your power sources. When we are on our knees in total dependence on the Spirit and filling our minds with Scripture, we are in the perfect posture to be filled. A heart that is bowed low before God in humility is prepared to be used greatly by God. Do you make it a regular practice to ask him to fill you each day? Do you confess sin, ask for wisdom, and express your total dependence on him to bear his fruit in your life? That may be the best step you've ever taken in your walk with the Lord. The Father sent the Spirit and Jesus said it would be to your advantage, so take full advantage of the Helper.

### 3. Reject Any Requirements for the Baptism of the Holy Spirit Except Grace Alone through Faith Alone in Christ Alone

Now that you have studied and seen that the baptism of the Holy Spirit is centered on bringing believers into the body of Christ, there can be no requirement for it except the same requirements for salvation: faith. Do not accept any theological position that calls for you to speak in tongues as evidence of Spirit-baptism or to speak certain phrases or have someone lay hands on you at an altar. The baptism of the Holy Spirit was never sought, never coerced, and never a human transaction.

### Questions for Reflection

1. What is the difference between the baptism of the Holy Spirit and the filling of the Holy Spirit?
2. Why should we hesitate to follow any teacher who says that speaking in tongues is the required evidence for the baptism of the Holy Spirit?
3. Should we treat those who hold different views on this subject as brothers and sisters in Christ even if we strongly disagree with them? What would this look like practically?
4. Have you ever prayed for the Holy Spirit to fill you? What was the evidence of his filling work in your life?
5. What are some steps you can take today to "be being filled" (Eph. 5:18) with the Holy Spirit?

6

# WHAT DOES SPIRIT-FILLED WORSHIP LOOK LIKE?

*God is spirit, and his worshipers must*
*worship in the Spirit and in truth.*
—JOHN 4:24 NIV

MANY OF US ARE FAMILIAR WITH THE OLD TESTAment story about the children of Israel building a golden calf while Moses was on Mount Sinai with God, but did you know there were other instances of such reckless worship and idolatry in the Old Testament? First Kings 12:25–33 unveils the drama that took place when Jeroboam, one of King Solomon's officials, made a big mistake because he was competing for the kingdom with Solomon's son, Rehoboam. What makes this story even more tragic is that God promised Jeroboam that he would experience blessing if he walked in obedience and followed in King David's footsteps (11:38). What started with so much promise was destroyed by sinful pride. It all started when Jeroboam's ego got the best of him. He competed with Rehoboam. Both of these men tried to get people to follow them, and in the process they turned people away from God and to idols.

Jeroboam was leading his followers in the Northern Kingdom and trying to keep them from following Rehoboam, who was leading his followers in the Southern Kingdom, which was where the temple was in Jerusalem. Even though the kingdom was divided, when it came to worship, all still had to obey God's commands regarding worshiping him at the temple. But can you guess the last place on earth where Jeroboam would ever want his followers to go? Jeroboam needed to replace Jerusalem and avoid God's laws to accomplish his self-serving agenda. He was worried that a trip to Jerusalem would rekindle the old flame of unity in the people's hearts. "Jeroboam thought to himself, 'The kingdom will now likely revert to the house of David. If these people go up to offer sacrifices at the temple of the LORD in Jerusalem, they will again give their allegiance to their lord, Rehoboam king of Judah. They will kill me and return to King Rehoboam'" (12:26–28 NIV). So what did he do? So that nobody would go to Jerusalem, he broke God's laws and set up a place of worship in the Northern Kingdom, complete with two golden calves (breaking the first and second commandments) and its own priests, who were not from the tribe of Levi (breaking God's laws about the Levitical priesthood). His motive was selfish ambition. And his insecurity caused him to ignore God's commands for worship.

In this story, Jeroboam was worshiping. But he had the wrong motive, the wrong method, and the wrong god. There was worship. There were worship leaders. There was a sanctuary. But God was nowhere to be found. Jeroboam thought he would do worship the way he wanted, rooted in his version of truth. And, oh, he had passion! But it was born of his manipulative vision. He worried about his influence. He couldn't stand the thought of anyone else getting the glory. In the same way that Moses' brother, Aaron, erected a golden calf in Exodus 32, Jeroboam ignored God's orders, treating them as nothing more than suggestions.

## DO WE THINK WE CAN WORSHIP HOWEVER WE WANT?

Similarly, many people in the church today might not say this, but they live it through their actions: I'll just worship my way. Much of our worship practices and our ideas about worship echo the abandonment of truth that began in the garden when the serpent came to Eve, whispering, "Surely, God didn't really mean that you'd die? Go ahead, have it your way." (See Gen. 3:4.) Now, as then, the lie that the enemy whispers (and at times roars) is that you can worship a holy God however you please. Just as Jeroboam's false worship damaged generations after he was long gone, today there are movements, habits, methods, and mindsets built on past errors and false beliefs that are also the origin of a dangerous future. No matter what tradition you come from, be it Baptist, charismatic, Lutheran, or nondenominational, much of worship has become about us and not so much about God. We can be glory hogs and preference obsessed, singing and preaching ourselves into every single song and sermon.

In many churches today, worship has become little more than a top-notch production filled with lip service and entertainment, or merely an empty routine of liturgical traditions.

The Bible teaches that there are both true and false worship and worshipers. Not all worship is acceptable to God. Not all worship *worships* God. Perhaps the worst judgment on this side of heaven is to be under the delusion that you're worshiping God when in reality you're only worshiping a god you created. That ought to cause us to tremble with fear but also to motivate us to proclaim the truth to lost souls. We must get back to, and fight for, God-honoring, Spirit-led worship in our churches. Doctrine matters more than our preferences. The glory of God is the focus, we aren't. God's holiness calls us to worship with reverence and order, not with a casual spirit or one of chaos. We need to go back to worship that is rooted in both Spirit and truth.

The Holy Spirit is with us now, indwelling, guiding, protecting, empowering, purifying, teaching, filling, and leading believers to live a lifestyle of God-honoring worship. Let's consider what that looks like.

## WORSHIP IS LIFESTYLE, NOT A PERFORMANCE

The most important consideration is how we define worship. When the word *worship* comes to mind, do you think about music? If you have been inundated by this generation's tactics, you might think worship includes these elements:

- A really creative backdrop
- Special lighting
- Light fog with a massive screen projecting abstract images
- Camera crews moving swiftly around stage, zooming in on keyboards, drums, and singers
- The latest radio hits
- Moody lighting over the congregation

These elements are fairly common today. After a highly entertaining musical set, you will hear people say things like, "Man!

I just love the worship here." Before planting Shepherd's House a couple of years ago, I visited a church near my house. They needed a new pastor and I thought I would get an idea of their needs. I wanted to plant a church, but a friend suggested I check out this one just in case God opened the door for me to pastor an existing congregation that needed new leadership. I sat in the second row with an open heart and no preconceived notions. I genuinely wanted to experience their worship gathering. Right on cue the band started playing. The room was blacked out except for the massive stage. The lighting scheme was very creative, with something of a scaled-down Coldplay-concert vibe. I know people worship in different creative spaces, so I tried to keep an open mind, but I couldn't get over the cameraman and the music leader's coordinated strategy. Over and over, the cameraman sprinted down the middle aisle and right up to the base of the stage, while the music leader (a male vocalist) timed his approach and stepped toward the camera to look into it like a stage performer. It felt more like a Taylor Swift performance at the Grammy's than the worship of a holy God. The elaborate show continued while people looked on, entertained. The entire experience was heartbreaking because it happened in a place that claims to be about worshiping and honoring the God of all creation. Instead, it felt like we were worshiping a rock band and a charismatic speaker. I tell you this story not to judge that church's final destination but to highlight what is happening too often in today's megachurches. This church is huge, possesses potential for influence, and has had seasons when five thousand people were in attendance. The way they present the worship of God matters because God's holiness matters, and God's people matter.

Worship is a lifestyle. It is not merely music. We must stop thinking of worship as the moment when the band plays and the lights go out. Worship is praying, preaching, singing, serving, giving, receiving, fellowshiping, counseling, baptizing, remembering, loving, and more. We are to live for the glory of God. We are worshipers in every moment of every day. We need to ask what we are worshiping and how we are worshiping. When we see worship as a lifestyle, we are ready to rightly assess the way worshipers engage God and each other when they gather.

For the remainder of this chapter, I want to lay out the marks of Spirit-filled worship so you can use discernment and wisdom in your life and church.

# THE MARKS OF
# SPIRIT-FILLED WORSHIP

## MODELED BY QUALIFIED LEADERS

If you wonder about the state of worship, simply look at the state of our leadership. It has been well said that the preacher is the worship leader. The church needs faithful elders who are bold and courageous proclaimers of truth, and those who stand with conviction on the front lines willing to lay aside Christian liberties and rights if it strengthens and protects the church. God's standard for church leaders is nothing less than fidelity to him above all else.

Today, we find leaders who are fighting and politicking for their preferences, their man-made traditions, and their power positions in their denominations, but are they fighting the good fight of faith? It has been well said and widely understood that everything rises and falls on leadership, meaning that people typically follow leaders' examples. If leaders are not qualified, faithful, and focused on the glory of Christ, the church veers off course. Our worship leaders need to be qualified according to Scripture. They are to be 1 Timothy 3:1–7 men of God who equip the saints for the work of service, raising up men and women to worship God faithfully. Paul clearly lays out the qualifications for church leaders. Imagine if our churches were led by leaders who lived this:

> The saying is trustworthy: If anyone aspires to the office of overseer, he desires a noble task. Therefore an overseer must be above reproach, the husband of one wife, sober-minded, self-controlled, respectable, hospitable, able to teach, not a drunkard, not violent but gentle, not quarrelsome, not a lover of money. He must manage his own household well, with all dignity keeping his children submissive, for if someone does not know how to manage his own household, how will he care for God's church? He must not be a recent convert, or he may become puffed up with conceit and fall into the condemnation of the devil. Moreover, he must be well thought of by outsiders, so that he may not fall into disgrace, into a snare of the devil.
>
> —1 TIMOTHY 3:1–7 ESV

With leaders like that, we'd have a worship revolution. But why do you think Satan attacks leadership positions in the church, seeking to infiltrate us where influence is most powerful? It seems you can be a worship leader or a pastor today by being a social-media influencer, leveraging relationships, playing politics, wearing the right clothes, and giving the culture what it wants rather than what it needs. Is everyone so busy trying to be famous they have no time to be faithful? Theological considerations regarding worship and the qualifications of leadership are viewed as "old school," and doctrine is mocked as just nitpicking.

It's no wonder so many churches are in a spin cycle of confusion. The Spirit of God has not called us to bow to the spirit of the age. The bride of Christ deserves qualified and courageous leaders, and that's what we must be committed to being or supporting. Spirit-filled worship begins with qualified leaders who serve the church like Christ calls them to.

## CONTROLLED BY THE HOLY SPIRIT

Our study in the previous chapter sets us up to put this section of this chapter into practice. Ephesians 5:18–20 reminds us, "And do not get drunk with wine, for that is debauchery, but be filled with the Spirit, addressing one another in psalms and hymns and spiritual songs, singing and making melody to the Lord with your heart, giving thanks always and for everything to God the Father in the name of our Lord Jesus Christ" (ESV). This passage's instructions can apply to worship gatherings and our need for Spirit-filled expressions. Drunkenness represents a lack of self-control, which is one of the fruit the Holy Spirit produces. Paul wants believers to be under the influence only of the Holy Spirit. Pagan worship in Paul's day was out of control. Pagan worship was under demonic influence; it sought its own pleasures. In the Old Testament some pagans sacrificed their babies to Molech (Lev. 18:21), while the prophets of Baal worked themselves into a stupor trying to call down fire from their false gods, cutting themselves and dancing around like lunatics as was their custom (1 Kings 18:28–29). False worship throughout Scripture was always out of control.

This does not mean we cannot express ourselves in worship, but it does mean that Spirit-filled worship will reflect the fruit of the Spirit. Jesus explained to the woman at the well in John 4:24 that there is a right way to worship and it included both spirit and truth. In Luke 19:45 he cleared out the temple because the money changers polluted worship and were out of control. Faithful, God-honoring expressions in worship are byproducts of a life under the control of the Holy Spirit. Galatians 2:20 speaks to believers' surrender to Christ when they are saved. Paul writes, "I have been crucified with Christ. It is no longer I who live, but Christ who lives in me. And the life I now live in the flesh I live by faith in the Son of God, who loved me and gave himself for me" (ESV). If you're a believer, you ought to approach worship with the whole idea of how God calls you to present yourself.

When it comes to expression in worship, I've spoken with Pentecostal pastors who have remarked that too much of what we're seeing in some services today is "soaked in the flesh." I've seen conferences that promote fire tunnels like the ones at Bethel Church in Redding, California (where people make a human tunnel and bounce off of each other's bodies while praying for each other), people shaking and convulsing, roaring like animals, and manifesting more like those possessed by demons than indwelt by the Spirit of the living God. Many people I converse with claim such expressions are the Spirit-filled experience. Some of the responses I have received include "don't put God in a box" and "don't quench the Spirit." But when I call us (myself included) to consider following God's order for worship, I am not putting God in a box or quenching the Spirit but proposing we stay within the boundaries that God himself has set. When we remain Spirit filled *and* orderly in our worship, you can rest assured that the Spirit is not shouting, "I wish you would let me out of this box!" He is pleased as Christ receives glory and the Word is obeyed.

But other noncharismatic expressions are just as disheartening. In some conservative theological circles, you may find unmoved stoicism among those who spend more time analyzing the environment than adoring Christ. They cling insistently to man-made rules and "the way we've done it is the way it always ought to be." They believe that the Holy Spirit is bound to do things the way they prefer. They pay no mind to how different cultures and languages and personalities express themselves. God forbid they should ever find themselves removed from their American church and put in the middle of a church in Africa or India. They don't know how to reconcile that while God's Word does have a standard for worship, various cultures have unique expressions of worship all within that standard. For example, when I was in India, the worship music was so loud we could hear it down the street as we drove toward the church. The instruments they used were unique to their culture, creating sounds localized to their context. They waved their hands, the children danced with joy, they sang songs written locally, and many had never seen an organ let alone had the money to purchase one. Some American theologians' ideas that worship music should be hymns sung by the congregation and that expressions such as handraising are nothing more than charismatic infiltration need to be put to rest. Many cultures express themselves in different ways.

The expression debate can be one of extremes. Some believe that worship isn't worship unless people are slain in the Spirit and rolling on the floor, while others see a hand or two go up or see someone move with joy and think, *Oh, no, we've got a charismatic in the house. It's one of those crazy people here to distract us all.* Both sides of the expression debate need to go back to the Bible. Psalms, hymns, and spiritual songs emanating from transformed lives will produce a variety of expressions that can be Spirit filled. Believers under the control of the Spirit and raising the highest praise to God can be possible in many different traditions.

Believers are those who sing out loud with thunderous praise like Psalm 95:1–2 declares, and who sing to the Lord a new song like Psalm 96:1 exhorts, and who lift their hands to bless the Lord while declaring they live for his name like Psalm 63:3–4 expresses or as a sign of humble surrender like the people did in Nehemiah 8:6 when Ezra opened the Word of God. Wouldn't it be amazing if people responded to the preaching of God's Word this way today? Oh, that the people of God under a new covenant of grace would even lift their hands in response to the declaration of the Word of God as Israel did in those times! Throughout the Bible, people stand, shout, sing, bow, kneel, clap, play an array of instruments, dance, and exalt God. Enjoy the freedom of expressing your love and joy for our God, yet always be determined to stay under the control of our God. Truth must always undergird our worship.

## PRIORITIZES TRUTH IN THE MIDST OF PASSION

Based on the Spirit's ministry of truth, we can rightly say that he does not lead the church into error. In John 16:13 Jesus says, "When the Spirit of truth comes, he will guide you into all truth, for he will not speak on his own authority, but whatever he hears he will speak, and he will declare to you the things that are to come" (ESV). When Jesus said this, he was explaining the Holy Spirit's job to his disciples. The Holy Spirit's coming led to incredible advantages, but notice one of the key statements about the Holy Spirit's work. Does he guide into error? Emotionalism? Rationalism? Not in the slightest. He guides into truth. The same Holy Spirit who led the disciples into truth as their pens flowed with the breath of God and as they worked miracles in his name and proclaimed his message to Jews and gentiles resides in you. You are his temple. Romans 8:14 says, "All who are being led by the Spirit of God, these are the sons and daughters of God." His leading into truth is synonymous with who our God is all throughout the Scriptures. Psalm 25:5 says, "Lead me in Your truth and teach me." Psalm 43:3 declares, "Send out your light and your truth; let them lead me; let them bring me to your holy hill and to your dwelling!" (ESV). Jesus says in John 14:6, "I am the way, and the truth, and the life." On and on the Scriptures point to our God as a God of truth. God leads his people into truth, and he is truth.

Can people get hyped up with passion they believe is of heavenly origin when it's actually earthly manipulation? Of course. Your passions can lie to you. Hitler was passionate. Criminals are passionate. False teachers are passionate. There is no shortage of passion in the church world. But there is nothing wrong with passion in and of itself. Who wants to follow an uninspiring leader? Who wants to worship a God whose followers look half dead? Passion just must be rooted in God's truth.

This is why we need to consider and pray about what we define as worship and the kind of music we think passes for worship. Does it sound passionate? Great! Is it soaked in truth? Don't get sucked into the notion that music is harmless and it's okay if the lyrics are a little off because they're poetic. We can worship with passion, but let's not compromise truth. I heard John Piper once say, "A congregation learns its theology by the songs they sing, not just by the preaching they hear." Passion, no matter how good it sounds or looks, must be rooted in truth.

## FOCUSES ON THE HOLINESS OF GOD

In Scripture one of the most gripping scenes of God's revealing his holiness is found in Isaiah 6:1–4, when the prophet Isaiah sees an incredible vision. "In the year that King Uzziah died I saw the Lord sitting upon a throne, high and lifted up; and the train of his robe filled the temple. Above him stood the seraphim. Each had six wings; with two he covered his face, and with two he covered his feet, and with two he flew. And one called to another and said: 'Holy, holy, holy is the LORD of hosts; the whole earth is full of his glory!'" (ESV).

This vision was part of Isaiah's commissioning from God, his being called as a prophet. We can learn so much from this glimpse. When the Bible gives you a glimpse of God, it's not about you. When we get a revelation from Scripture of who God is, we see his holiness, and that should change the way we approach him in worship. We tremble at his majesty. We are humbled by his glory. He is the God of the universe who is so holy that he gave the seraphim four extra wings so they could cover their eyes and their feet from his explosive glory. Holy, holy, holy. Worship is not about us, it is about God.

When God met Moses on Mount Sinai, he said, "Do not come near; take your sandals off your feet, for the place on which you are standing is holy ground" (Exod. 3:5 ESV). When he met Joshua in Jericho, he told him the same thing (Josh. 5:15). When the Holy Spirit spoke through the pen of Peter to the church scattered throughout Rome, he commanded them to be "holy for I am holy" (1 Peter 1:16).

Do you focus on God's holiness in your worship? Are your prayers marked by adoration even more than by supplication? Oftentimes our songs are a reflection of our hearts. Do the lyrics point to us? Is God a means to our end? How many repeated choruses are about us, how we feel, what we want, what we need, going on and on about ourselves? What God can do for you is wonderful, and the fact that he has made you his beloved child is marvelous, but it's even more wondrous who he is. We often overlook God's holiness in our worship and replace it with ourselves. Let's commit to getting over ourselves and more into him.

## INVOLVES CONFESSION AND ADMITS TO BEING A SINNER

In his vision, Isaiah continues, "And the foundations of the thresholds shook at the voice of him who called, and the house was filled with smoke. And I said: 'Woe is me! For I am lost; for I am a man of unclean lips, and I dwell in the midst of a people of unclean lips; for my eyes have seen the King, the LORD of hosts!'" (Isa. 6:4–7 ESV).

Notice how a revelation of God's holiness ignites a humble response in Isaiah. He suddenly understands the holiness of God and it causes him to see how sinful he is. He quickly and humbly declares he is unworthy before a holy God. Everything gets put in perspective. This is the foundation of all worship. I see who God is, and in light of who I was and what he has done I cannot help but praise him. Spirit-filled worship erupts from a humble heart that realizes God is fine without us, we are not fine without him. God is holy without us, we can never be without him. God was glorified without us, we can never be without him. Spirit-filled worship causes us to realize who we are in light of who God is, which leads to us revel in his glory and goodness. If we are not being led to a place of clarity on the gospel, sin, redemption, and God's work on our behalf through Christ, we need to double check what we're singing about.

David's perspective is helpful because he was such a great example of worship, yet he was sinful and human—many would even say that he was known for sinning worse than you and I ever have:

> Create in me a clean heart, O God,
>     and renew a right spirit within me.
> Cast me not away from your presence,
>     and take not your Holy Spirit from me.
> Restore to me the joy of your salvation,
>     and uphold me with a willing spirit.
>
> Then I will teach transgressors your ways,
>     and sinners will return to you.
> Deliver me from bloodguiltiness, O God,
>     O God of my salvation,
>     and my tongue will sing aloud of your
>         righteousness.
> O Lord, open my lips,
>     and my mouth will declare your praise.
> For you will not delight in sacrifice, or I would
>         give it;
>     you will not be pleased with a burnt offering.
> The sacrifices of God are a broken spirit;
>     a broken and contrite heart, O God, you will
>         not despise.
>                                    —PSALM 51:10–17 ESV

Do you focus on the grace of God, having never confessed your sin to him? Do you treat music like entertainment, to make you feel good, or do you use it to praise God? Have you had your moment of trembling before the Lord yet? Has your life been changed by an understanding of how a holy and perfect God could be a loving, personal, and gracious Father to you?

I forget who said it to me once, but I was told, "You will spill out what you're filled with." Are a high view of God and the right view of man coming out of you? Is your worship saturated with the marks of Spirit-filled worship? When you consider your lifestyle, church services, personal time with the Lord, and view on worship, does it reflect faithfulness, truth, passion, a high view of God and the right view of sin, the gospel, and God's glory?

## DECLARES THE GLORY OF CHRIST

One line in the Holy Spirit's job description in John 16:14 could summarize this entire book and all of what worship should be: Jesus said of the Spirit, "He will glorify Me."

The Holy Spirit didn't come to put the spotlight on us, he came to put the spotlight on Christ. That is where all Spirit-filled worship begins and ends. The Spirit is fully God, equally God, and working in our lives with God. One of his roles while the redemptive plan of God is unfolding and more lost sheep are being saved is to bring glory to the Son, Jesus. He takes the minds, hearts, and attention of believers and shifts all of the focus onto Christ. Even as I write this book I am consistently praying, *Holy Spirit, help me to faithfully honor your ministry of glorifying Jesus, because I know that even you don't want attention on yourself.* That may seem odd to pray, but it's exactly what Scripture teaches. So when charismatic services go on for hours, repeating phrases again and again, calling down the Spirit, calling down fire, chasing signs and wonders, and focusing on manifestations, putting little attention on Jesus, they have missed the point of worship.

Spirit-filled worship honors the Spirit by making much of Jesus Christ.

# LEARNING TO LIVE

## 1. Recognize Worship as a Lifestyle, Not Merely Music at Your Church or on the Radio

I'll never forget when I was first taught that worship is a lifestyle. My relegation of worship to Sunday singing and car rides with my Spotify playlist pumping was only a small part of the whole picture. For the believer, all of life is worship. What are you compartmentalizing? Are there areas of your life that you think belong to you and God isn't privy to? Do you think some things are just yours to enjoy and that terms like *Spirit-filled* and *worship* are more of a church experience you'll try to make it to on Sunday? Commit to seeing worship as a lifestyle. It will change the way you worship and live.

## 2. Require a Biblically High Standard for Anyone Leading Ministry at Your Church

Church leaders who get away with spiritual abuse and misleading the body can do so for two reasons. First, they manipulate and deceive people. Second, people's standards are not biblical. Leaders in many circles today prefer terms such as *influencer, relevant, cool, appealing, talented, innovative, creative, visionary, builder,* and on and on. What if we put less stock in those terms and more in the terms in 1 Timothy 3:1–7? What if people rose up biblically to remove leaders from powerful positions who are not leading us in worship the right way? Don't cower in fear. Step out in faith.

## 3. Remember That the Glory of God Is the Highest Goal of Worship

If someone comes up to me and says, "Wow! I just love your sermons. You are so funny!" I am deeply disappointed. If someone leaves church and says, "The music is so cool!" We have failed. What do you say about gatherings for worship in the church? How do you lead worship in your home? Where is your focus when you worship God through your life? If you are the star of your own show, it's time to reroute the glory to where it belongs.

## Questions for Reflection

1. Worship is a sensitive topic for people and churches. Are there certain truths or examples in this chapter that convict, encourage, or challenge you?

2. In your own words, write a biblical definition of worship.

3. Read Isaiah 6:1–7. What should our response be to the holiness of God?

4. Do you think we need to be careful of extremes when it comes to expression in our worship? Some insist that raising your hands is little more than charismatic manipulation, while others insist that if you don't manifest expressively in a church service, you haven't experienced the Spirit. How might you live in biblical balance?

5. Are there specific things you should talk about with a church leader when it comes to worship conduct at your church, without being unbiblically opinionated or rude? If a church leader is abusive and domineering, how might your approach be different than if a church leader were to kindly disagree with you on some aspects of this chapter?

## 7

# WHAT ARE THE GIFTS OF THE SPIRIT?

*There are different kinds of gifts, but the same Spirit*
*distributes them. There are different kinds of service, but the*
*same Lord. There are different kinds of working, but in*
*all of them and in everyone it is the same God at work.*
—1 CORINTHIANS 12:4–6 NIV

IMAGINE A WEDDING. PICTURE THE BRIDE AND THE groom enjoying each other during the ceremony, the photoshoot, or the reception. What is the groom's focus supposed to be on? His bride, of course. What is the bride's focus supposed to be on? The groom, of course. Now a commotion erupts that pulls the bride and groom apart. It's the wedding party. They are arguing about something at the wrong time and in the wrong way. The groom urges the bride to stay focused on themselves, to enjoy the moment and allow others to handle the commotion. But the bride is a hothead, and she leaves the groom to engage in the argument without knowing what's going on. All she knows is that she has an opinion too and it's time to let everyone know it. The conflict intensifies, and soon the groom sits at their table alone while the bride's combative attitude and love for quarrelling are on full display. The only thing worse than her ill-timed temper is her ignorance of the matter at hand.

My feeble attempt at a parable is a picture of how the church looks on this important subject of the gifts of the Holy Spirit. We are supposed to be focused on the Lord, and we ought to give proper attention to having a proper understanding of the Spirit, but we get pulled away by heated arguments about the gifts of the Spirit without ever having given attention to the work of the Spirit. As a result, we make ignorant statements, expose our love for quarrels, and armed with little more than what we learned once in a YouTube video, enter the ring for the battle royale.

Let's slow down and understand the gifts biblically. Then let's expect reasonable applications of those gifts to be based on the gifts' biblical definitions and purposes. It's vital to study the Scriptures and come to conclusions faithfully.

Paul begins one of the major chapters on spiritual gifts with words that ought to ring in our ears every time this subject comes up: "Now about the gifts of the Spirit, brothers and sisters, I do not want you to be uninformed" (1 Cor. 12:1 NIV). Let's be informed.

## EXTREMES, OPINIONS, AND HUMAN TENDENCIES

There is perhaps no more hotly debated subject in Christendom today than the gifts of the Holy Spirit. The reason for hot debate centers on which gifts have ceased and which are active. Debate and differences in doctrinal beliefs are normal for Christians when it comes to matters outside of the gospel, but I believe it's not only the "what" but the "how" that stirs much of the animosity that often arises during these discussions. Adding fuel to the fire is today's culture of Twitter wars and some people's inclination to think that because they watched a teaching or sermon on YouTube, they're experts on the subject. Many of us would be lying if we said we haven't been guilty of this to some degree.

That being said, many abuses and deceptions regarding the gifts of the Spirit go well beyond debate between Christians who are unified on the essentials of the gospel. I am passionate about this subject because of the years I spent growing up witnessing abuses of the prosperity gospel and charismatic extremism. Having seen every kind of parlor trick and excessive claim you can imagine, I came to a point where I simply wanted Scripture to define my view on the gifts of the Spirit.

Some of the extremes that rightfully deserve critique derive from the extreme emotionalism and exaggerated claims often found in prosperity-gospel movements. The leaders of these ministries strategically do and say things that work their followers into a spiritual frenzy. A family member who leads a worldwide ministry once claimed to me that he possessed "all nine gifts of the Spirit" and could operate in them at any time. Others were not as anointed or as gifted, according to his theological view on the gifts. I was in my late teens or early twenties at the time, and I hadn't studied the topic but just took his word for it because he seemed to be a supernaturally gifted and powerful man of God. Years later, after studying the Bible, it was clear to me that while there are some debatable ideas regarding the gifts of the Spirit, the belief that someone can possess all nine is neither founded on Scripture nor touted by even the most passionate charismatic today.

In addition to unbiblical teaching about the gifts, wild claims about dreams and visions tend to dominate the headlines of certain ministries and draw people who are enamored by such power as well as well-intentioned people who want to encounter God in meaningful ways. These ministries rightfully draw criticism for their antics, no matter how well-intentioned they may seem. People get hurt when leaders are not prudent in their teaching. James 3:1 is a sobering reminder that not many should become teachers lest they incur a stricter judgment. God takes leadership seriously, and any leader who teaches anything that steers people into chaos will find themselves answering to God almighty, no matter how noble their intentions. Irresponsible teaching has led to many unbiblical practices in the charismatic movement, and many of the criticisms that are leveled against those practices are merited.

Conversely, I have seen the dangers of extreme rationalism. In an effort to avoid the extremes and abuses of the charismatic movement, some Christian teachers will explain away every aspect of the supernatural at work in our lives and in our worship. For example, when rationalism takes over the prayer meeting or pulpit, you may hear a teacher squelch prayers for healing or dismiss any claim that God moves in power through prayer. When rationalism takes over the worship service, you may also hear some teachers dismiss all emotion, feelings, and passion within Christian ministry as merely "charismatic emotionalism" or fleshly expression. While I understand the need for order in a worship service and that Paul prioritizes order in his instructions in 1 Corinthians 14, to squelch any form of passionate expression is out of balance with Scripture. When it comes to these subjects, we ought to let Scripture speak and not our man-made rules and preferences.

If there is one goal of this chapter, it is that we let Scripture speak definitively on the nature of the gifts before making statements about what we believe to be the Spirit's normative pattern. Let's start with understanding the biblical definitions of the gifts so we can appreciate the revealed Word of God for all that it says. Only then will we be as accurate and faithful as we can possibly be. No one can claim to have perfect knowledge on all of these matters except in what Scripture reveals. In God's Word we have perfect revelation, so we ought to hold that as the unmovable standard, then be gracious in our differences over how to apply the Word to our lives.

## WHAT EXACTLY IS A SPIRITUAL GIFT?

Here's a basic definition of the gifts of the Spirit in my own words: spiritual gifts are undeserved special abilities that the Holy Spirit gives to all believers for the purpose of building up the church.

I formulated this definition with specific words used in Scripture to describe spiritual gifts. In 1 Corinthians 12:4 Paul says, "There are different kinds of gifts, but the same Spirit" (NIV). The word he uses for "gifts" is the Greek word *charisma*, which literally translates as "grace gift." The Greek word for "grace" is *charis*, which means "unmerited favor," so we know that spiritual gifts are undeserved gifts of grace from the Spirit. In 1 Corinthians 12:1 Paul uses the word *pneumatikos* for "spiritual gifts,"[1] which contains the word *pneuma* (the word for "spirit" or "spiritual"). We get more understanding of what spiritual gifts are when Paul continues in 1 Corinthians 12:7, saying, "But to each one is given the manifestation of the Spirit for the common good,"

---

1. Frederick William Danker, ed., *A Greek-English Lexicon of the New Testament and Other Early Christian Literature*, 3rd ed. (Chicago: Univ. of Chicago Press, 2000), 837.

which tells us that every believer is given a spiritual gift, and they manifest or put on display the work of the Spirit for the common good of the church.

## WHAT IS THE PURPOSE OF THE GIFTS OF THE SPIRIT?

If spiritual gifts are grace gifts, undeserved, given by God for the common good, it's safe to say that spiritual gifts involve you but are not about you. We're given much of what we need to understand the purpose of spiritual gifts in the first seven verses of 1 Corinthians 12:

> Now concerning spiritual gifts, brothers and sisters, I do not want you to be unaware. You know that when you were pagans, you were led astray to the mute idols, however you were led. Therefore I make known to you that no one speaking by the Spirit of God says, "Jesus is accursed"; and no one can say, "Jesus is Lord," except by the Holy Spirit.
>
> Now there are varieties of gifts, but the same Spirit. And there are varieties of ministries, and the same Lord. There are varieties of effects, but the same God who works all things in all persons. But to each one is given the manifestation of the Spirit for the common good.
>
> —1 CORINTHIANS 12:1–7

From this passage we can gather at least four key truths about the purpose of spiritual gifts and why they are so important.

1. *They are used by God to lead the church into truth.* Paul begins by demonstrating that not all spiritual experiences are rooted in the Holy Spirit when he says that he does not want the

Corinthians to be uniformed. They need to use discernment regarding their spiritual experiences. Pagans have spiritual experiences as well, but the Corinthians are to reject them since the pagans are led by idols.[2] The Corinthians used to be deceived and engaged in pagan worship. To put it lightly, they were a little wild back in their unsaved days. When Paul brings up the Corinthians' past pagan beliefs, he is in the middle of a long letter of correction. The Corinthians had been causing confusion with their use of the gifts of the Spirit, yet they were supposed to be leaving their former ways behind. He says they once "were led astray to the mute idols" (v. 2) perhaps to highlight the way they were ignorant and gullible before, but he says they now needed to be wise and discerning, specifically regarding the gifts and how they served each other in worship. This is on the heels of his correcting their sexual immorality (1 Corinthians 5), reminding them that they are the temple of the Holy Spirit (6:19–20), and several other corrections, including their abuse of communion (11:17–34). They were notorious for their misuse of spiritual gifts, which is why Paul had to explain the gifts so extensively in chapters 12–14. No other group of Christians in the entire New Testament got this kind of attention on spiritual gifts. In light of this background information within the letter, it's safe to say that spiritual gifts are to be used to lead people into truth and not into the confusion that some in Corinth were causing with their misuse of the gifts.

2. *They give everyone in the body of Christ a special part to play.* There are "varieties of gifts" and "varieties of ministries" (12:4–5) and "to each one is given" (v. 7). These verses show

---

2. Thomas R. Schreiner, *1 Corinthians: An Introduction and Commentary*, Tyndale New Testament Commentaries (Downers Grove, IL: InterVarsity Press, 2018), 253.

us that God spreads out his gifts. God doesn't give only a select group of people spiritual gifts and call everyone else to be spectators. He is a God of variety in the way he beautifully designed creation, and he is a God of variety in the way he gifted his body, the church. Spiritual gifts are given so everyone has a purpose. Every body part is meant to be used by God.

3. *They foster unity in the Spirit.* No matter what our giftedness is, we all receive our gifts from the "same Spirit" (12:4) and we have the "same Lord" (v. 5), and "the same God" is working all things in all of us (v. 6). Evidently some in Corinth were spiritually arrogant, boasting in their gifts as though they didn't need others or looking down on those who had different gifts than they did. Verses 20–21 remind them, and us, that "as it is, there are many parts, but one body. The eye cannot say to the hand, 'I don't need you!' And the head cannot say to the feet, 'I don't need you!'" (NIV). Plain and simple: we need each other. Spiritual gifts foster unity and get the whole body working together. That is a major part of their purpose.

4. *They are for the common good.* Spiritual gifts are for the "manifestation of the Spirit for the common good" (12:7). That phrase "common good" literally translates "to bring together." The Spirit works through the gifts to bring the body together into one purpose and build it up. We are to use our gifts to minister to others in the church and help each other.

5. *They are given only to believers.* Nowhere in Scripture are unbelievers addressed with regard to spiritual gifts. Furthermore, one must be baptized with the Holy Spirit into the body of Christ to be considered a part of the body of Christ (as we saw in the last chapter), which means faith in Christ precedes being given a spiritual gift to function in the body of Christ.

If we take this list to heart, it is obvious that gifts are for glory, but not our own. Gifts bring glory to God as people serve, give, help, preach, teach, love, and care for others. The purpose of spiritual gifts is Philippians 2:3–5 in action: "Do nothing from selfishness or empty conceit, but with humility consider one another as more important than yourselves; do not *merely* look out for your own personal interests, but also for the interests of others. Have this attitude in yourselves which was also in Christ Jesus."

The body of Christ is called to imitate Christ. We do that best when we use our spiritual gifts for the purpose they were intended for.

## WHAT ARE THE GIFTS OF THE SPIRIT IN SCRIPTURE?

Gifts are mentioned in Scripture in several places, but not all of the lists of gifts in Scripture are the same and others are repeated. For example, 1 Corinthians 12:7–10, 13:1–3, and 13:8–9 all have some similarities (Paul lists eight gifts) because Paul is addressing the Corinthians and mentioning the gifts in multiple places. In other places, such as Romans 12:6–8, he mentions seven. In Ephesians 4:11 he gives a list not mentioned anywhere else, and then Peter (1 Peter 4:10–11) breaks all of the gifts up into just two: speaking gifts and serving gifts. Last, some believe that the gift of singleness (or celibacy) that Paul speaks about in 1 Corinthians 7 is a gift, though it is not considered to be widely given throughout the body of Christ. All of these variances tells us that God has given us a general framework for categorizing gifts, but that the way each person is gifted may vary. Thomas Schreiner, in his helpful book *Spiritual Gifts: What They Are and Why They Matter*, shows the variations in how the gifts are listed in at least four different places in the New Testament. (See table 7.1.) If you're looking for an easy-to-understand book about the spiritual gifts, I highly recommend you read his book. I find this table to be especially helpful for understanding the categories of the gifts.

## Table 7.1: Spiritual Gifts in the New Testament

| Romans 12:6–8 | 1 Corinthians 12:7–10 | 1 Corinthians 12:28 | Ephesians 4:11 |
|---|---|---|---|
| *Having gifts that differ according to the grace given to us* | *To each is given the manifestation of the Spirit for the common good* | *And God has appointed in the church* | *And he gave* |
| | | Apostles | Apostles |
| Prophecy | Prophecy | Prophets | Prophets |
| | | | Evangelists |
| | Ability to distinguish between spirits | | |
| Teaching | Word of wisdom and word of knowledge | Teachers | Pastors and teachers |
| Exhorting | | | |
| | Working of miracles | Miracles | |
| | Gifts of healing | Gifts of healing | |
| Service | | Helping | |

| Romans 12:6–8 | 1 Corinthians 12:7–10 | 1 Corinthians 12:28 | Ephesians 4:11 |
|---|---|---|---|
| Leading | | Administration | |
| | Various kinds of tongues | Various kinds of tongues | |
| | Interpretation of tongues | | |
| Giving | | | |
| | Faith | | |
| Mercy | | | |

Source: Thomas R. Schreiner, Spiritual Gifts: What They Are and Why They Matter (Nashville: Broadman and Holman, 2018), 18.

Some theologians and commentators differ on the number of gifts they list because they merge gifts like "word of knowledge" and "teaching" or "pastor" and "teaching," and they may differ on how they define certain gifts, but the following definitions can give us a foundational understanding of these gifts.

## 1. TEACHING

The gift of teaching is the God-given ability to explain and interpret Scripture clearly and accurately. This ability is unique because it is about not merely transferring basic information but instructing, feeding, and guiding the flock in understanding and applying the Word of God. Someone could possess a Harvard degree in theology but not be able to make the Scriptures clear, while someone could have no theological degree but excel in teaching because they are gifted. Charles Spurgeon was one such example. Though he had no formal degree, he was called "the Prince of Preachers." Some theologians include "word of wisdom" and "word of knowledge" in the gift of teaching because Paul mentions teaching in every list except in 1 Corinthians 12:8–10. There he uses "word of wisdom" and "word of knowledge"[3] to describe what teaching is. Whatever the case, teaching provides knowledge from the revealed Word of God and builds up the body in truth. When the gift of teaching is operating in someone's life, people who hear them will experience understanding and clarity under that ministry. It's important that pastors possess this gift because they regularly teach God's Word. Not everyone who has the gift of teaching is a pastor, but every pastor should have the gift of teaching.

## 2. EXHORTATION

The gift of exhortation is the God-given ability to encourage people to do good deeds and to take godly action. It is considered to be a practical gift because people who have it excel at telling you what to do based on God's truth. Someone with this gift may comfort, correct, counsel, plead, urge, and call people to obedience to Christ in a variety of formats, including preaching, counseling, one-on-one discipleship, Sunday school, small groups, and casual settings. Exhortation has also been translated "encourage" in the NIV because of its close relation. People who have been exhorted by a gifted individual typically feel a sense of purpose and clarity about what to do in light of the truth they were taught.

## 3. FAITH

The gift of faith is the God-given ability to trust the Lord in all details of his work, even when the outcome seems uncertain. This gift produces stellar assurance that God will accomplish all his purposes.[4] This gift has nothing to do with the gift of salvation

---

3. Ibid., 19.

4. John MacArthur and Richard Mayhue, eds., *Biblical Doctrine: A Systematic Summary of Bible Truth* (Wheaton, IL: Crossway, 2017), 385.

(as in believing by faith in Jesus) but has everything to do with confidently moving forward in belief that God will work powerfully in any situation. I saw this gift on display this past year when we planted Shepherd's House Bible Church. A year before our first Sunday gathering, a number of people asked our planting team big questions that required big faith, including, "How in the world will you pay for the church plant? Where will people even come from? Where will you find the resources you need? Only a few of you have ever been a part of a church plant, and you were very young; are you sure you know what you're doing? How will it even work?" Our team was stacked with people who have the gift of faith. Their response was, "We don't know, but we are going to keep our hands to the plow and trust the Lord to do what only he can do." In January 2022 the Lord had gathered approximately 150 people from all over the Phoenix, Arizona, valley. We had made phone calls, put the word out, and told people that this venture was not for the faint of heart. On February 20, 2022, we launched, and within six months there were almost six hundred people gathering every week, we had more than thirty baptisms, new believers were getting saved, people were sharing the gospel with their neighbors, Bible studies were launching at car dealerships and homes all over the valley, and God's Word was working in hungry hearts. Our team never boasted in anything they did. If you ask them, they will tell you that they felt like the Lord was going to do something great whether there were six people or six hundred. We prepared as best as we could, but we felt certain that God was going to handle the details and make it all happen. He did. People with the gift of faith often are criticized as living in denial, not being realistic, and dreaming too big. The truth is that people with the gift of faith don't deny facts and are very aware of the realities but smile with confidence in God because the bigger the mountain, the more glory he receives when human fears, doubts, worries, and wisdom are put to shame by his great power.

## 4. LEADING (ADMINISTRATION)

The gift of leadership is the God-given ability to lead, organize, and mobilize the other gifts in the body of Christ. People with this gift rally believers toward the will of God, since that is what the Spirit desires to bring about in the lives of believers. The church is a body that must accomplish its mission, and the Spirit uses people with this gift to move that mission forward. One of the great needs of churches is godly and visionary leadership, so this gift plays a key role in getting the church on track and keeping it there.[5] When this gift is operating in the church, the church executes its mission effectively. People who have this gift often excel at team building, launching new ministries, delegating to others, and galvanizing people. Churches that have pastors and leaders who excel in this gift are often well organized and well protected. Like a family with a strong, loving, and courageous father who has a plan for their future, they experience the joy, security, and clarity that come from being well led (Eph. 4:14).

## 5. HELPING (SERVING)

The gift of helping is the God-given ability to enthusiastically and joyfully do whatever is needed to serve and help others and is often accompanied by a submissive heart. While everyone struggles at times to sacrifice for the needs of others, those with the gift of helping rarely linger in those feelings for long. They eagerly say yes to opportunities to serve. Though this gift is not limited to deacons, it is one of the essential qualities of a deacon (1 Tim. 3:8–11). People with the gift of helping see it as a privilege to serve and assist others. Everyone is commanded to serve others (1 Peter 4:7–11), but those gifted with helping embrace this role and thrive in it over the long term.

5. Thomas R. Schreiner, *Spiritual Gifts: What They Are and Why They Matter* (Nashville: Broadman and Holman, 2018), 24.

## 6. MERCY

The gift of mercy is the God-given ability to understand, care for, and empathize with people who are hurting. We should all be thankful this gift exists in the body of Christ because we need merciful people. As with the gift of helping (serving), all believers are called to be merciful and bear one another's burdens (Gal. 6:2), but people with the gift of mercy take the initiative to help and they excel at this ministry. Where others have to work hard to have empathy or be patient with hurting people, those with the gift of mercy exude compassion with ease and know how to walk alongside people going through difficult seasons. The gift of mercy may also manifest as gentleness with people who are struggling with sin. Again, we are all commanded to be gentle with those who are repentant (Gal. 6:1), but merciful people have an enduring patience and love that in Spirit-empowered ways bears, believes, and hopes all things (1 Cor. 13:7).

## 7. GIVING (GENEROSITY)

The gift of giving is the God-given ability to dedicate resources such as wealth and possessions to assist others and fuel gospel work with eager joy. Giving is an essential part of the Christian life, but those gifted with giving can't get enough of it. I remember meeting with a generous individual who was supporting a ministry project and I said, "Thank you so much for your generosity," to which the response came, "No, thank *you* for the opportunity." That is the way a person with the gift of giving responds.

Another time I was sitting with a couple of friends who have an incredible gospel perspective. When I wanted to know how they feel when people ask them for money to support ministry work, the wife asked me, "Do you get uncomfortable when people ask you to preach the Word?"

I said, "No."

She responded, "Because you are gifted for it, correct?"

I nodded.

"Well," she continued, "giving is one of our primary roles and contribution to the body of Christ. We don't possess many other gifts, but we know this is our role. It's a joy to be needed and useful in whatever way the Lord would have us be. In our case, God blessed us financially, and we know that comes with a responsibility to give generously to ministries."

You don't have to be wealthy to have the gift of giving, but God doesn't give a gift without granting the means to use it. If you continue to give generously and God keeps giving you more, it's not the prosperity gospel that's making you rich, it's God trusting you with the gift of generosity to keep on funding his kingdom work. You are blessed to be a blessing for his purposes. It's a gift for his glory.

## 8. HEALING

The gift of healing is the God-given ability to heal the sick immediately regardless of disease or injury, the level of faith of the person being prayed for, or even the proximity between the healer and the person being healed. For example, Jesus healed the centurion's servant with just a word, having never gone to where the sick servant was (Matt. 8:8–13). In a supernatural display, the sick were being healed by handkerchiefs that the Bible says had "merely touched" Paul's skin (Acts 19:12). Throughout the New Testament, people who have this gift display a consistent ability to heal the sick on command. Since this gift is sovereignly given by the Spirit and he is the power source, there is no denying its authenticity. Immediate, undeniable, supernatural healings are the telltale sign of this gift. The genuine gift of healing as defined in the Bible looks completely different from today's faith healers parading themselves across stages and using music and manipulation to hype up a crowd of desperately sick people. If someone claims to have this gift, they would be able to verifiably heal people anywhere, including in hospitals, just like someone with the gift of evangelism can see conversions on a street corner or in a church setting. Many of today's "practitioners" claim to heal minor aches and pains like back spasms and a ringing in the ears, or to perform the infamous "leg lengthening" trick.[6] Whereas in the Bible the gift of healing addressed incurable disabilities and diseases such as leprosy (2 Kings 5:9–14), uncontrollable bleeding (Matt. 9:20–22), total blindness (John 9:1–12), and the inability to walk (Acts 3:1–10). Just seconds after Peter said to the lame man in Acts 3, "I have no silver and gold, but what I do have I give to you. In the name of Jesus Christ of Nazareth, rise up and walk!" (v. 6 ESV), the man began walking and leaping and praising God.

## 9. MIRACLES

The gift of miracles is the God-given ability to perform powerful works that through divine intervention defy the laws of nature. When Moses parted the Red Sea, water changed shape and location, and then stayed that way for the people of Israel to cross (Exodus 14). When Elijah made an axe head float (2 Kings 6:2–7), that was outside the laws of nature. It was a miracle when Lazarus was raised from the dead (John 11:1–44). And it was unnatural when Philip was teleported (Acts 8:38–40). Yes, that is in the Bible! Luke records this event: "And [Philip] gave orders to stop the chariot. Then both Philip and the eunuch went down into the water and Philip baptized him. When they came up out of the water, the Spirit of the Lord suddenly took Philip away, and the eunuch did not see him again, but went on his way rejoicing. Philip, however, appeared at Azotus and traveled about, preaching the gospel in all the towns until he reached Caesarea" (NIV). Now that is a miracle!

Such miraculous power is clearly outside anything a person can do without divine intervention and authority. If someone claims to

---

6. American Gospel, "Leg Lengthening—American Gospel: Christ Alone," YouTube, February 15, 2019, www.youtube.com/watch?v=dD7YtCTkdPc.

have the gift of miracles today, they would need to be consistently making limbs to grow, causing medically verified barren women to conceive, raising the dead, stopping storms, commanding water to come from rocks, or calling down rain or fire from heaven. Miracles always defy the laws of nature and cause onlookers to be awestruck.

## 10. TONGUES

The gift of tongues is the God-given ability to speak in a foreign language you have never learned. This gift was effective in the early church (it never appeared in the Old Testament) especially for exalting God (Acts 10:46), prophesying and revealing mysteries (1 Cor. 14:2), edifying the church through interpretation (1 Cor. 14:4–5), and spreading the gospel to people groups who had never heard it before by evangelists who needed to be able to speak their language or dialect (like on the day of Pentecost). Tongues also served as a sign to the Jews who did not believe (1 Cor. 14:21–22). Tongues are quite obviously human languages in the book of Acts where Luke records the various languages that were being spoken: "When they heard this sound, a crowd came together in bewilderment, because each one heard their own language being spoken. Utterly amazed, they asked: 'Aren't all these who are speaking Galileans? Then how is it that each of us hears them in our native language? Parthians, Medes and Elamites; residents of Mesopotamia, Judea and Cappadocia, Pontus and Asia, Phrygia and Pamphylia, Egypt and the parts of Libya near Cyrene; visitors from Rome (both Jews and converts to Judaism); Cretans and Arabs—we hear them declaring the wonders of God in our own tongues!'" (Acts 2:6–11 NIV).

More than a dozen languages and dialects were spoken and heard at Pentecost. In 1 Corinthians 12–14, Paul explains the gift of tongues, along with certain rules for using it because the Corinthians were out of control. Based on what he teaches them, tongues in a service or gathering are to be used in order, and there can only be "two or at most three, and each in turn, and let someone interpret. But if there is no one to interpret, let each of them keep silent in church and speak to himself and to God" (14:27–28 ESV). Some use 1 Corinthians 14:2 as an argument for tongues not only being known languages but also being ecstatic utterances (as many charismatics practice today). Paul writes, "For one who speaks in a tongue speaks not to men but to God; for no one understands him, but he utters mysteries in the Spirit" (ESV). But I do not find the arguments for this very convincing since the mysteries can simply be defined as that which was never known before, much like prophesying, not to mention that Paul's overall point is to explain how prophecy is more helpful for the Corinthians than tongues anyway, because it can actually be understood (v. 3). Some people will use their experiences to argue for tongues as ecstatic utterance. I used to do the same thing when I spoke in tongues and believed that it was a repetitious, ecstatic phrase I would say over and over.

Experience is subjective, whereas Scripture can give us objective clarity. Besides the fact that Luke lists the languages and dialects spoken on the day of Pentecost, there are several key reasons that the tongues at Pentecost and the tongues in 1 Corinthians 12–14 are referring to known languages and not ecstatic utterances. First, Paul never disconnects the gift of tongues from interpretation (1 Cor. 12:10; 14:26, 28). So even if someone were to say they were speaking in ecstatic utterance to God, those tongues would have to be interpreted into a clear, intelligible message in line with the purpose of the gift. Second, when Paul describes the gift of tongues as "kinds of tongues" and "varieties of tongues" (1 Cor. 12:28), he uses the Greek word *gene*, which can refer to a family, offspring, race, nation, kind, sort, or class.[7] Dr. Robert Gromacki, Distinguished Professor Emeritus of Bible and Greek, who taught at Cedarville

---

7. Robert Gromacki, *The Holy Spirit: Who He Is, What He Does* (Nashville: Word, 1999), 230.

University for more than forty years, explains this scholarly point in such a simple way: "[*Gene*] always depicts things that are related to each other. For example, there are many 'kinds' of fish, but they are all fish (Matt. 13:47). There are many 'kinds' of demons, but they are still demons (Matt. 17:21). There are many 'kinds' of languages and tongues in the world, but they are all known languages. Paul could not have possibly combined known foreign languages with unknown ecstatic utterances under the same classification. They are simply not related."[8]

In summary, the gift of tongues was for the purpose of communicating truth from God (prophesying), communicating truth about God (praising), communicating the gospel (proclaiming), and as a sign to the Jews (proving). Regardless of your position on whether tongues are active today, one must accept certain truths that Scripture declares.

First, tongues had a specific purpose in the Scriptures and were not required for salvation. It's 100 percent false to teach that someone must speak in tongues to be considered baptized in the Holy Spirit and saved. Nowhere does Scripture teach this, and as we've covered in this section and in the previous chapter, Scripture teaches the opposite. In 1 Corinthians 12:30 Paul makes it clear that not all will speak in tongues.

Second, there must be order in our services. The mass crowds in charismatic services and churches who speak in tongues through ecstatic utterances must submit to 1 Corinthians 14:27–28 and cease from abusing what they claim to be the gift. Only two or three may speak, and only in turn and with interpretation. Anything outside of this disobeys God's Word, even if one believes the ecstatic utterance is the gift of tongues.

Third, if tongues are uninterpreted or merely a private prayer language without interpretation and engaging the mind as some

---

8. Ibid.

claim, this is "unfruitful" according to 1 Corinthians 14:14 and should not be divorced from the standard Paul sets:

> Therefore let one who speaks in a tongue pray that he may inter-
> pret. For if I pray in a tongue, my spirit prays, but my mind is
> unfruitful. What is the outcome, then? I will pray with the spirit
> and I will pray with the mind also; I will sing with the spirit and
> I will sing with the mind also. Otherwise if you bless in the spirit
> only, how will the one who fills the place of the ungifted say the
> "Amen" at your giving of thanks, since he does not know what
> you are saying? For you are giving thanks well enough, but the
> other person is not edified. I thank God, I speak in tongues more
> than you all; however, in the church I desire to speak five words
> with my mind so that I may instruct others also, rather than ten
> thousand words in a tongue.
>
> —1 CORINTHIANS 14:13–19 (NASB 1995)

The Corinthians are told to sing and pray with clarity, and even Paul would rather use fewer words and make sense ("with the mind") than to speak ten thousand words in a tongue. Paul's point is about clarity. Tongues is a sensitive and personal subject for some people, but we all do well to surrender even our strongest opinions to Scripture. (See appendix 1, "Common Questions about Tongues, Quenching, Grieving, and Blaspheming the Holy Spirit," for more on tongues.)

## 11. INTERPRETATION OF TONGUES

The gift of interpretation is the God-given ability to interpret what is being spoken by someone with the gift of tongues. The interpreter requires this gift from the Holy Spirit because they don't know the language being spoken. This is different from hearing someone speak your own language. Then you would be just a normal translator like we use today in many different countries.

An example of the gift of interpretation would be if an American who never spoke Chinese began to proclaim the gospel in Chinese through the gift of tongues and a Persian who did not speak Chinese began to interpret the Chinese language being spoken by the American. Supernatural! To say the least.

## 12. DISTINGUISHING BETWEEN SPIRITS (DISCERNMENT)

The gift of distinguishing between spirits is the God-given ability to discern true revelation from false revelation, and true teachers from false. The early Christians relied on this spiritual gift because of the fragility of the infant church and the devil's constant attacks through subtle deception. In 2 Corinthians 11:13–15 Paul explains the threat that the Corinthian church was facing when he writes, "For such men are false apostles, deceitful workers, disguising themselves as apostles of Christ. No wonder, for even Satan disguises himself as an angel of light. Therefore it is not surprising if his servants also disguise themselves as servants of righteousness." Today, some people believe the gift of discernment is the supernatural ability to see what is happening in the supernatural realm (as in the activities of angels and demons), while others maintain this gift was unique to the apostles and prophets in the foundational era of the church as they discerned genuine revelation from God and false prophets posing as God's servants. Regardless of one's view of this gift, every Christian can test all things by the Word of God and should be able to distinguish between true and false teachers because we have "the prophetic word made more sure" (2 Peter 1:19–21) and can test everything against God's revelation in Scripture (1 Thess. 5:20–21; 1 John 4:1).

## 13. PROPHECY

The gift of prophecy is the God-given ability (*and* office of prophet: 1 Cor. 12:28; Eph. 4:11) to communicate to people direct revelation from God. Like some gifts, such as miracles, prophecy and prophets also appear throughout the Old Testament, and prophets were expected to be 100 percent accurate in their prophetic words, lest they be labeled as false prophets. In the New Testament, prophets were held to the same standard, though falsely prophesying did not lead to death as it did in the Old Testament (Deut. 18:15–22). Contrary to many who claim to be prophetic today, New Testament prophecy was not a loose "word from the Lord" about something you felt. It was a definitive revelation from the Lord and was totally accurate. I have heard far too many self-proclaimed prophets stand on stages or at the altar and tell people things like this: "I feel like God told me that there is something going on in your life that is very difficult, and I am here to tell you that a breakthrough is coming." This is not prophecy. Prophecy is specific, providing details and instructions that come directly from God. When I was younger I had numerous prophetic words spoken over me that were wildly inaccurate but sounded amazing at the time. One man who claimed to be a prophet spoke as though he were speaking the words of God, saying, "I, the Lord, declare over you, Costi, that you will take over your father's church in Vancouver, Canada, and take it to heights never seen before." He was weeping uncontrollably while several others laid their hands on me. In another event, a well-known person whom at the time I'd held to be equally as prophetic prophesied that I was next in line for what was often called the "anointed mantle" of my uncle Benny Hinn. This person prophesied over me that I would have a global healing ministry and see miracles beyond anything he'd ever seen. I have been prayed over and prophesied over by countless men and women, including Oral Roberts, Paul Crouch (founder of Trinity Broadcasting Network), Benny Hinn, Kim Clement, and a host of others, yet no one ever mentioned in their prophecies my becoming a pastor in Phoenix, Arizona, or gave even the slightest hint about desert sand. I write this with no animosity toward them but only a desire to see people walk in truth. One of the more recent wake-up calls and falling out of the modern prophetic movement was regarding Donald Trump's reelection attempt. Countless charismatics were prophesying that he would get a second term, and when he didn't, some claimed it was because the election was stolen, while others apologized for being wrong.[9] In the midst of the debates over what had happened, people failed to see that any prophet who fit the biblical standard would have been able to foresee the entire situation and the conflict that arose because of it. Biblical prophets were able to hit the bull's-eye every time. They did not miss once. Prophecy was a miracle, not a human attempt to share something encouraging. God directly spoke revelation to someone who then declared that information to their audience. When a prophet heard from God, there was no doubt it was God. Prophecy was not human words or wisdom, it was divine. Therefore, a false prophet is someone who claims to hear from the Lord but speaks inaccurately on behalf of the Lord. "Fallible" prophecy has become popularized in today's world because so many people are starting online ministries and claiming to be prophets. Furthermore, schools like the Bethel Supernatural School of Ministry in Redding, California, offer training for people to become prophets. There is no need to train to be a prophet or learn how to use your prophetic gift, if you have it, because prophecy, according to Scripture, is simple: God speaks directly to someone with undeniable clarity and power, then the prophet declares the undeniable truth that God revealed with pinpoint accuracy and calls God's people to heed the word of the Lord. The true prophet is never wrong, never misses, and never sees a prophecy not come to pass. To falsely prophecy is not akin to bumping someone's car door when you open yours, or spilling a bit of your coffee while walking down a stairwell. To miss on just one prophecy is to be a false prophet.

9. Julia Duin, "The Christian Prophets Who Say Trump Is Coming Again," *Politico*, February 18, 2021, www.politico.com/news/magazine/2021/02/18/how-christian-prophets -give-credence-to-trumps-election-fantasies-469598.

## 14. APOSTLESHIP

The gift of apostleship is the God-given ability and office (1 Cor. 12:28; Eph. 4:11) of men who were commissioned by Christ or by the apostles themselves, as was the case with Matthias (Acts 1:21–23). There is some debate whether Barnabas was an apostle, but there is general agreement that Titus and Timothy were apostolic delegates and not apostles based on the way Paul repeatedly gives them instructions to help him organize and mobilize the churches he had started, while never leaving them there permanently or speaking to them like fellow apostles. For example, Paul calls Timothy "my true child in the faith" (1 Tim. 1:2 ESV) and left him at Ephesus to set some things straight (1 Tim. 1:3). Paul also calls Titus a true child in the faith and left him on Crete to do as he instructed (Titus 1:4–5). Titus was also eager to help in Corinth (2 Cor. 8:16–18). Neither of these men fit the New Testament description of the apostles.

The Greek word for apostle is *apostolos* and can describe a messenger or a commissioned ambassador. In one sense, many church planters and missionaries today are apostolic, but we see the gifting of apostleship in the truest sense in the twelve apostles of Christ and in Paul, who was later commissioned by Christ through a supernatural visitation (Acts 9). The ministry of the apostles was authenticated by signs and wonders (Acts 5:12), and Paul tells the Corinthians that "the signs of a true apostle were performed among you" (2 Cor. 12:12), making it clear that there were true and false apostles and that one could tell the difference.

## 15. EVANGELISM

The gift of evangelism is the God-given ability to boldly, clearly, and effectively deliver the gospel to unbelievers. If you've ever known people in the church who seem to have a special ability to make the gospel clear and conversions seem to erupt from their ministry efforts, that is what an evangelist looks like operating in their gifting. As with some of the gifts, all believers are commanded to make disciples and live out the Great Commission (Matt. 28:16–20), but the evangelist has a special enablement by the Spirit for the work of delivering the gospel. Missionaries often have this gift along with the courage and unction to use it in stressful circumstances, even during imprisonment and persecution.

## 16. PASTORING

The gift of pastoring is the God-given gift of shepherding. To pastor is to feed, lead, teach, care for, protect, correct, and nurture God's flock. In Ephesians 4:11 the gifts of pastor and teacher are listed sequentially, and there is good evidence in the grammatical construction that links them to form the gift of pastor-teacher. This is why many churches have men who excel as the primary teaching pastor, though all of the other pastors and elders should be able to teach (1 Tim. 3:2). All church leaders are required to rightly handle God's Word, but some are especially gifted to both preach and teach.

At least three major questions on the gifts of the Spirit need to be addressed now. First, how do you get them? Second, how do you know what your spiritual gift is? And third, have some gifts ceased because they were for specific purposes in the past or do all the gifts still operate today just like they did in the early church?

The next chapter will answer those questions and more.

# LEARNING TO LIVE

### 1. Define the Gifts the Way the Bible Does

The most important question is, What does God say about this? Christians may disagree on aspects of the gifts, but it's vital we define the gifts according to Scripture. If someone says they can teach, we would expect them to teach the Bible with clarity and accuracy. All who sit under their teaching would say, "The Scriptures make sense when you explain them." In like manner, if someone says they can heal, they must operate in that gift regularly, unequivocally, and normatively. They should be visiting hospitals and going room to room healing incurable diseases, then leading people in mass salvations as they are awestruck by the one true God.

### 2. Be Respectful of Those You Disagree With

Refrain from pettiness in your passion for your position. We can have strong convictions or believe we are right without being ugly about it. Most of those you disagree with will be your neighbors in heaven for eternity, unless they are false teachers or believe in a false gospel. In-house debates are just that, in-house—meaning we are family. Let's keep that in mind. There is nothing wrong with choosing a new church to fellowship with and be a member of because you have unity on issues you find important, but be careful to speak well and tastefully even about those you disagree with.

### 3. Be Unashamed and Unafraid of Defending What the Bible Says

When it comes to those who make truth relative and make a mockery of spiritual gifts, do not be ashamed or afraid to defend biblical truth. Even though Paul considered the Corinthians his family in Christ, he rebuked them for their abuses of the gifts and unrepentant sin. That is what drives the entire letter of 1 Corinthians. You are not helping anyone by shoving truth under the rug to avoid uncomfortable conversations. Speak the truth in love (Eph. 4:15). God's Word is worth defending, and it is loving to challenge lies with his truth for the good of his people and his glory.

## Questions for Reflection

1. Does the number of spiritual gifts or the definition of certain gifts surprise you? Why or why not?
2. How would you summarize the purpose of spiritual gifts?
3. What would you say to someone who believes they have a spiritual gift but show no evidence of operating in that gift?
4. Have you ever had a disagreement with someone regarding spiritual gifts? How did you maintain respect and a charitable spirit in the midst of disagreement?
5. Name a situation in which you may speak more strongly to someone, even rebuking them, in a disagreement on spiritual gifts.

# HOW DO YOU OPERATE IN THE GIFTS OF THE SPIRIT?

*Each of you should use whatever gift you have*
*received to serve others, as faithful stewards*
*of God's grace in its various forms.*
—1 PETER 4:10 NIV

A BOY WHO LOVED FOOTBALL DECIDED TO TRY OUT for his high school football team. He looked forward to tryouts, hoping to find a place in the sport he had grown so fond of.

The boy's father, on the other hand, nervously loathed tryouts. He wasn't sure his son would even make it through them, let alone make the team. The father was a former athlete, and he saw his son as more of a bookworm and a math nerd. The boy wasn't exactly a fine physical specimen. He lacked size and strength. He did not have the aggressiveness to give and take hits. The father could not think of one respectable position that his son could compete for.

Tryouts came. Each day the boy went to the football field and returned after the day's drills. The father could not believe his son was making it through.

Finally the day came when the results from the tryouts were to be released. The father nervously waited for his son to get home.

The boy excitedly burst into the house and shouted, "I made it! I got a spot on the team!"

The father asked him what in the world kind of position did they think he was a good fit for?

The boy said, "You're looking at the official statistician for the varsity football team!"

The father tried to hide his disappointment.

The boy explained. "By the second day the coaches knew I wasn't physically ready to play on the field, but they saw my love for the game and how well I understood it, so they said I was a perfect fit for analyzing the data on the field and providing them with reports all season long. I'll be giving them play-by-play analyses and scouting reports, setting up film sessions to watch certain players, organizing position-by-position data from previous games, and more. I will travel with the team and serve the coaches and the players all season long!"

It took some time, but eventually the father realized what all loving fathers do. His son had found his place, was using his gift, and was full of joy as he pursued what he loved. It wasn't about position, it was about fulfilling a purpose.

Too many Christians treat the body of Christ like a cutthroat dad who thinks any position but starting quarterback is a disappointment. We look at the preacher, teacher, singer, artist, influencer, galvanizer, and even just the physically attractive person as the honorable parts of the body. We look at the merciful counselors and the meek servants who clean the church, mix the sound, administer the finances, organize spreadsheets, and coordinate the visitation and meals for sick and needy families as the B team and not really very important.

When it comes to spiritual gifts we need to remember these words above all else:

> The eye cannot say to the hand, "I don't need you!" And the head cannot say to the feet, "I don't need you!" On the contrary, those parts of the body that seem to be weaker are indispensable, and the parts that we think are less honorable we treat with special honor. And the parts that are unpresentable are treated with special modesty, while our presentable parts need no special treatment. But God has put the body together, giving greater honor to the parts that lacked it, so that there should be no division in the body, but that its parts should have equal concern for each other. If one part suffers, every part suffers with it; if one part is honored, every part rejoices with it.
>
> —1 CORINTHIANS 12:21–26 NIV

What if we approached our view and use of the gifts with that section of 1 Corinthians 12 in mind? What if in all of our oohing and aahing over the more noticeable parts of the body of Christ we recognized that all the parts have significance and should be celebrated? I know that pushes against our human response. Our human nature, which we still possess on this side of heaven, wants to glorify what we see as the greater and more powerful gifts. Pastors, perhaps above all else, need to teach themselves and people not to think of the gifts in such a way. As Paul Washer put it at a conference I attended in 2021, "There is no such thing as a great man of God, only weak, pitiful, faithless men of a great and merciful God." I was so deeply convicted as he preached about Christ that night. I walked away with a deep stirring in my heart to think of my role in the body of Christ in a renewed way. We are not that impressive. God is. He does great things not because of us but in spite of us.

That is the attitude we must approach this chapter with.

# HOW DO YOU GET THE GIFTS OF THE SPIRIT?

Three passages give us insight into how the gifts of the Spirit are given to believers and should humbly remind us of God's sovereignty, no matter how gifted we might be. These examples from Scripture put to rest any notion that a man or woman can get the gifts through any other means. A large number of ministries and teachers around the world teach what is called "the impartation of the gifts" because they believe you can have a certain spiritual gift imparted to you by the laying on of hands. They take the biblical occurrence of the laying on of hands to unbiblical lengths with this teaching.

## NOTHING YOU HAVE IS YOURS (1 COR. 4:7)

To the exceptionally gifted and spiritually arrogant Corinthians, Paul writes, "For who makes you different from anyone else? What do you have that you did not receive? And if you did receive it, why do you boast as you though you did not?" (1 Cor. 4:7 NIV). Like all human beings, the Corinthians struggled with spiritual pride because they had all sorts of supernatural gifts in the church, including healing, tongues, interpretation of tongues, and prophecy. Paul's reminder to them is really a reprimand that we all would do well to receive. We cannot ever take credit for our spiritual gifts, we did not earn our spiritual gifts, and anything great we do is only because our great God chose to use us for his glory, not ours. Nothing we have is really ours. Gifts are from him, for the good of the church and for his glory.

## THE SPIRIT GIVES GIFTS AS HE WILLS
## (1 COR. 12:7–11)

Spiritual gifts are given according to the will of God, not the will of man. This is so important for us to know and remember. Envy is a constant temptation because we might look at others and think, *Why am I not gifted like him or her?* We also might go a step farther and think, *God must not love me as much because he did not gift me like him or her.* These thoughts are not from the Spirit of God but are lies and doubts coming from the kingdom of darkness. Satan is the "father of lies" (John 8:44), and one way he breeds division is by pitting us against each other. Where jealousy and selfish ambition are, you will find "every evil thing" (James 3:16). In 1 Corinthians 12:7–11 Paul explains that each believer is given a different gift and that "all these are the work of one and the same Spirit, and he distributes them to each one, just as he determines" (v. 11 NIV). It is plain to see that the Spirit determines how the gifts are given according to his sovereign will.

## GOD ARRANGES THE BODY OF CHRIST AS
## HE WANTS (1 COR. 12:18, 28)

The final passages that will give you great peace and confidence regarding how the gifts are given are 1 Corinthians 12:18, where Paul writes, "But in fact God has placed the parts in the body, every one of them, just as he wanted them to be" (NIV), and verse 28, where Paul begins his explanation of certain gifts by saying, "And God has placed in the church . . ." (NIV). We do not need to compete with others in the body of Christ because God never made it a competition. He decreed diversity and wants the body to have different parts functioning in different ways. Like the human body, we as the body of Christ function in the healthiest way when we each embrace our own gifting but also celebrate the giftings of others.

# HOW DO YOU KNOW YOUR
# SPIRITUAL GIFT?

One of the most common questions I receive as a pastor is, How do I know what my spiritual gift is? My answer is always just to begin serving in your church. Why? All Christians should serve and be willing to do anything that's needed because that's the example we are given by Christ. Above all else we should have a heart to serve. No follower of Christ is above any menial task. At the same time, discovering your spiritual gift is important because I believe the Scriptures give us permission to place people in roles that align with their giftedness. For example, in Acts 6:1–7 the early church had to begin identifying gifted leaders and servants to keep up with the growing needs of the church. Giftedness and specific tasks had to be prioritized. This is the difference between churches that function with excellence and those that seem a little short on organization and clarity.

Here are a few ways to identify your spiritual gifting:

*1. Pray for the Spirit to open doors and make it clear.* Why wouldn't we go to the source of the gifts for guidance? I am not saying that if you pray, the Spirit will appear to you visibly and speak to you audibly, but I guarantee that if you pray in accordance with his will that you will see him open doors, provide opportunities, and bring your gift to light. I do believe the most important question you should ask after praying is, Has God already provided me with a church to serve, opportunities to connect in the body, and loving leaders who will guide and disciple me? If he has, you should stop praying for the Spirit to open doors and lead you into opportunities to know your gifting. He already has. It's time to obey.

*2. When you begin to serve, your God-given abilities will manifest.* If someone has leadership or administrative gifts, they tend to start pushing the pace, asking "why do we do this?" a lot and inspiring others with their zeal. Misplaced zeal can cause problems if not discipled, of course, even if you have a particular spiritual gift, so this is another reason to serve. When we serve, our gifts come out and wiser believers and leaders can direct and correct us. Eventually, in the Spirit's timing, we find ourselves thriving in Christian service and spending much of our time in the area of our giftings.

*3. Get confirmation from qualified and mature Christian leaders.* Early on in my conversion I wasn't exactly sure what my spiritual gifts were. After about a year of serving in my church, I had a hunch that my spiritual giftedness involved some aspect of leadership, teaching, and exhortation because as I served, I tended to galvanize people, build teams, teach, and encourage people forward in our mission. Before even two years had gone by, I felt I was ready to plant a church since it *seemed* that I was gifted to lead people.

Boy, was I was in for a lesson in humility, training, and submission. God graciously taught me that before you can receive authority to lead, you must learn how to submit to authority and to follow. Self-appointed rogue leaders are ministry implosions waiting to happen. Thankfully, the Lord put men in my life who at that time sat me down, slowed me down, and simmered me down. None of their wisdom or counsel was meant to squash my desire for ministry. Rather, they wanted to shape me and allow my gifts to grow and deepen. More than anything, they expressed a desire to see me walk in God's will, not merely according to my own way.

Our desires, no matter how noble, need to be assessed. Our motives, no matter how pure we think them to be, need accountability and examination. No matter our gifts or desires, finding our spiritual gifts and thriving in them includes receiving confirmation, affirmation, and guidance from qualified and mature Christians.

What do I mean by qualified? Whenever possible, I recommend speaking with your elders who have the character qualifications described in 1 Timothy 3:1–7 and Titus 1:5–9. Women who match the description given in Titus 2:3–5 or Proverbs 31 are excellent sources of guidance. Don't avoid accountability because of fear that others will slow you down. People who love you and want God's best for you will want to help you, not hurt you. They want to launch you, not limit you.

## WHAT ABOUT THOSE WHO AREN'T ACCOUNTABLE TO A CHURCH?

I would like to offer a word of encouragement and caution that can help you use wisdom and discernment in a world where online ministries and traveling apologists thrive. Based on everything we have gathered from Scripture thus far, do you believe it's wise for an online influencer or author or apologist to use their spiritual gifts to operate ministries while being personally disconnected from a church? Anyone serving any ministry should stay connected to a body where they can be supported, sharpened, encouraged, *and* held accountable.

The heartbreaking example of Ravi Zacharias comes to mind. He was knowledgeable and celebrated and seemed to be a stalwart ministry leader. His influence spanned denominational and religious lines, and he sat with the likes of Albert Mohler and R. C. Sproul. Celebrities and influencers were so greatly impacted by his ministry that when he died, the popular hashtag #ThankYouRavi was posted by people like Tim Tebow, Lecrae, Louis Giglio, and countless others. As a successful traveling apologist operating a global ministry, he seemed to have all the right pieces in place. He had a board of directors for the nonprofit Ravi Zacharias International Ministries (RZIM) and was ordained by his denomination at the Christian and Missionary Alliance, and from the outside everything appeared to be in order.

Only after his death did the global scandal of his sexual exploits come out, and it suddenly became more newsworthy to ask, Was

Ravi a part of a church where qualified elders could speak into his life and ask hard questions? Did he submit to anyone, or was he the unchallenged front man for a global ministry? There was no denying the facts and eventually his denomination revoked his ordination[1] and RZIM released a statement confirming that the worst was true.[2]

I bring up this illustration because it hit so close to home for me. When I was in the prosperity gospel, we would travel constantly and attend church sparingly, if at all. When challenged, we made a number of excuses, such as:

- I am the church; I don't need to go to church.
- We are so famous that if we go, people will just bother us.
- We just spent a week on the road ministering to the church; we don't need to go.
- We give people church globally; it's not necessary for us to always go to a church locally.
- I can't sit under some pastor who isn't as anointed, because he'll kill my faith.

These statements and ways of thinking are one of the main reasons we end up with evangelists, pastors, teachers, apologists, influencers, and communicators making headlines for their lack of accountability. It is because we were never meant to be rogue in our ministry endeavors, without church leaders keeping us accountable. Based on 1 Corinthians 12 and Ephesians 4, and following Paul's

---

1. Daniel Silliman, "Ravi Zacharias's Denomination Revokes Ordination," Christianity Today, February 19, 2021, www.christianitytoday.com/news/2021/february/ravi -zacharias-cma-investigation-revoke-ordination.html.

2. International Board of Directors, RZIM, "Open Letter from the International Board of Directors of RZIM on the Investigation of Ravi Zacharias," accessed 2022, https:// rzim.org/read/rzim-updates/board-statement.html. This document can be found here: https://context-cdn.washingtonpost.com/notes/prod/default/documents/2719acf9-859e -43e4-8ccc-cbae5222cd97/note/5ff473a3-44c7-4f68-98d5-ed715ec38129.

example of taking time to learn, grow, and get affirmation from the other disciples (Acts 9:19–30), we can humbly admit that no matter how gifted we think we are, no one is above accountability. The Holy Spirit doesn't just give you a spiritual gift, he also baptizes you into the body of Christ to use that gift and be accountable for how you use it.

Be cautious concerning any ministry or influencer who is asking for your monetary support and ministry loyalty yet does not belong to a church or have an accountability system in place. More than that, be very careful of anyone who is "ministering" at a large and public level, yet is a new convert. No matter who it is or how famous they are for what they used to do (athlete, rapper, actor, etc.), ministry is not a worldly enterprise where your social status gets you a fast track. Use your gifts wisely and expect a high standard of faithfulness from the ministries you support.

## ARE ALL THE GIFTS THE SAME AS THEY WERE IN THE BIBLE?

A lot of well-respected theologians and Bible-minded Christians disagree on whether all of the gifts are the same now as they were in the Bible. Some will say yes. Others will say that most of them are, but that certain gifts were foundational but not permanent gifts. They say that the Spirit sovereignly gave these gifts to authenticate the apostles as those who had been with Christ and their revelation as being directly from Christ, so that the church can build on their foundation. On the spectrum of this debate, from "continuationist" (all the gifts continue) to "cessationist" (some gifts cease), there are claims and extremes of all kinds. Adherents of certain movements claim they can raise the dead and that they talk with Jesus personally all the time, and adherents of others claim that God does not do any miracles and does not heal people at all today.

As with most theological debates, extremes add to the fog. My prayer is that even if we don't agree on this issue, this section of the book will help bring clarity. There are five prominent views on the gifts of the Spirit that we need to understand. Entire books have been written on this one aspect of the Spirit's work, but I am attempting to explain it in only one chapter. It's likely that more questions will arise after reading this chapter, so I have added extra content in the appendix for those who want to dig deeper. I've done my best to represent each view with fairness and charity.

## VIEW 1: THIRD WAVE CHARISMATIC AND NEW APOSTOLIC REFORMATION[3]

The view of the Third Wave charismatic movement and the New Apostolic Reformation is that there are apostles and prophets today who are a continuation of the original apostles and prophets in the Bible. These leaders believe that they can not only do signs and wonders like raise the dead and command prosperity to come into your life but also impart gifts to others. This movement reaches back to some fringe characters like William Branham, whose followers kept his body from burial for months, believing he would rise from the dead.[4]

As the era of famous televangelists' ministries, like those of Oral Roberts, Aimee Semple McPherson, Kathryn Kuhlman, Kenneth Hagin, Kenneth Copeland, and my uncle Benny Hinn, took some of the charismatic excesses global, the belief spread that the apostolic era was restarting. Up to that point, most of the more extreme

---

3. Several years ago I coauthored with Anthony Wood a book titled *Defining Deception: Freeing the Church from the Mystical-Miracle Movement* (El Cajon, CA: Southern California Seminary Press, 2018). In this book we address numerous claims from teachers named in this section, present the history, theology, and extensive false teachings of the New Apostolic Reformation and the roots of the Third Wave. It is not possible to treat this issue in its entirety in this book, but *Defining Deception* provides a much deeper study along with sections on well-known false teachers and a plethora of quotes from their teachings.

4. Douglas C. Weaver, *The Healer-Prophet: William Marrion Branham (A Study of the Prophetic in American Pentecostalism)* (Macon, GA: Mercer Univ. Press, 2000), 104.

charismatic movements were categorized as the Third Wave and linked to figures like the late John Wimber (Vineyard Church) and John Arnott (leader of the "Toronto Blessing"). To be fair, some of my friends who are sympathetic to some aspects of Wimber's ministry would argue that if he were alive today, he would call out many of the charismatic excesses. While this may be true, the offshoot of extremes can still be addressed here. The Third Wave movement was often seen manifesting wildly in church services with people having convulsions, crawling on the floor, barking like dogs, weeping uncontrollably, and speaking in tongues through ecstatic utterances, and with very little discernment. This movement has accepted and platformed physically abusive false teachers like Todd Bentley (who has been banned from the UK)[5] and was responsible for the #WakeUpOlive incident in which a family who lost their little girl held services to raise her from the dead at Bethel Church in Redding, California. They claimed that Jesus had paid for her healing, so they commanded her to rise from the dead. The story was so widely known that every major news outlet covered it.[6] The Third Wave brand of beliefs and the New Apostolic Reformation may be well intentioned on a case-by-case basis, and there is nothing wrong with parents asking God to raise their sweet little girl from the dead, but this represents a consistent pattern in the movement.

The troubling element of this view is that adherents teach they can demand healing and that Jesus somehow guarantees that they can perform these signs and wonders at any time. They also often run education centers like the Bethel Supernatural School of Ministry, charging tuition to teach people how to either get or use the gifts of the Spirit. In addition, they offer guidance on how

---

5. Lizzy Davies, "Revivalist Preacher Todd Bentley Refused Entry to UK," *The Guardian*, August 21, 2012, www.theguardian.com/world/2012/aug/21/todd-bentley -refused-entry-to-uk.

6. Marisa Lati, "After a Toddler's Death, a Church Has Tried for Days to Resurrect Her—with Prayer," December 19, 2019, www.washingtonpost.com/religion/2019/12/19 /after-toddlers-death-church-has-tried-days-resurrect-her-with-prayer/.

churches can start their own supernatural schools, so the movement continues to grow rapidly across the globe. Having grown up in this movement, I would surmise that it is the most misleading and dangerous because it takes the gifts of the Spirit far beyond what Scripture teaches.

When I was young, both my father and my uncle founded their own Signs and Wonders School of Ministry in the nineties and sold material promising to impart the anointing of God into people's lives. Countless people signed up, paid tuition, and attended classes that promised they would become just like their heroes in the faith. Today, this movement has still failed to put forth a leader who regularly heals people, raises the dead, and controls the weather, though many claim to have these powers. There is no leader who regularly prophesies with 100 percent accuracy (like Isaiah, Jeremiah, Ezekiel, Daniel, etc.), performs miracles like teleporting (Philip), heals on command (Peter), parts waters (Moses), calls fire down from heaven (Elijah), shakes off snakebites (Paul), or turns water into wine (Jesus). This goes against everything we've studied thus far. The Spirit is sovereign in giving the gifts.

## VIEW 2: TRADITIONAL PENTECOSTAL

Traditional Pentecostalism holds that all of the gifts of the Spirit are fully operating today and that speaking in tongues can also include ecstatic utterance and teaches that the baptism of the Holy Spirit is a twofold experience in which one is first brought into the body of Christ and subsequently experiences the second baptism of the Holy Spirit through speaking in tongues. Traditional Pentecostalism also places a high emphasis on evangelism, typically combining gospel preaching with experiential prayer meetings and altar calls where people can receive spiritual gifts such as tongues.

A primary example of this view is the Assemblies of God denomination, which has an estimated 65 million people in it. They have long been the tip of the spear for the Pentecostal and charismatic movements, and both my father and my uncle were ordained Assemblies of God pastors for years. There are still excesses in the movement, but it also must be said that Assemblies of God churches are autonomous, and I have spoken with many who have differed with me on certain aspects of the gifts of the Spirit but have insisted we do not differ on much beyond that. I have lost count of how many Assemblies of God pastors have said to me, "For years I have sounded the alarm on the same excesses that you have, and I believe your uncle is a false teacher and dangerous to our movement." This is one reason why I am cautious when making blanket statements about Pentecostals and charismatics. Many of them would agree with my concerns, many of them repudiate the prosperity gospel, and many of them distance themselves from the New Apostolic Reformation, while disagreeing with other views on speaking in tongues.

Teachers in the Pentecostal movement can be known for going too far and teaching that one must speak in tongues as evidence of baptism in the Holy Spirit and to experience the fullness of the Spirit. I speak with dozens of people each year who share stories about being told as a young person in a Pentecostal church that they had to speak in tongues as evidence of having the fullness of the Spirit or even as evidence of salvation. Just recently I was talking to a friend who is still in the Assemblies of God. He shared that when he was growing up, his pastor frequently tried to force him to speak in tongues lest he not be saved or not have the Holy Spirit. He is kind and respectful to fellow Pentecostals, but he no longer holds the belief that one must speak in tongues as evidence of the baptism of the Spirit.

For a fuller treatment on the Assemblies of God and the New Apostolic Reformation (NAR), I highly recommend the work of writer Holly Pivec.[7]

---

7. Holly Pivec, "The Assemblies of God and the NAR," blog post, May 21, 2013, www.hollypivec.com/blog/2013/06/the-assemblies-of-god-and-the-nar/3246. Holly has written extensively on this topic on her blog at https://www.hollypivec.com.

## VIEW 3: OPEN-BUT-CAUTIOUS CONTINUATIONIST AND REFORMED CHARISMATIC

The view of open-but-cautious continuationists and Reformed charismatics is exactly what the names describe. These continuationists are open to supernatural gifts such as healing, miracles, tongues, interpretation of tongues, and prophecy being normative today, and they seek them out, but outside of their pneumatology (doctrine of the Holy Spirit), they are mostly Reformed in their soteriology (doctrine of salvation). Some (perhaps with the best of intentions) will try to operate in the sign gifts without knowing for sure whether they have them. Leaders and teachers who hold this view typically are reliable in their gospel preaching, are known for their faithful teaching ministries, and are not known for many excesses. When the debate about the gifts surfaces, some people raise concerns that this view leaves the door open too wide for charismatic behaviors without biblical backing, while the open-but-cautious warn against suppressing the work of the Spirit.

An exemplar of the open-but-cautious view is John Piper. For years he has prayed for tongues and prophecy, and advocated for people to operate in those gifts, while also being honest that he has never received them.[8] As open-but-cautious continuationists, his church generally looked similar to the church pastored by John MacArthur, who is a well-known cessationist. Both men's churches sing hymns, are conservative theologically, preach the Word verse-by-verse, emphasize the holiness and glory of God, and model faithful Christianity. Other notable theologians and pastors who hold this view are Wayne Grudem, D. A. Carson, and the leaders of Sovereign Grace Music, which is headed up by Bob Kauflin. It is important to note that Sovereign Grace Music headlines Reformed conferences like G3, which is staunchly cessationist, and that Bob

---

8. Desiring God, "What Is Speaking in Tongues?" YouTube, January 30, 2013, www.youtube.com/watch?v=jzipsG3-S6A&t=241s.

Kauflin headlines the music at the Shepherd's Conference, where John MacArthur pastors Grace Community Church, exemplifying the way brothers and sisters can dwell together in unity while still holding their respective lines on the gifts of the Spirit.

Even still, I would like to say there are times I believe that the open-but-cautious view does leave the door a little too open. This can lead to confusion and a lack of discernment. With the best of intentions, perhaps, some who hold this position will mix with those in the NAR, or friends whom I love may argue that my uncle or another divergent preacher has been wrong at times but is still in the faith and has been used by God mightily. I believe that such openness may seem like gracious prudence, but in my opinion it leaves the door open for too much acceptance of false teaching and not drawing clear enough lines.

I do not fear the open-but-cautious viewpoint for its desire for miraculous gifts. By all means, pray for them if you'd like. Should someone suddenly heal like Peter could, raise the dead or genuinely speak in tongues like Paul did—with interpretation—I will cheer that on and give glory to God. What concerns me is when the open-but-cautious view does not offer clarity when it ought to. This is why we are now seeing more teachers willing to partner with churches and ministries like Bethel Church (Redding, CA) and other movements that teach unbiblical theological views. It seems that once the door is open, they have a difficult time closing it, even when Scripture does.

## VIEW 4: CLASSIC-AND-NUANCED CESSATIONIST

The view of classic-and-nuanced cessationists is that God still heals and can do miracles anytime he pleases, but that the gifts of healing, miracles, tongues, interpretation of tongues, prophecy, and apostleship were given by the Spirit specifically to authenticate the message of the apostles and establish a strong foundation for the church (Eph. 2:20). Therefore, the adherents of this view believe that the gifts that enabled the New Testament leaders to perform signs and wonders at will have ceased to be normative. This means that you can pray for healing, ask God to do miracles, and embrace God's supernatural action wholeheartedly but not look around your church for a specialized healer to rid your body of cancer. This view seeks the Lord in sickness or weakness and accepts God's will in the prayer of faith (2 Cor. 12:7–10; James 5:14–16), while rejecting the notion that anyone can wield these gifts the way the apostles did.

The classic cessationist defines miracles in a literal way. Whereas some people call everything good that happens to them a miracle, cessationists look at the eras throughout biblical history in which miracles were prevalent and conclude that miracles were special occurrences to accomplish God's purposes through special servants like Moses, Elijah, Elisha, Daniel, Jesus, and the apostles. Church history is a go-to source for most cessationists after they have mined the Scriptures. In all of church history there is no record of a leader who went about doing verified miraculous works as the normative pattern of his or her life. The cessationist view sees this as clear evidence for the foundational role of the apostles and prophets and for the unique purpose of genuine miracles.

Even so, the most respected cessationists are wise to clarify that a sovereign God can do as he pleases (Ps. 115:3). Thomas Schreiner is once again so helpful here when he writes about healings, miracles, and God's working powerfully in people's lives:

> I tend to think these gifts [miracles and healings] don't exist today. If a person has a gift of healing, it seems there would be a pattern of healing. And the healings should be on the same level that we see in the New Testament: healing of the blind, of those who are unable to walk, of those who are deaf, and of those who are near death. Claims to healing are quite often subjective: colds, the flu, stomach and back ailments, sports injuries, etc.

Now, I am not denying that God may heal in such instances, and we thank God for it! The issue is that it is often difficult to prove that a miracle has truly taken place. It isn't clear to me that particular people have a *gift* of healing or miracles. This certainly does not mean there aren't miracles today! God can still heal and do miracles according to his will, and he does! Cessationism doesn't mean there are no miracles in the present age, nor does it mean we don't pray for healings or miracles. I pray for them regularly. But charismatics must show that miracles are really happening to the same extent today as in the New Testament, and that there are people who have the gifts of healing and miracles. . . . Is this truly the regular and normative feature in the lives of our churches? I think not.[9]

Notable modern-day cessationists include Thomas Schreiner, John MacArthur, Paul Washer, R. C. Sproul, Michael Horton, Justin Peters, Voddie Baucham, Charles Swindoll, Norman Geisler, and Al Mohler. Historically speaking, notable church fathers and leaders who held this view include Augustine, John Chrysostom, John Calvin, Martin Luther and the rest of the Reformers, John Owen, George Whitefield, Charles Spurgeon, and Jonathan Edwards.

## VIEW 5: FULL CESSATIONIST

Full cessationists typically believe everything that classical-and-nuanced cessationists believe but take it one step farther by saying both that the supernatural gifts have ceased and that God has ceased from working miracles in this age. Notable theologians who held this position include B. B. Warfield and Francis Nigel Lee.

---

9. Thomas R. Schreiner, *Spiritual Gifts: What They Are and Why They Matter* (Nashville: Broadman and Holman, 2018), 164.

# MY VIEW OF CESSATIONISM VERSUS CONTINUATIONISM

My convictions on the cessationist versus continuationist debate derive from what I have presented in the previous chapter and in this one:

1. *I believe the office of apostle and the gift of apostleship have served their purpose to establish the church and are no longer operating.* There are no more apostles. The apostles were the foundation of the body of Christ, which continues to grow as a holy temple. We are living stones being built upon the foundational work of the apostles and prophets and ultimately rest on the cornerstone of Christ (Eph. 2:20–22; 1 Peter 2:5).

2. *I believe the office of prophet and the gift of prophecy have served their purpose as foundational for the church and are no longer operating.* The prophets declared divine revelation to the church for its edification and direction. They delivered Scripture to the saints and preserved the Scriptures by the sovereign power of God. We have no need for a new word from the Lord because we have been given the Word of the Lord. There is no such thing as "fallible prophecy," as some would claim. The standard for prophecy never changed in the new covenant except that false prophets, instead of being put to death (Deut. 18:20), are marked by the church and avoided (Rom. 16:17–18; Eph. 5:6–13; 2 Peter 2:1–3; 2 John 10).

3. *I believe that the gift of healing was wielded at will by the disciples and by appointed individuals for the authentication of their ministry and the establishment of the church.* The Gospels and the early church are filled with evidence of gifted healers. From Jesus himself to the apostles and disciples, undeniable healings were a normal pattern. These people

required this level of giftedness to lay a solid foundation because they faced Jews who needed miraculous healings to show them that God was doing something new. The church also did not yet have the canon of New Testament Scripture, and so the gentiles and other people groups needed to know that the apostles and disciples had the same power and message as Christ. They could raise the dead, teleport like Philip, heal the blind, and command crippled limbs to work like new. There is also evidence in James's model for seeking out prayer for healing that the gift of healing was slowly fading into the background (James 5:13–16). I believe that this serves as evidence for God's invitation to us to seek and ask for healing, and also to follow Jesus' model to pray "not my will but yours be done" (Luke 22:42). If anyone possessed the gift of healing today, we would know it because they would regularly heal without monetary offerings, music, and special services. They would clear the hospital rooms and be widely known for their undeniable ability to heal incurable diseases and ailments.

4. *I believe that God gave the gift of miracles to certain individuals during certain eras throughout history to showcase his power at work through their ministries.* The miracles in the Bible were different from the ones faith healers and self-proclaimed miracle workers today claim to do, who "heal" only minor ailments like ringing in the ears, back pain, joint issues, or other things that cannot be proven to be healed. Many people say, "I heard some stories about amazing things." What they've heard may or may not be true, but even if it were, the gift of miracles is a gift, so someone who has it would be known widely as a miracle worker. Pharoah and all of Egypt knew that Moses had miraculous power. Jezebel hated Elijah, and her false prophets feared him because he called down fire from heaven. Jesus put on such a display of

miraculous power that even his most hated enemies finally resolved just to say it was the devil who made it possible (Matt. 12:24). God can and still does work miracles today. First and foremost, the miracle of raising dead sinners to life (Eph. 2:1–10) is one of the greatest of all miracles still pouring out around the world.

5. *I believe that tongues were known languages and required interpretation, and were given as a sign to Jews during the birth of the church and for the spreading of the gospel.* The Bible teaches explicitly that tongues were known languages which were interpretable. Not everyone will speak in tongues (1 Cor. 12:30), so no one should ever teach that everyone ought to. Regarding unclear references to tongues that some argue is evidence for ecstatic utterance, I believe that even if Paul is referencing angelic tongues when he says, "If I speak with the tongues of mankind and of angels, but do not have love, I have become a noisy gong or a clanging cymbal" (1 Cor. 13:1), this is hypothetical, since he says "if." But even if he did speak in tongues, the tongues of angels were understandable, for even when the angels came to declare the message of God to Mary, Joseph, and the shepherds keeping watch, the angels spoke in an understandable language so they could understand (Luke 1:26–38; Matt. 1:18–25; Luke 2:8–20). There is no clear indication that ecstatic utterance is the genuine gift of tongues, and since all spiritual gifts are for the common good and all tongues must be interpreted, it does not make biblical sense to have a private prayer language without interpretation.

6. *I believe that anyone claiming to operate in the spiritual gifts should be tested and required to match the biblical description of the gifts, just as was expected in the early church; otherwise they ought to cease from their deceptive claims.* Since godly theologians have landed differently on spiritual gifts, I believe

it is best to avoid petty disputes over subjective experiences and let the biblical description and authority of Scripture govern all definitions and uses of the gifts. If someone claims to have a certain gift, they ought to be tested (1 John 4:1). Since even Paul the apostle's message was tested by the discerning and diligent Bereans (Acts 17:11), any claim to operate in miraculous gifts must pass the biblical test. It is not acceptable to make a serious claim to operate in these gifts by merely saying, "I have seen some things" or "I have heard some wild stories."

Regarding the Holy Spirit speaking today, I will answer that in-depth in chapter 10, providing you with practical tools for hearing from God.

# LEARNING TO LIVE

## 1. Call Out False Teachers and Dangerous Movements Who Threaten the Church's Witness

This practical step might be the most uncomfortable one, but it's necessary. The Bible does command that false teachers be marked (Rom. 16:17–18) and that evil deeds be exposed (Eph. 5:11), but who should do that and how should it be done? When ministries and pastors have already blasted something or someone, how do you determine your own course of action? Should what others do factor into what you do?

Many questions arise, but these five from John Piper can be especially helpful when determining whether to name someone publicly:[10]

1. *The seriousness and deceitfulness of the error.* You might not want to go after everyone who teaches an eschatology different from yours or who holds a differing view unrelated to salvation. At the same time, you would be wise to deal strongly with those who malign Christ, the gospel, Scripture, the character of God, the work of the Holy Spirit, and other essentials of the Christian faith.

2. *The size of the audience.* Is it growing? When someone with a massive following says suspect things, it behooves the Christian to mention the troubling theology and the troubling person propagating it.

---

10. John Piper, "Should We Call Out False Teachers or Ignore Them?" *Desiring God*, October 4, 2019, www.desiringgod.org/interviews/should-we-call-out-false-teachers-or-ignore-them.

3. *The duration of their ministry.* Did they make one blunder or are they constantly doing it? Major teachers who have been consistently deceiving people for years, yet repeatedly making excuses, avoiding accountability, "repenting," and reappearing in the news for ridiculous antics ought to be called out.

4. *The vulnerability of the people for whom you are responsible.* If you're an elder or a church leader, a small group leader, or God has given you broad influence, the sentiment of "I just stay in my lane" is unacceptable and disobedient. You don't have to blast every false teacher all over your social media every week, but when mainstream false teachers pound podcast platforms, YouTube, and social media and you say nothing, I would lovingly challenge you to consider what Christ would have you do. God has called you to be a protector, shepherd, caregiver, watchman or watchwoman, and a herald of truth.

5. *Your role in influencing shepherds who need to learn to discern false teachers.* Are you a leader of leaders? Do you train church planters, pastors, small group leaders, or seminarians? Do you have a large online platform or a greater reach than others? If so, you ought to think deeply about speaking up and naming dangers. Your platform, like your body and your life, is not yours. It belongs to God (Luke 14:25–35; 1 Cor. 6:19–20; 10:31).

In your calling out false teaching, do keep in mind that slinging mud all over the place is not a spiritual gift. The best protection against the darkness of error is the light of truth, so call out error in obedience to God, but major on edifying truth so that people learn about their God.

## 2. Be Accountable to a Faithful Church as a Way to Thrive in Your Christian Service

Your spiritual gift may have been given to *you*, but it's for the benefit of the *church*. If you're not plugged in to a church, you ought to be. Your spiritual gift is not limited to Sunday use only, but connecting with the body every Sunday is going to stir up your heart (Heb. 10:24–25), help you bear burdens with others (Gal. 6:1), and discover new ways to serve. Are you more of a spectator these days? It's time to embrace this truth: God the Holy Spirit has gifted you to bring value to the body of Christ. When you aren't functioning in your gifting, you're missing out on the joy of purpose, and the body is missing out on what you bring to it.

## 3. Study Carefully before Coming to Dogmatic Conclusions

One of the best ways you can bring glory to God and walk in the Spirit is to apply yourself to studying his Word before coming to dogmatic conclusions. I may seem sure of what I believe, but I have been studying these issues for more than ten years, and I must be ready to admit that I can be wrong. The best we can do is study the Word, submit to what is clear, ask the Spirit for help, and weigh every claim against the truth of God's Word. Whether you agree or disagree with my convictions on miraculous spiritual gifts, I hope you'll be diligent in your own study.

Though we needed to wade into the waters of debated doctrinal views in these last two chapters, I hope you come away seeing the bigger picture of spiritual gifts and the importance of unity, despite disagreement. When it comes to false teachers and fighting the good fight, study the issue before naming names and check your heart. Do you want to care for souls, or just crush

opponents? I haven't always been perfect and sinless in my calling out of false teaching, and sometimes it's tempting to share
things that aren't theological but would end the debate by expos-
ing people's lifestyle choices. However, we must use wisdom so
that when we look back one day on our lives and ministries, our
regrets about what we've said and how we've said it are minimal.
Chuck Swindoll's famous advice comes to mind here: "We can be
right, but we don't have to be ugly about it."

## Questions for Reflection

1. Why is it important to research and verify what certain
   teachers and movements teach about spiritual gifts?
2. How do you discover your spiritual gift?
3. When using our spiritual gifts, why is the local church
   incredibly important for our accountability?
4. How do you receive a spiritual gift?
5. Which view do you hold on spiritual gifts and why?

# 9

# IS BEING SLAIN IN THE SPIRIT BIBLICAL?

*For those who are led by the Spirit of*
*God are the children of God.*
—ROMANS 8:14 NIV

IT HAD BEEN MORE THAN THREE HOURS SINCE THE
*service started, and I was really starting to feel God's presence in the*
*building. As I stood next to my friend, the music was deep and intense.*
*The lighting made everything feel so intimate, and a slight fog danced*
*through the air. The lead singer's voice was so beautiful—Bethel's music*
*is so anointed. The voices around me rose in unison, and I felt myself*
*slipping into a deep, rhythmic trance as I swayed to the song. The pastor*
*had been continuously telling us to expect an encounter with God and*
*that God was going to touch us all in some special way. Could this be*
*the solution to my problems in life? I'd been through so much heartache*
*and insecurity. I was tired of being told that God's Word and prayer are*

enough. *Maybe this was the real deal. Maybe this was the encounter I needed.*

*Just then, the pastor interrupted the singing and shouted, "Jesus is here! The anointing is yours! If you want a fresh touch from God, get down here to the front of the stage!" I looked at my friend quickly and said, "Are you coming?! This is it!" He shrugged nervously and stayed put. I think he was skeptical of this sort of thing—he's a Baptist. Oh well, I thought, his loss. Bodies poured out into the aisles as people just like me hurried down to the stage. As I got closer to the front, I felt adrenaline pump through my veins and soon found a spot just a few feet away from the pastor. Looking up at him I felt like God was telling him who to lay hands on. His eyes scanned the sea of young people below his platform. Then my moment came. He told one of his assistants, "Get that girl right there! The power of God is all over her!" I felt so special that he picked me, it caused me to sob uncontrollably. I was pulled up on the platform and it felt like I had made it to the holy of holies. My hands were shaking from the nerves, my breaths were short but heavy, and I sensed the catchers getting into place. Then he shouted, "Fire! on you . . ." The emotion of the moment was too much for me to take as I felt something take hold of my body. I abandoned all control and felt powerfully forced to the ground. My body began to convulse and contort while I was lying on the stage; sounds poured out of my mouth that I'd never made before. I could hear and feel other bodies beginning to fall around me and on me. Some people were laughing hysterically, others touched me and groaned deeply, and some were screaming while crawling on all fours. I have heard some Christians say this sort of experience is demonic, while others say it's just hypnosis. To be honest, I haven't seen it in the Bible and don't really know what it is, but I really feel like it's the Holy Spirit.*

Experiences like this are taking place all over the world every single week in tens of thousands of charismatic churches, healing crusades, youth groups, kid's camps, Third Wave revivals, and conferences. Many conservative Christians are scared to death of their children going to one of these services, but when asked what the issue really is, most cannot explain it except to say "It's unbiblical" or "It's not God."

We need a better answer than that.

## A MAINSTREAM PHENOMENON

So what exactly does someone mean when they say, "I got slain in the Spirit"? This phrase describes what many believe to be a touch from the Spirit that sends them falling to the ground. I used to work as a catcher for people who were falling, and it's as simple as it sounds, unless they are hard to catch! Those who ardently defend this practice claim that it's God's manifest presence in a service that causes people to fall over. According to them, God's power is usually imparted to people by a pastor who lays his hands on them, blows his breath on them, waves his hand, waves his jacket, or shouts a word like "Fire!" or "Touch!" These gestures cause people to go flying in all directions. Sometimes it even occurs when a certain song is sung by the worship band or because people are overcome with emotion during a portion of the service. Oftentimes those being slain in the Spirit will manifest on the ground by making animal sounds, crawling, slithering, or shaking. Some say they feel electricity when the pastor touches them, others feel warmth, while others are not able to stand under their own strength for hours afterward. All of this is believed to be the work of the Holy Spirit as he refreshes and renews spiritually empty and broken people. With more than 500 million charismatics and 1.5 billion Hindus[1] practicing some type of behavior that is like slaying people in the Spirit, it is no exaggeration to state that nearly a quarter of the entire world has beliefs tied to falling or shaking under the power of some sort of spirit. This is not fringe behavior. This is now mainstream spiritualism and considered normative. It's everywhere.

But does the Bible portray the Holy Spirit causing people to shake, slither, laugh, bark, crawl, or convulse in the church? When God interacts with people in the Bible, does he electrocute them into a seemingly drunken state in which speech is slurred and the body uncontrolled? Can a preacher shouting "Fire!" really cause heaven to invade your life on earth? Is there a chance that when some of these charismatic experiences are identical to manifestations found in Hinduism there is a demonic aspect to them?

The best way to understand the charismatic practice of being slain in the Spirit is to understand the position of those who support and practice it.

## WHAT DO SLAIN IN THE SPIRIT ENTHUSIASTS CLAIM?

Claims regarding being slain in the Spirit vary depending on which charismatic group is explaining it. That in itself proves how much confusion surrounds the practice.

Here are several key claims:

- Slain in the Spirit experiences are the result of the manifest presence of God the Father.
- Jesus is the one doing the slaying.

---

1. Hindus practice Kundalini awakening, which is described by yoga experts as a type of divine energy connected to the spine.

- The Holy Spirit is a force who cannot be stopped. When he touches people, they fall.
- People who are empty need to be slain in the Spirit to get filled with the Spirit.
- When God touches human flesh, something will happen.
- When heaven touches earth, things shake.
- The power of God is overwhelming. When it shows up, people fall.

To support these general claims and explanations, charismatic enthusiasts use Bible passages as prooftexts for being slain in the Spirit. Christians who aren't biblically literate won't usually notice the interpretive gymnastics involved in using these passages, but when we study what the Bible actually says, the myths behind being slain in the Spirit get biblically busted.

## MYTH 1: IT HAPPENED IN THE OLD TESTAMENT

*Prooftext Used:* "It happened that when the priests came from the holy place, the cloud filled the house of the LORD, so that the priests could not stand to minister because of the cloud, for the glory of the LORD filled the house of the LORD" (1 Kings 8:10–11).

*Context:* The context of this passage is the completion of Solomon's temple, after which the manifest glory of God descended on the temple. God's presence dwelled in the temple, as was consistent throughout the Old Testament. A similar experience happened to Moses when he was unable to enter the tent of meeting because of the glory of the Lord (Exod. 40:34–38).

*Myth Busted:* God's glory descended upon the temple to signify his residence in the temple. The priest could not to stand to minister (1 Kings 8:10; 2 Chron. 5:13) and Moses was unable to enter the tent of meeting because of the cloud of glory that filled it, not because they were laid out on the floor or slain in the Spirit. There is nothing in these verses that is remotely close to today's slaying in the Spirit that provides evidence for the practice. God's presence did not once slay people in the Spirit, nor did he cause people to fall hysterically, burst out into holy laughter, nor manifest with strange noises. None of what the Old Testament says about God's presence or about experiences at the temple has anything to do with the practice of being slain in the Spirit today.

If charismatic enthusiasts insist on using these texts as proof for their antics, then they must reconcile how the Old Testament priests were unable to stand or serve in the manifest presence of the Lord, while modern-day preachers, catchers (including me!), organ players, singers, and the rest of the audience are able to stand, clap, use the restrooms, and film the event with their cellphones, while only people being "touched" are slain in the Spirit.

If the glory of God shows up, nobody will be filming for YouTube. All will be face down.

Other Old Testament texts that are often twisted in an attempt to justify being slain in the Spirit:

- Genesis 15:12: Abram fell into a deep sleep.
- Exodus 19:18: Mount Sinai shook from the presence of the Lord.
- 1 Samuel 16:13: The Spirit of the Lord came mightily upon David.
- Judges 6:34: The Spirit of the Lord came upon Gideon.

There is not a reputable theologian on earth who can make any of these passages mean that being slain in the Spirit is biblical. Did God move in powerful ways throughout the Bible, and does he still today? Absolutely. Is there a single instance in the Old Testament where he slays someone in the Spirit or instructs a prophet to form a fire tunnel and knock people down in a heap? Absolutely not.

## MYTH 2: IT HAPPENED IN THE NEW TESTAMENT

*Prooftext Used:* "They answered Him, 'Jesus the Nazarene.' He said to them, 'I am He.' And Judas also, who was betraying Him, was standing with them. Now then, when He said to them, 'I am He,' they drew back and fell to the ground" (John 18:5–6).

*Context:* Jesus, the Son of God, stood face to face with a betrayer and a mob of soldiers and high priests, then sent them straight to the ground with a declaration of who he was. This was the ultimate sign of power and authority and a clear display of his divine sovereignty over those he was allowing to kill him.

*Myth Busted:* When we observe Jesus sending these men falling to the ground, several things cannot be overlooked:

1. They were his enemies.
2. He did not impart his anointing to them.
3. They did not have a euphoric encounter with God.
4. They did not manifest by barking, shaking, convulsing, or sobbing.
5. They were not filled with the Spirit.
6. They were not healed while lying on the ground.
7. They carried on with arresting him.

The events of this text offer no support for modern-day practices.

Other New Testament texts that are often twisted in an attempt to justify being slain in the Spirit:

- Acts 8:17: Peter and John laid hands on people and they received the Holy Spirit.
- Acts 19:12: Handkerchiefs that had touched Paul were used to heal and deliver people.
- Acts 26:13–14: Paul was knocked off his horse by light from heaven.
- Revelation 1:17: John fell on his face before Jesus out of fear. Jesus said, "Do not be afraid."

To use any of these examples of God's power in the New Testament as proof to support the practice of slaying people in the Spirit today is beyond overreaching. It's dangerous hermeneutics.

## WHAT DOES THE BIBLE SAY ABOUT BEING SLAIN IN THE SPIRIT?

Nothing in the Bible supports the practice of slaying people in the Spirit or being slain in the Spirit. The Bible doesn't even use those terms. Some may argue that the term *Trinity* is not in the Bible either, yet we believe in the Trinity. This is not a good argument because the doctrine of the Trinity is proven through numerous texts that describe the Father, Son, and Holy Spirit, and we apply it exactly as the Scriptures teach it. Terminology is not the issue, but finding biblical evidence for the practice is.

Even the most important chapters that we have studied on spiritual gifts (1 Corinthians 12–14) do not at all deal with the practice. Instead, Paul works to tone down the chaos of Corinth rather than to invoke further antics that would confuse the church. The burden of proof to legitimize this unbiblical practice lies with those sympathetic to being slain in the Spirit.

So now we'll attempt to make sense of what is happening when people engage in this practice.

## WHAT HAPPENS WHEN PEOPLE ARE SLAIN IN THE SPIRIT?

Since being slain in the Spirit is clearly not found in the Bible, there must be other factors at work in the practice. After twenty-six years of experiencing or being a part of tens of thousands of "slayings," and after later studying Scripture as a genuine Christian, I've come to five conclusions that might explain what in the world is going on when people fall under this supposed power.

1. *People think they have to fall down.* Peer pressure at this sort of service is intense. Nobody wants to look bad or make the preacher look bad. It is widely believed that there is something wrong with you if you don't feel God's presence and have a manifestation of some sort, so peer pressure plays a huge factor in falling. Sadly, kids end up being the biggest losers as they seek to please and soon are brainwashed into the system. In many cases, people see other people falling and just follow suit. Finally, it is common for seekers who come to these services to think they have to fall down to get the experience that the preacher is promising.

2. *People are told they are going to fall down.* The power of suggestion and hypnosis are real. Documentaries like *Miracles for Sale*[2] have proven that the power of suggestion and hypnosis

---

2. Derren Brown produced one of the wildest exposés of faith-healing tricks with his documentary *Miracles for Sale* (April 2014). He trained a total novice to mimic a faith healer and deceive people, then pulled off a miracle healing service. The documentary can be accessed through his website: https://derrenbrown.co.uk/shows/miracles-for-sale/.

can be used to make complete strangers do whatever the hypnotist commands. This isn't news to those who understand psychology and social science, but many Christians are unaware that many charismatic extremists who slay people in the Spirit are experts at hypnosis and manipulation. Three hours of sensual and soothing music, countless bursts of saying, "Jesus is here! He is going to touch you! You are going to feel something you've never felt before! Just receive it!" primes people. Then they are ripe for the picking. Hypnosis is also proven to put people into a trancelike state—something which is common at these services.

3. *People want to fall down.* Reverence is a big deal in Third Wave, New Apostolic Reformation, and charismatic extremist circles. People are taught to honor leaders in a godlike fashion. Many former followers in these movements have admitted that they wanted a deeper connection with God and the anointing that was being promised by the leader, so they chose to fall in the hope of having a spiritual experience. This desire often leads to the weeping, praying, and emotional responses seen after the pastor lays his hands on people.

4. *People are faking it.* I know of friends, family, and followers who have faked it. By the grace of God, people who don't grow up in charismatic chaos have no idea this happens, but when you grow up with a special anointing service week in and week out, and it lasts four hours, sometimes you start falling just to get it over with. I once asked someone close to me why he threw himself back and acted so crazy on the platform, and he said, "Come on, man, we gotta make him look good and get this over with." Make no mistake about it, people fake it.

5. *It is demonic.* In many cases when a false teacher is involved, modern-day slayings in the Spirit are akin to the biblical

accounts of someone who is experiencing demonization and demonic possession (Mark 9:17–18). One of the most disturbing clips I have ever witnessed captures a young man seemingly being controlled like a puppet on a string. He convulses and screams in what appears to be torment, while the teacher, Heidi Baker, continues to call out phrases.[3] Being seized, thrown to the ground, and convulsing are all things that demon-possessed people experienced in the Bible. This isn't a blanket statement to say that all slaying in the Spirit practices today are demonic, but it is to say that when the previous reasons aren't in play, you can bet it's not innocent charismatic behavior. Some may wonder how anyone could dare attribute this practice to demonic behavior, but think about it for a second. Can a false teacher, teaching a false gospel, being used by Satan (2 Cor. 11:13–15), lay hands on someone and cause them to experience the true Holy Spirit? No. It's an imposter, a demonic spirit.

At best, well-meaning people are seeking an encounter with God in the wrong way and will end up confused and disappointed. At worst, desperate people are being overtaken by hypnosis, the power of suggestion, demonic forces, or a false spirit that they believe to be the Holy Spirit.

If it doesn't match the Bible, isn't found in the Bible, or can't be backed up by proper interpretation of the Bible, you're not missing out on anything. The Holy Spirit is accessible today through the power of the gospel, and he glorifies the Lord Jesus Christ (John 16:14–15) and does not put on a show. If people surrender to Christ, embrace the true work of the Spirit in their lives, and submit to the

---

3. Lynda Kuni, "Heidi Baker @ Bethel Redding," iBethel.tv, October 9, 2014, www
.youtube.com/watch?v=kQHsgY5EzVc.

Bible as sufficient and final revelation, a sign like being slain in the Spirit is neither necessary nor important.

No matter what a person's position is on spiritual gifts today, discerning Christians can confidently say "I'll pass" when it comes to being slain in the Spirit.

# LEARNING TO LIVE

### 1. Keep the Goal of Winning People above the Goal of Winning Arguments

The topic of being slain in the Spirit can turn up the heat in a lot of theological circles because people are attached to their experiences or the leaders they have looked up to. Stick to the truth and be careful of getting sucked into character assaults and petty arguments. The Word of God stands on its own, and it doesn't change the truth when people do not submit to the truth. You do not need to get emotionally charged and crush opponents. Just keep speaking the truth in love (Eph. 4:15).

### 2. Face the Uncomfortable Reality of Spiritual Warfare

The demonic realm is real. Spiritual warfare is real. Satan and his kingdom of darkness attack people, use false teachers (2 Peter 2), and seek to steal, kill, and destroy (John 10:9–10). Satan's goal is to possess and dominate as many people as he can. He hates God, he hates the true work of the Spirit, and he hates you. Facing this reality lessens the shock of false teaching to the point where you are able to handle it and not be caught off guard. Think of Peter's goal as he wrote 2 Peter 2, or Jude in writing his letter. They wanted the church to face the dark reality of false teachers so that they could stand firm in the faith. No need to run in fear. Stand in faith!

### 3. Be Discerning about What Conferences or Events to Go To

Wouldn't it be easier if everyone who claimed to be a Christian or every conference that our teens went to were truly gospel focused? Discernment is a spiritual gift for a reason. We desperately need it. As believers, we are called to be like the Bereans (Acts 17:11) and take responsibility for the spiritual well-being of those entrusted to our care. Don't be like Eli, who was lazy as a father and refused to correct his sons (1 Sam. 3:13). Do the work of being discerning, both for yourself and for those you love.

## Questions for Reflection

1. What are some lessons to learn from this chapter about biblical interpretation?
2. Why do you think so many people get taken in by teachers who practice slaying in the Spirit?
3. What would you say to someone who doesn't care whether it's in the Bible, they just like the way being slain in the Spirit makes them feel?
4. Have you or someone you know ever experienced being slain in the Spirit? Describe the experience. What do you think happened?
5. What role does spiritual warfare play in our daily lives? How does Ephesians 6:11–18 instruct us to operate?

# DOES THE SPIRIT
# SPEAK?

*For those who are led by the Spirit of*
*God are the children of God.*
—ROMANS 8:14 NIV

THE CRACKING OF THE ENIGMA CODE MACHINE WAS one of the greatest victories of World War II. The Enigma machine was an encryption device that the Germans used to transmit messages containing war strategies, orders, and more. The machine was so complex that there were billions of possible settings to sift through each day before that day's messages could be decoded. It was thought to be impossible to crack the Enigma machine, and even if someone could, they would hardly be able to do so in time to stop German plots being transmitted through it. The Germans seemed to have their enemies beat in the impossible task of trying to decipher the code. Theirs seemed an inevitable victory if their steady progress continued. Then Alan Turing ruined everything. He, along with a team of brilliant minds, created a machine that could find the daily settings being used by operators of the Enigma machine and began decoding German messages and thwarting numerous attacks. Because of their work, countless lives were saved, and the Allied forces turned the tide on the Nazi war machine.

When it comes to hearing the Holy Spirit speak, countless Christians today feel like those who first encountered the Enigma. Between thoughts, feelings, impressions, teachings, grand claims, and even guarantees from well-known teachers that claim they can show you how to hear God's voice just like they do, well-meaning Christians are left with a million different possibilities to sift through. Which thought was from God? Was that feeling the Spirit? If I get goosebumps while listening to a song, *Spirit, is that you?* If I suddenly have a strong impression or a conviction to deal with something, *Spirit, are you telling me I am supposed to drive over there right now? It's 2:00 a.m.!*

Important questions must be answered if we are to accurately and consistently heed the voice of God and walk in his will. If you're baptized by the Spirit, filled with the Spirit, and walking by the Spirit, how do you hear the Spirit? If we're yielded to him, will we not hear directly from him?

## MISGUIDED BUT WELL-INTENTIONED IDEAS

A host of Christian and non-Christian teachers provide guidance that is supposedly helpful for hearing from a deity. I must admit that in my former years within the charismatic movement I tried all of these in my ignorance. Not once did I heard from God audibly, though like all humans, I had thoughts and wondered which ones were from God. This all led to my making confused or knee-jerk decisions, claiming, "I feel like God told me to do this." Thankfully, God graciously opened my eyes to how I could hear from him with 100 percent confidence and never wallow in confusion again. But first, let's walk through four unsuccessful and unbiblical approaches I used to use.

## 1. SITTING IN SILENCE

I learned the strategy of silence from mystics who believe that sitting in silence until God audibly speaks is a type of wrestling with God like Jacob did (Gen. 32:22–32). Sitting in silence may be good for slowing down our busy lives, meditating on Scripture, or processing thoughts, emotions, and ideas so that we can respond wisely to situations. But sitting in silence until God speaks as a protest or a battle of wills, as though we can beat God in a waiting game, is not at all what Scripture teaches us. When Jacob wrestled with God, it was not about winning a battle of wills to make God do what he wanted, it was about Jacob's stubbornness, God's testing him, and Jacob's need to submit to the Lord.

## 2. LISTENING FOR THE STILL SMALL VOICE

Listening for the still small voice was not always my go-to strategy, but it was there when I needed it. What did it mean? I don't completely know, but it worked wonders with my Baptist friends because it's not as wildly charismatic as "God appeared in my room and told me . . ." but it was still supernatural enough to make everyone believe I was hearing God in a special way. The still small voice could be a feeling, a subtle perception, or a thought that popped into my head, but the expression was meant to convey the idea that God was whispering direction into my ear and I had to really focus to hear it. It's as though the volume was turned almost completely down on my phone and I was saying, "God, is that you I hear?" Recently Justin Peters was sharing thoughts on this topic and he lamented, "Evangelicals have created an entire theology of hearing God's 'still small voice' from a verse that has been completely taken out of context and misinterpreted."

The still small voice has one reference in Scripture, though the interpretation that I employed was 100 percent wrong. Queen Jezebel and King Ahab hated the prophet Elijah. They wanted him dead. After Elijah called down fire from heaven to consume the sacrifice on the altar and beat the prophets of Baal in their supernatural competition (1 Kings 18:20–40), he then prayed down rain upon the land (vv. 41–46), and pretty soon Jezebel sent word to Elijah that she was going to kill him the next day (19:1–2). Elijah fled for his life. While he was staying in a cave, the Lord called to Elijah to come out from the cave to hear from him. We find the phrase "still small voice" in the King James translation:

> And, behold, the LORD passed by, and a great and strong wind rent the mountains, and brake in pieces the rocks before the LORD; but the LORD was not in the wind: and after the wind an earthquake; but the LORD was not in the earthquake:
>
> And after the earthquake a fire; but the LORD was not in the fire: and after the fire a still small voice.
>
> And it was so, when Elijah heard it, that he wrapped his face in his mantle, and went out, and stood in the entering in of the cave. And, behold, there came a voice unto him, and said, What doest thou here, Elijah?
>
> And he said, I have been very jealous for the LORD God of hosts: because the children of Israel have forsaken thy covenant, thrown down thine altars, and slain thy prophets with the sword; and I, even I only, am left; and they seek my life, to take it away.
>
> And the LORD said unto him, Go, return on thy way to the wilderness of Damascus.
>
> —1 KINGS 19:11–15

One thing to note is that the the still small voice ("gentle whisper" in most modern translations) was an actual voice and not a feeling or an impression as some will say today. Another thing to note is the conversation that took place between Elijah and the Lord. This was a back-and-forth dialogue, as was the case when God spoke audibly with certain people in the Scriptures. There was no doubt that he spoke to Elijah. Finally, it is important that we be faithful students of the text and see the lesson God taught Elijah. God had consistently moved in powerful ways through sensational events throughout Elijah's ministry. In this passage the writer mentions the wind, the fire, and the earthquake, yet the Lord was in none of those. Finally Elijah heard God's voice in a whisper. God was showing Elijah that he was still with him and still working in his life even when he wasn't using signs and wonders as he'd previously done. Perhaps a healthy reminder for us: God works in simple and subtle ways and not always in the sensational. God regularly spoke to Elijah, and the still small voice was part of a bigger lesson God was teaching him.

## 3. READING THE TEA LEAVES

"Reading the tea leaves" is an English idiom that comes from an ancient fortune-telling practice that sought to find significance in the patterns tea leaves make in the bottom of a teacup. If that sounds like sketchy superstition, it is. I used to "read the tea leaves" by seeing any little event as a sign from God. For example, I might be sitting at a red light and say, "God if you want me to do [blank], then you'll turn the light green . . . right . . . now!" The light would still be red—thank God for that in hindsight! Reading the tea leaves is really just superstitious guesswork that can lead to disastrous decisions. As believers, we have a "prophetic word made more sure" (2 Peter 1:19). Therefore, we don't need to engage in this type of hit-or-miss mysticism. God does not make it his practice to work through fortune cookies, mysterious messages, and hidden signs.

## 4. PLAYING THE BIBLE THUMB GAME

Maybe you've never played the Bible thumb game, but I did it all the time. Take your Bible, hold it like you are going to open its pages, then close your eyes and just put your thumbs together and pull it open. Look at the first passage that catches your eye, and that's what God wants to say to you. Sound crazy? You might be shocked to know how many people I have talked to who did the same thing until they understood how to hear the voice of the Spirit. My hope is that by my admitting it in this book, more people will be encouraged to join me in moving on. We're all works in progress, right? Thank God help and clarity are never too far away. He's good about opening our eyes and putting our feet on solid ground.

# TAKE OUT THE GUESSWORK

There are several ways to take the guesswork out of hearing the Spirit speak to you. Maybe you're thinking, *But what about the mystery of the Spirit so many teachers talk about? Shouldn't there be some mystery to hearing from him?* No. While the Spirit's working through an infinite number of details, people, and circumstances is a mystery to our finite humanity, there is no instance in the Scriptures in which the Spirit spoke and believers had to wonder, *Spirit, is that you? Can you be more specific? I think I am having an impression but am not sure exactly what you are saying.* In the apostle Paul's life we see there is constantly clarity when the Spirit speaks. In 1 Timothy 4:1 Paul writes, "The Spirit explicitly says . . ." How's that for clarity? The Spirit spoke and it was explicitly clear. In Acts 8:29 we read, "And the Spirit said to Philip, 'Go over and join this chariot'" (ESV). There was no doubt what the Spirit was saying to Philip. In Acts 13:2 we see a moment in which the Spirit wants to advance the work of the gospel, so he tells the Christians at Antioch what to do:

"While they were worshiping the Lord and fasting, the Holy Spirit said, 'Set apart for me Barnabas and Saul for the work to which I have called them'" (ESV). None of those church leaders had to read tea leaves, decipher an impression, sit silently and outwait the Spirit, or discern which of their thoughts was the Spirit and which was their own bad idea. Acts 21:11 describes another instance when the Spirit speaks: "And coming to us, he took Paul's belt and bound his own feet and hands and said, 'Thus says the Holy Spirit . . .'" (ESV). Again, there was no doubt that the Spirit was speaking.

Charles Spurgeon, the notable nineteenth-century preacher, was known to remark about impressions from the Spirit. He was not one to live by them, nor did he make much of them, though he said he sometimes had strong impressions in the pulpit to say certain things and believed those impressions to be from the Spirit. It's vital to define impression as nothing more than a strong feeling. I would call it a "conviction based on Scripture" to avoid confusion or put too much stock in anything else. Spurgeon warns,

> To live by impressions is oftentimes to live the life of a fool and even to fall into downright rebellion against the revealed Word of God. Not your impressions, but that which is in this Bible must always guide you. "To the Law and to the Testimony." If it is not according to this Word, the impression comes not from God—it may proceed from Satan, or from your own distempered brain! Our prayer must be, "Order my steps in Your Word." Now, that rule of life, the written Word of God, we ought to study and obey.[1]

In another sermon, Spurgeon offers excellent insight for his congregation and warns them not to live by impressions. We can

---

1. Charles Spurgeon, "A Well-Ordered Life," quoted in Nathan Busenitz, "Spurgeon, Impressions, and Prophecy," Cripplegate, November 15, 2012, https://thecripplegate.com /spurgeon-impressions-and-prophecy/.

take his advice to heart today and avoid so much confusion. He taught them,

> "If I feel it impressed upon my mind," says one, "I shall do it." Does God command you to do it? This is the proper question. If he does, you should make haste, whether it is impressed upon your mind or not; but if there be no command to that effect, or rather, if it diverges from the line of God's statutes, and needs apology or explanation, hold your hand, for though you have ten thousand impressions, yet must you never dare to go by them. It is a dangerous thing for us to make the whims of our brain instead of the clear precepts of God, the guide of our moral actions.[2]

# THE SPIRIT SPEAKS THROUGH SCRIPTURE

Based on what the Bible shows us time and time again, when the Spirit speaks there is no guesswork or ambiguous messaging that one must decipher. There is no Enigma machine in the spirit realm pumping out messages that have a billion different possibilities and your job is to figure out which one is his voice so as not to run your life off course.

The Bible not only shows us how clearly the Spirit spoke but also tells us how he speaks to us now. Hebrews 1:1–2 declares, "In the past God spoke to our ancestors through the prophets at many times and in various ways, but in these last days he has spoken to us by his Son, whom he appointed heir of all things, and through whom also he made the universe" (NIV). In this passage the

---

2. Charles Spurgeon, "Intelligent Obedience," quoted in Busenitz, "Spurgeon, Impressions, and Prophecy."

author of Hebrews puts Christ above everything and everyone. The prophets did their jobs as proclaimers of God's revelation, and from Abraham to John the Baptist God used various means to speak to his people, including a burning bush when he spoke to Moses (Exod. 3:1–17) and even a donkey when he spoke to Balaam (Num. 22:21–39). But in these last days, he has spoken through his Son, Jesus Christ. Jesus is superior to any voice, and the Spirit reveals him through the Scriptures. The word of Christ is "heard" through the proclamation of the "word of Christ" (Rom. 10:17). God's word through the Son is final and complete. The apostles are but additional spokesmen for Christ, for in their letters they only expand his subject matter and do not add any new teachings or insights.[3] When we preach the gospel of Jesus Christ according to the Scriptures, when we preach the Scriptures in their plain and pure meaning, when we read the Scriptures, and when we pray the Scriptures, the Spirit is speaking because the Scriptures are his voice revealed. The voice of the Spirit and the revealed Word of God are never to be divorced from one another. They are one and the same. This is why 1 John 4:1 tells the believer to "test the spirits." There will be many false spirits that breed deception and attempt to distract and deceive believers and unbelievers alike (though John is specifically writing to believers). The only way to combat such spiritual warfare is by trusting in the Word of God as your only source for his voice.

My brothers and sisters, if there is one thing you take from this book, I plead with you to live your life by this truth: the Spirit's leading, guiding, and directing of our lives will never be divorced from the Word. The Scriptures are where his voice is revealed. If you want to hear the Spirit speak, read the Bible. If you want to hear the Spirit speak out loud, read the Bible out loud.

---

3. Ray C. Stedman, *Hebrews*, IVP New Testament Commentary Series (Downers Grove, IL: IVP Academic, 1992), Heb. 1:1–3.

Naturally, practical questions will arise. I get these all the time as a pastor and they are important to address in a biblical way. Here are several I've heard over the past year:

- "What about that thought I had about calling that person to check on them and it happened to be perfect timing?"
- "How do you explain that time I felt an impression about not going to the store and there ended up being a bad accident on the street I would have driven on?"
- "When I felt like God spoke to my heart about confronting someone in their sin, and then they repented, how can you deny I heard from the Lord?"
- "One time I just knew in my heart that a friend of mine was dating the wrong person, so I told him and he ended up breaking up with her. Turns out she is now divorced. The Spirit obviously spoke to me and I saved his future from pain."

I believe the answer to all of these questions is so simple. Are believers the temple of the Holy Spirit and the holy dwelling place of God? Yes, according to 1 Corinthians 3:16, 2 Corinthians 6:16, 1 Peter 2:4–5, and a number of other passages. Are believers those who possess the mind of Christ and have been given spiritual eyes to see what the spiritually blind cannot? Yes: according to 1 Corinthians 2:10–16 all believers have the ability to discern spiritual things, be indwelt by the Spirit, be controlled by the Spirit, be filled with the Spirit, and as a result, be led by the Spirit. Romans 8:14 says, "For those who are led by the Spirit of God are the children of God" (NIV). Therefore, if we are filled with the Spirit, have the mind of Christ, and are under the powerful influence of the Spirit, why wouldn't we think thoughts in line with what Scripture calls us to? Why wouldn't we be saturated with God-honoring perspective when making decisions? If we are filled with the Spirit and walking by the Spirit, would we not be consistently thinking of other believers, how we can serve, how we can give, where we can help, what ways we need to grow, what sins we ought to confront, who we should disciple, and when we should use wisdom? Even if we believed that a thought came to mind because the Spirit has filled our minds, that is still not him speaking audibly to us. That would still fit perfectly into the category of being under the influence of the Spirit (Eph. 5:18) and walking by the Spirit (Gal. 5:16). There are 100 percent reliable ways to be led by the Spirit and never wonder or wander in confusion again.

1. *Let the Word of Christ dwell in you richly (Col. 3:16).* If you want to take the guesswork out of hearing the Spirit speak, fill up your life with Scripture until it's coming out of your pores. Colossians 3:16 says, "Let the word of Christ richly dwell within you, with all wisdom teaching and admonishing one another with psalms, hymns, and spiritual songs, singing with thankfulness in your hearts to God." If you are richly filled with the word of Christ, you don't need to seek out a still small voice or try to tap into the whisper of God. You can rest assured that if you know the Word, you will know how to live the Word. As Paul Washer said once, "Be so saturated with the Scriptures that when they cut you, you will bleed the Bible." When the word of Christ dwells in us richly, we overflow with the divine truth that provides us with divine direction. Consider the words of Psalm 119:15–16: "I meditate on your precepts and consider your ways. I delight in your decrees; I will not neglect your word" (NIV). Give yourself to the Scriptures and the Spirit will speak to you through them.

2. *Ask the Holy Spirit to fill you, and yield to him in obedience (Eph. 5:18).* Have you ever interacted with a believer who

seems to consistently make good decisions, is growing in truth, and is experiencing the blessings of God that money can't buy and this world can't steal? It is likely that they have a strong prayer life in which they ask the Spirit to fill them and enable them to obey him. I have several people in my life who are inspiring examples of what it looks like to live the Spirit-filled life. They bear his fruit (Gal. 5:22–23), make consistently biblical decisions, and have very few regrets. They stay accountable, are thankful, and are generally worry free. One would look at their lives and think, *They must be hearing from the Spirit daily because there is no way it's possible to make so many right and wise decisions without him.* I believe they are this way because they look to the power of the Spirit through the illumination of the Word to guide their daily decisions. The Spirit-filled believer is going to be hungry for God's Word and will have no problem hearing his voice through his Word—and obeying it.

3. *Pray for the wisdom of God in faith (James 1:5–8).* If there is one prayer I pray more than any other, it's this one. Like all of us, I need an abundance of wisdom every day. You can't get anything you want just by praying in faith, but God does promise wisdom to the one who asks in faith and without any doubting. James writes, "If any of you lacks wisdom, you should ask God, who gives generously to all without finding fault, and it will be given to you. But when you ask, you must believe and not doubt, because the one who doubts is like a wave of the sea, blown and tossed by the wind. That person should not expect to receive anything from the Lord. Such a person is double-minded and unstable in all they do" (NIV). We should take advantage of this promise more often because he will pour out wisdom through the Spirit in our lives. People chase a word from the Lord in so many of the wrong places, yet have they even paused to consider

asking for wisdom from the Lord straight from his Word? Many people who are hungry to hear from God might feel that a special service or a communal experience is an opportunity to tap into some special insight about hearing the voice of God, but God has already given all believers access to his voice any time they want. Simply ask for wisdom, saturate your life with God's Word, and watch as the decisions you make consistently become godly ones that align with his will.

Do you notice a common denominator in hearing the Spirit speak? Scripture! Everything goes back to the Word of God revealed through the apostles and the prophets so that we will be built up as living stones upon the bedrock foundation of Christ (Eph. 2:20). When you resolve to look to Scripture to hear the Spirit speak, you will always end up heading in the right direction.

## WHEN YOU DON'T KNOW WHAT OR HOW TO PRAY

Weakness is a fantastic place to be. Why? Because when you are weak, the Spirit is strong. When you reach your breaking point, the Spirit has barely even begun. Many people get sucked into chasing supposed words from God because they are desperate and the televangelist capitalizes on their vulnerable moment, only to end up disillusioned by that word not being remotely accurate. You do not ever need to suffer that kind of spiritual abuse. Romans 8:26–28 has a word from the Lord that will change your life. Paul writes, "Now in the same way the Spirit also helps our weakness; for we do not know what to pray for as we should, but the Spirit Himself intercedes for us with groanings too deep for words; and He who searches the hearts knows what the mind of the Spirit is, because

He intercedes for the saints according to the will of God. And we know that God causes all things to work together for good to those who love God, to those who are called according to His purpose."

This passage opens up a whole new perspective.

First, the Spirit helps us in our weakness. Therefore, we look to him for direction.

Second, when we don't know how or what to pray, the Spirit is praying for us. Perhaps we get distracted or we are focusing on only one thing in our prayers or maybe we don't know how or what to pray. Like the groans of creation longing for redemption (Rom. 8:22), the Spirit groans on our behalf as weak and frail humans who are in great need of divine help. As believers, we don't get saved and left alone to figure out the rest for ourselves. The Spirit is our helper every step of the way, including the ministry of intercession on our behalf. He brings our needs before the throne of God even when we don't. When the Scriptures call the Spirit our helper (John 15:26), remember that this means he is helping in ways we may not even realize.

Third, he is praying for and working out the will of God in our lives. God the Father is the one who "searches the hearts" of man and "knows what the mind of the Spirit is." Because the Holy Spirit is God and an equal member of the Godhead, you don't ever have to wonder whether the Father is getting the message from the Spirit or whether the Spirit knows exactly what to pray for. He not only intercedes according to the will of God but he and the Father are in perfect unity as they work out all things for the good of those who love him and are called according to his purpose.

The plain meaning of Romans 8:26–27 has nothing to do with mystical groanings from human beings, as a great number of charismatics teach and I used to believe. Furthermore, your feelings of abandonment and anxiety because you don't think you are hearing from God can be sent back to the pit of hell, where lies like that come from. You are known, loved, secured, and prayed for by the Spirit of the living God.

## BRINGING CLARITY TO
## MISLEADING PHRASES

There are three confusing phrases that do more harm than good. I do not presume to know the motives of people who use them, nor would I mock anyone for saying them, since they were a part of my spiritual practice before I did more study. Ignorance, a lack of solid teaching, and poor semantics lead to the use of these phrases to express how we feel the Spirit is leading us to act:

- "I feel like God told me . . ."
- "The Lord spoke to me through an impression . . ."
- "God spoke to my heart and he said . . ."

You might think I'm being nitpicky, but each of these phrases conveys more of a subjective fog than biblical clarity. We all pick up practices or sayings throughout our Christian lives, but it's important to express things accurately lest we misrepresent God or cause others to stumble into ignorance or error. Remember, the goal is not to be culturally relevant or to make light of how people express their understanding of God's speaking. The goal is to know the Spirit's voice and be led into his will with accuracy. If you have been seeking his direction through Scripture regarding a decision you have to make, there is absolutely no need to say you feel like God told you, because you *know* God told you, and he did so through his Word. He didn't speak to your heart and say anything, he spoke through his Word and your heart was stirred with passion to obey him. Consider replacing any such phrasing with one simple phrase any time you are stirred to do something in line with Scripture that you believe is the leading of the Spirit. Confidently say, "I have a deep conviction about [blank] because of God's Word, and I believe this is what the right decision is." By using this approach, you will not only find yourself feeling more confident about your decisions, you will also help others through your example of Spirit-led living.

But what about when you aren't reading the Bible and you think a thought or dream a dream and wonder, *Did that idea come from the Spirit of God?* Always, and I mean always, go to the Scriptures and filter it through his voice there. If it turns out your thought lines up with Scripture, then thank the Lord for the way his Word is saturating your life so greatly that your thinking has become aligned with his Word. He has spoken—through the Word. I remember a few years ago I was reading in the Scriptures about unity and living at peace with others. Romans 12:18 jumped off the page as I read it again. It says, "If possible, so far as it depends on you, be at peace with all people." Almost immediately after I read that passage and meditated on it, two individuals came to my mind. I thought of a few reasons why they should reach out to me first, since in my opinion they had been the guilty party. But there was no excuse for me not to initiate contact with them, since I felt convicted about making things right as the Word pierced my heart. I picked up my phone and texted both of them, asking for a phone call so we could come to an understanding and make things right. One never wrote back, while the other did, and we reconciled our differences and walked forward in unity. Did God tell me to text them? Had the Spirit spoken to my heart? I wouldn't say that. I read the Word (which I believe to be God's clear and revelatory voice) and truth hit me squarely between the eyes. God did tell me something— through his Word. I have the Spirit living inside of me and the mind of Christ (1 Cor. 2:16), and I know the will of God is for me to obey his commands (1 John 5:1–5), and so I want to act on the truth he's given. I encourage you to give yourself to the Scriptures, be submissive when conviction hits your heart because of the Scriptures, and act on that conviction when it is in line with the Scriptures. There is no need to mystify hearing God's voice. Walk in the Word. He is talking to you through it.

# CHRISTIAN LIBERTY AND THE LEADING OF THE SPIRIT

If you are saturating your life with the Word, walking by the Spirit, filled with the Spirit, and bearing the fruit of the Spirit, it is safe to say you are hearing the Spirit with clarity through the Word. But there are still questions that Scripture does not speak to specifically or that may fall into the category of Christian liberty. One of the most helpful resources I have ever read on this subject is *Ethics for a Brave New World* by John Feinberg and Paul Feinberg, in which they lay out eight questions for making decisions in line with God's Word regarding gray areas. For example, is it sinful to get a tattoo? Can Christians drink alcohol? Is it materialistic to purchase a nice home? How nice of a car is too nice? Does the Spirit endorse moving to a new state for a high paying job? Should you send your kids to a Christian school or homeschool them instead of putting them in public school? There are endless questions that the Bible doesn't address, but it provides us with truths that help us make Spirit-led decisions. No matter how desperate you may be, you don't ever have to wander in confusion.

Here are the eight questions and a brief explanation of each:[4]

1. *Am I persuaded that this is right?* When it comes to decisions about areas that the Spirit has not revealed in the Word exactly what to do about, you can trust that Romans 14 has revealed what you should do. Paul writes, "One person values one day over another, another values every day the same. Each person must be fully convinced in his own mind. . . .

---

4. These questions and explanations are taken from the excellent work of John S. Feinberg and Paul D. Feinberg, *Ethics for a Brave New World*, 2nd ed. (Wheaton, IL: Crossway, 2010), 52–55. I have also outlined their questions and offered further commentary in Costi Hinn, "Eight Questions for Christian Decision-Making," *For the Gospel*, podcast episode 93, August 15, 2022, www.forthegospel.org/listen/8-questions-for-christian-decision-making.

I know and am convinced in the Lord Jesus that nothing is unclean in itself; but to the one who thinks something is unclean, to that person it is unclean. . . . But the one who doubts is condemned if he eats, because his eating is not from faith; and whatever is not from faith is sin" (Rom. 14:5, 14, 23). Paul, using the example of how people considered certain foods sinful to eat and set apart certain days as holy, explains that we have liberty but must be convinced in our own minds what we should or shouldn't do. Consult the Word, ask the Spirit to fill you, lead you, and guide you, then make the decision that aligns with your convictions. Don't overthink things. If you are fully persuaded that something is right and acceptable to God, do it. If your conviction is that such a decision is not, do not do it.

2. *Can I do it as unto the Lord?* Everything we do must be as unto the Lord (Rom. 14:6–8). If what are you are doing can be seen as serving God's greater purpose and honoring him, then move forward. If not, do not engage in that activity.

3. *Can I do it without being a stumbling block to my brother or sister in Christ?* We are not lone rangers. We are connected to the body of Christ. If you are unsure what the Spirit would have you do in a certain situation, think of how the Spirit has instructed you not to be a stumbling block to your fellow believers. Will what you are doing offend someone needlessly? Might someone with a weaker conscience be led astray? Could someone watching you misunderstand the reason for your decision? We have a responsibility to consider such a person above ourselves, just as Christ did (Phil. 2:3–8). Even so, we do not need to bind our conscience where God has given us liberty. Paul says in Romans 14:22, "The faith which you have, have as your own conviction before God. Happy is the one who does not condemn himself in what he approves." This means

that while you might not indulge in something publicly, it may be perfectly acceptable for you to enjoy it privately according to the conviction you have in your liberty before the Lord.

4. *Does it bring peace?* This is a convicting question! We might get lost in the weeds regarding what to do, but the Spirit has given us clear evidence for making wise decisions with our liberties. Paul says, "Therefore do not let what is for you a good thing be spoken of as evil; for the kingdom of God is not eating and drinking, but righteousness and peace and joy in the Holy Spirit. . . . So then we pursue the things which make for peace and the building up of one another" (Rom. 14:16–17, 19). There will be numerous times in life when an acceptable decision will not bring peace but instead stir up unnecessary strife. A believer must take this into consideration and ask the Spirit for wisdom.

5. *Does it edify my brother or sister?* The command to consider what will build up one another means we will pause to think about how our decision might encourage, strengthen, and spur on our brothers and sisters in the Lord. A believer seeks to bring peace and to edify others with their decisions surrounding Christian liberty.

6. *Is it profitable?* Regarding the constructiveness of Christian liberty, Paul says, "'I have the right to do anything,' you say—but not everything is beneficial. 'I have the right to do anything'—but not everything is constructive" (1 Cor. 10:23 NIV). There is a time and a place for everything. For example, one might engage in an activity allowed by Christian liberty in their yard, while the same activity would be unprofitable during a church service or a funeral. I believe the Spirit gives us the word and leads us into common sense when we are walking closely with him through prayer and truth.

7. *Will it enslave me?* The Spirit gives us liberty to decide according to our convictions on many things, but we must wisely ask for the Spirit's help with our blind spots. Our hearts are deceitful (Jer. 17:9); we can be good at convincing ourselves that what we are doing is good, when in fact it has us captive. Whether it be liberties regarding material goods, money, drinking, or any other decision that requires wisdom, we have to be honest about our attachment to it. If we didn't get our way, how would we react? If we cannot have or indulge that thing we want, do we lose our temper or react with defensiveness? Regarding Christian liberty and enslavement, Paul says, "'I have the right to do anything'— but I will not be mastered by anything" (1 Cor. 6:12 NIV).

8. *Does it bring glory to God?* Paul succinctly sums up Christian liberty when he says, "So whether you eat or drink or whatever you do, do it all for the glory of God" (1 Cor. 10:31 NIV). How do you know whether your actions bring glory to God? If you answer all of the other seven questions negatively, you can be sure your decision will not bring glory to God if you indulge. Conversely, if the decision is acceptable on those other grounds, it will bring glory to God to indulge.

# LEARNING TO LIVE

## 1. Trust God's Word as the Source of the Spirit's Voice

My prayer for you is that after reading this chapter you are even more eager and confident to approach God's Word, knowing that the Spirit will give you clarity through it. Remember what we've learned in earlier chapters. Illumination is the opening of our eyes to his truth. He can and will give you eyes to see and ears to hear. Look to his Word and embrace Psalm 119:15–16. Meditate on his precepts and do not neglect his Word.

## 2. Look to the Spirit in Times of Weakness

We all go through times of despair and seasons when we don't feel close to God. Instead of looking for mystical signs of his presence, look to the Spirit through prayer. Cry out to him as in the examples we have from Scripture. Ask him to fill you, to bear fruit in you, to pour out his wisdom upon you. Instead of being lured by the temptation of mystical signs and superstitions, thank the Spirit for interceding for you in your weakness. Embrace your limitations and relish his role to help you when you cannot help yourself. We love to try to make it on our own to build up our human ego. Lay ego aside and look to his strength. You will find perfect peace.

## 3. Use Wisdom with Christian Liberty

When you can't find a verse that gives the Spirit's clear guidance for a decision, remember that he has given clarity on Christian liberty. You *can* be confident in decisions even when there is no definitive answer in Scripture because the one answer that outweighs all the rest is that you and I ought to bring glory to God in every area of our lives.

## Questions for Reflection

1. Have you ever claimed that God told you something, or have you ever felt you received an impression from the Spirit? How would you express or clarify that in light of this chapter?

2. Many rationalists get uncomfortable with the idea of the Spirit leading, while many emotionalists believe every thought could be the Spirit speaking. How do you stay balanced in biblical truth when discerning what the Spirit is leading you to do?

3. What danger is there in believers' seeking out a special word from the Lord outside of Scripture?

4. How should we reason with someone who frequently tells us they feel like God is telling them things?

5. Do you agree with my conclusions in this chapter? Why or why not? Is there anything you would express differently? (Use Scripture to explain.)

# HOW TO PRESERVE THE UNITY OF THE SPIRIT

*As a prisoner for the Lord, then, I urge you to*
*live a life worthy of the calling you have received.*
*Be completely humble and gentle; be patient, bearing*
*with one another in love. Make every effort to keep*
*the unity of the Spirit through the bond of peace.*
—EPHESIANS 4:1–3 NIV

THERE'S AN OLD PASTOR'S JOKE: A MAN ONCE PUT A dog and a cat in a cage together as an experiment, to see if they could get along. They did, so he put in a bird, a pig, and a goat. They too got along fine after a few adjustments. He thought perhaps he was onto something, so he took things to the next level. He put in a Baptist, a Lutheran, a Presbyterian, and a Pentecostal, but after just a few minutes there wasn't a living thing left! Unity can be achieved in many facets of life, but some things never seem to change.

No subject stirs up debate among Christians like the topic of the Holy Spirit. Christians across denominational lines can get along splendidly on topics like the gospel, global missions, and the attributes of God, only to explode into a full-scale theological war when the Spirit's work comes to the forefront. Brothers and sisters, it ought not be this way. We can have strong differences on secondary theological matters, while taking care not to destroy each other in the process. I say this not to encourage us to downplay the truth, but Scripture describes characteristics all believers ought to possess so that we cause more good than harm when speaking the truth to others. Believers should use truth to build others up rather than to crush those we disagree with.

Recently I was fellowshiping with some friends who are faithful members of another local church. Their pastor is a close brother and we agree on most everything doctrinally, though we differ slightly on methodology. As the conversation unfolded, one of the men in the group asked for my thoughts on his grandmother's practice of praying with a private prayer language. She was a godly woman who had been deeply involved with the Assemblies of God for years alongside her husband, who was widely respected for his decades of gospel faithfulness in ministry. My friend shared that in his past he had been coerced to speak in tongues after an altar call. In the end he had never received the gift of tongues and hadn't been convinced by the coercion at the altar.

As we talked, he and I didn't land on the same position regarding the use of tongues today, but we enjoyed our fellowship and dialogued like brothers in Christ. Despite his concerns about excesses, he wasn't going to throw his grandparents out of the faith or even hint that their ministry was not legitimate. In fact, their ministry had been significant. I came away from that conversation sensing nothing but mutual respect, love, and unity with him as a family member in the faith.

But that is not always the case in the body of Christ, is it? My friend and I could have thrown a few jabs at each other. He could have accused me of "quenching the Spirit" by not practicing tongues the way others do, and I could have fired back that he was throwing Scripture out the window. Of course, neither one of us wanted to do those things. I do not desire to quench the Spirit, nor does my friend throw Scripture out the window by holding to a different view than me. If we each read and study the text, consult helpful commentaries, and above all else pray and we come to different convictions, then what? War? I don't believe it should be.

People will have a wide variety of differing scriptural interpretations, personal experiences, relationships, and backgrounds that deserve to be navigated with maturity when we have conversations about the Holy Spirit. If genuine Christians have done their work in study and differ on how the Spirit works today, our discussion should not be a destructive conflict but rather feature a mutual love and an understanding that we simply differ in our views.

We may choose to worship with one congregation over another because of doctrinal distinctives, but unity is possible across the entire body of Christ even in the midst of theological disagreement. In this chapter, I want to provide a framework for our unity, because it is the will of the Spirit of God that we be unified, and I'll also provide some qualifiers for doctrinal unity so that we know which doctrinal differences put someone outside of the family of God and which ones do not. This is an important aspect of the Spirit's work in the church.

## WHAT YOU SAY AND HOW YOU SAY IT MATTER

Often when Protestant Christians celebrate the Reformation, they quote a statement widely attributed to Martin Luther: "Peace if possible, truth at all costs." I agree with this sentiment, and I am sure you would too. We want to seek peace whenever possible, but that does not mean we ever sacrifice truth. In Romans 12:18 Paul writes, "If it is possible, as far as it depends on you, live at peace with everyone" (NIV). Sometimes people will not want to be at peace with you, but when possible, seek peace. At the same time, two people can speak the exact same truth yet people resonate with one person over the other because he or she seems more reasonable. Why? I believe much of it has to do with not only what we say but how we say it. The Scriptures have much to say regarding how we are to speak and conduct ourselves with wisdom (Col. 4:6), and Jesus was a perfect example of how one may speak the truth in various tones of voice depending on the context. Consider these situations and audiences:

- Jesus kindly invited himself to Zacchaeus's house, even though Zacchaeus was a cheating tax collector (Luke 19:5).
- The disciples panicked during a storm, failing to realize that their leader was the Creator and could calm the storm. Jesus firmly rebuked them (Matt. 8:26).
- Early in Jesus' ministry, large crowds followed him and he patiently taught them (Matthew 5–7).
- A rich ruler who confidently told Jesus that he kept all the commandments was hit with hard truth when Jesus called him to sell everything, give it to the poor, and follow him. Jesus did not coddle the rich. He called them to give lavishly to kingdom work (Mark 10:17–27).
- Jesus aggressively and sharply rebuked the Pharisees, calling them vipers and other unflattering things (Matt. 23:33).

Jesus' example is an excellent one for us today. We can see that there was balance in his ministry. He could have blasted every person he met with hard truth because it all would have been true. Yet he tactfully and perfectly spoke unwavering truth in a variety of tones depending on the audience or person he was speaking to. There is one caveat here, and it's that Jesus could read minds and hearts. We cannot. We will speak truth the wrong way some-times, but if we aim to follow Christ's example, we can minimize how often we miss the mark. Perhaps more important, we will not be tempted to excuse ourselves from sinful antics in the midst of speaking the truth. I have been guilty of this a time or four!

My friend Jonny Ardavanis said it like this recently: "Truth disseminators disqualify themselves when the wisdom they offer is divorced from gentleness/humility. You can be doctrinally right but be way wrong. When you present truth in a snarky, slanderous and maligning manner, God is dishonored." I love the conviction that statement brings upon my soul, because when I see false teaching, abusive leadership, and hypocrisy in the church, it can be tempting to fire off about it. James 3:13 becomes paramount in those moments: "Who is wise and understanding among you? Let them show it by their good life, by deeds done in the humility that comes from wis-dom" (NIV). Hasty and aggressive reactions are not wise. Such behavior is not how the Spirit would have us deal with every issue, most especially when we're dealing with fellow believers. Wisdom from God "is first of all pure; then peace-loving, considerate, submis-sive, full of mercy and good fruit, impartial and sincere" (v. 17 NIV). That kind of wisdom leads to powerful unity and less regret from using our words unwisely, even when we're on a crusade for truth.

If you're interested in seeing the church maintain unity on the bedrock foundation of biblical truth, what you say matters. If you're interested in seeing the church maintain unity despite our differ-ences on secondary matters, how you say it matters too.

# FOUR CHARACTERISTICS
# TO FOSTER UNITY

Unity is hard to come by in the Christian faith, but it's impor-tant to our fulfilling our calling. And it's achievable, no matter what secondary differences we may have, so long as everyone in the household of God walks in a manner worthy of their calling (Eph. 4:1).

When Paul the apostle wrote to the Ephesian believers about unity, he was writing to people who came from different backgrounds, experiences, and opinions. Jews and gentiles had been brought together as one body, through one Spirit, under one Lord, and were to live an entirely different way than the world around them because they shared one faith (Eph. 4:4–6). A distinct mark of the church is unity. Despite all of our differences, if we hold to the faith that leads to heaven, we'll be family for eternity. After laying a gospel-rich foundation in the first three chapters of Ephesians, the apostle Paul told the church how they were to live in light of the fact that God's grace had changed them. Pride, factions, and self-interest dominated their former way of thinking. Now, with the Holy Spirit having taken residence inside of their hearts, they were to live out their faith in submission to God, not to their fleshly impulses. This new way of living would lead to unity.

In Ephesians 4:2–3 Paul writes, "With all humility and gentleness, with patience, showing tolerance for one another in love, being diligent to preserve the unity of the Spirit in the bond of peace" (NASB 1995). These two verses are loaded with four characteristics and one major truth I don't want you to miss. Let's break down each one.

## 1. HUMILITY

Paul tells the Ephesians that walking worthy of their calling includes walking "with all humility" (Eph. 4:2). *Humility* means "modesty or lowliness" and it is a Christian idea. Greeks and Romans at the time that Paul wrote this letter celebrated cockiness, arrogance, and pride. They looked down on humility as weakness. Of course, Jesus modeled humility. Paul writes elsewhere, "Do nothing from selfishness or empty conceit, but with humility consider one another as more important than yourselves; do not merely look out for your own personal interests, but also for the interests of others. Have this attitude in yourselves which was also in Christ Jesus, who, as He already existed in the form of God, did not consider equality with God something to be grasped, but emptied Himself by taking the form of a bond-servant and being born in the likeness of men. And being found in appearance as a man, He humbled Himself by becoming obedient to the point of death: death on a cross" (Phil. 2:3–8).

Jesus had the glory of heaven, was above us all, and was truly God. He came to earth and took on human form, never ceasing to be God but lowering himself by becoming man. He veiled his full glory, limiting himself when he could have destroyed all enemies, taken vengeance at every turn, and settled every score by fighting his holy war right then and there as equal to God the Father. Instead, he didn't see his equality with the Father as a thing to be grasped but submitted to the Father willingly so that he could redeem sinners through a brutal, humble death on a cross.

Because of Christ's example, we ought to run every attitude and ambition, every fight-or-flight response, and every thought and word through one filter: Does this look like my Lord? The next time you speak with a brother or sister in Christ who holds a different view on secondary doctrinal issues, ask yourself that question.

## 2. GENTLENESS

Paul then says, "And gentleness" (Eph. 4:2). *Gentleness* comes from a Greek word that closely correlates to *meekness*. Gentleness is being courteous toward and considerate of others and is an important Christian quality because if we are not gentle, we end up destroying and tearing down rather than building up.

I remember the early days of my conversion out of the prosperity

gospel when I could have used this advice. I recall not always knowing when to rebuke someone for being a false teacher and when to
gently dialogue with someone who was ignorantly just following a
long-held belief. There were times when I failed to be gentle and
caused relational damage that took years to repair. As the years
went on, the Lord graciously helped me to develop relationships
with friends who were not false teachers or even remotely dangerous
in their doctrinal teachings but who held different views than I did.
Being able to get to know them and see their example of gentleness
despite doctrinal differences was pivotal for me.

Gentleness in the life of Christ looks like strength under control. Jesus possessed a steel spine *and* a soft heart. For a Christian,
meekness isn't weakness. The gentle person may still be a mover
and a shaker, but the way they go about it is wise, gracious, and
Christlike. They aren't a bull in a china shop, smashing into
everything to achieve a result. As Christians, we should not be a
thorn that stabs but a soothing balm that heals, even if the truth
stings. Healing and purity are the result of that approach. Gentle is
Christ's offer to sinners who, seeking peace in all the wrong places,
are weighed down by the destructive burden of sin: "Come to Me,
all who are weary and heavy-laden, and I will give you rest. Take
My yoke upon you and learn from Me, for I am gentle and humble
in heart, and you will find rest for your souls. For my yoke is easy
and My burden is light" (Matt. 11:28–30 NASB 1995).

Are you known for being gentle? Do people with whom you
disagree still enjoy your company, or are you abrasive like sand-
paper? If you end up being right, are you pompous, or mature?
Think of a wild stallion that has been tamed but still has spirit,
fight, and drive to run. The stallion is fierce and strong, yet runs
where the master directs and runs only when the master directs.
A gentle church makes the devil tremble because it is strong yet
disciplined, and difficult to lure into divisive traps and schemes.

## 3. PATIENCE

Ephesians 4:2 also includes "with patience," which comes from the Greek word *makrothumia* and is "a state of remaining tranquil when waiting for an outcome." It's slowness to react, endurance, being long-tempered in challenging circumstances. How I wish I'd embodied this quality ten, five, and even three years ago! We are always a work in progress, so we ought to be patient with others. This attitude is key to unity in the church because it makes us less reactive during disagreement. It is difficult to offend a patient person. Patience is often linked to faith and trust in the Lord. That's the example of many of the heroes of the faith—they were patient, even when enduring challenges, being sinned against, and not having everything they wanted right away.

1. Noah built an ark for approximately seventy-five years without any sign of a global flood.
2. Joseph endured decades of hardship before ruling over Egypt.
3. David was anointed long before becoming king, then was attacked all the way to the throne by his predecessor, Saul.

God is patient with us. Instead of giving us what we deserve as sinners, he is slow to anger and adopts us as his own beloved children. Do we trust the Lord despite people not seeing doctrinal truths the way we do? Are we combative and pushy? Do we believe that the Holy Spirit is working in other believers like he works in us—slowly but surely?

## 4. FORBEARANCE IN LOVE

Finally, Paul writes, "Showing tolerance for one another in love" (Eph. 4:2 NASB 1995). Showing tolerance in love is not overlooking truth, it is continuing to love, serve, and care for someone who bothers you, displeases you, or disappoints you with their decisions. Love is so important to unity because when our feelings drive us into hasty decisions or harsh words, love keeps us grounded. Colossians 3:14 says, "Above all these put on love, which binds everything together in perfect harmony" (ESV). Love is the glue holding the body together and all of these characteristics flow from love. You cannot have these characteristics if you do not have love. This is why Paul prayed for the Ephesians to be "rooted and grounded in love" (Eph. 3:17) and to know Christ's love and be filled with it.

Armed with these four characteristics, believers are to be "diligent to preserve the unity of the Spirit in the bond of peace" (Eph. 4:3 NASB 1995). What happens when people live the Christian life with these character qualities pouring out toward each other? Unity! We ought to be constantly concerned with our unity, protecting it. And I don't want to miss one of the most important details in this passage. Does Paul tell the church to "make unity"? No. Does he command that they "find unity"? No. Does he tell them to "create unity"? No. He says to "preserve" what has already been provided. Christ has unified us through his work on the cross, bringing together a people who were once far off and divided, and given us the Spirit, who now dwells in us as a holy temple unto God. If the body of Christ lacks humility, gentleness, patience, and forbearance in love, we will find ourselves plagued by division. If we embody these characteristics, we will be able to preserve what Christ has provided. Unity is available, but sometimes it is lying dormant underneath layers of pride.

When believers walk in a manner worthy of their calling, unity is always the result because God has designed his body to work that way.

# PRINCIPLES THAT PROTECT OUR UNITY

Principles are one of the most valuable assets to the body of Christ, because when times change, people change, and feelings change, principles keep our ship from capsizing. Following are four principles that I keep in mind when navigating the topic of unity. You could add more and edit these, but they provide a healthy starting point for making wise decisions to protect unity.

## 1. DOCTRINE MATTERS

We ought to preserve unity with those who hold different doctrinal views that do not lead people to hell. However, to say that a doctrine is nonessential does not mean that doctrine is not important. We do well to remain prudent and balanced. Yes, we can experience beautiful unity with those with whom we have doctrinal differences, but that does not mean we throw doctrine out the window. This is especially important when we're dealing with doctrines pertaining to the gospel. I've often said that the devil loves unity that ignores the truth. If he can get us to lay aside doctrine altogether, he can wreak havoc in the church. Without any emphasis on doctrine, we will eventually unify with false religions and those who hate God, and the purity of the church will be destroyed. Protecting unity is important, *and* doctrine matters. Those ideas can coexist.

I think of one dear brother who has been a close friend for years now. He has advised me on major decisions and spoken encouragement to my weary soul in seasons of trial, and he's a fierce competitor on the basketball court too. He holds to a completely different view of eschatology (study of the end times) than I do, and we differ on some finer points of theology and philosophy of ministry, but we still have exceptional unity and share a friendship. In the church where I serve as a pastor, though, he and I would eventually come to a point of difference if we served together as leaders and would have to navigate that, because doctrine matters to both of us. We would consider each other to be wrong on some aspects of theology, yet still maintain gospel unity. In today's world of Twitter wars and cancel culture, we need to recover the glorious tension of declaring, "Doctrine matters! But I can find common ground with you in the gospel." This keeps our collective efforts unified when we share the same gospel, while understanding that our churches may have distinct differences.

## 2. PRESUMPTION IS UNWISE

Remembering that presumption is unwise protects our unity because it ensures we do our due diligence before making conclusions about others who hold different theological views than we do. In times of theological difference, we can be guilty of jumping to conclusions or making wild presumptions about people, assuming things about them instead of going to them directly. Presumption is tempting because it's fast and gets results, though the results are not godly ones. Presumption happens because we get impatient and make impulsive decisions because we're lazy. Unity takes discipline, love, self-sacrifice, and a slower pace that involves conversation, questions, and prudence.

I remember seeing a woman get hurt in a church context when she shared an experience about speaking in tongues with a pastor who quickly responded, "That was probably demonic." Even though I'm not a Pentecostal and am vocal about abuses, I found the response to be hasty. Instead of presuming, the pastor should have asked questions, sought to understand the context, and discerned her spiritual condition before firing off about the experience being demonic.

## 3. BROAD-BRUSHING STIRS UP STRIFE

How much trouble could be avoided if we refrained from making broad-brush statements? Most of us have done this at one time or another, and it nearly always leads to strife. Some in the more Reformed or Baptist traditions will make comments like "Pentecostalism is nothing more than emotionalism and a bunch of people dancing up and down the aisles." Pentecostals or charismatics might say, "Reformed folks are nothing but a bunch of stuffy Pharisees who quench the Spirit and insist that any expression of passion is unbiblical chaos." Round and round the broad-brush statements go, each side labeling the other in a way that wins the theological war instead of works to preserve unity. With social media mobs rewarding inflammatory statements and conference Q&A hosts baiting big names to drop "truth bombs," we end up saying things without any nuance that get lots of attention. But is Christ pleased with that approach? It takes hard work and patience to categorize people and their teachings appropriately, but it doesn't get as big of a reaction from those we're talking to. Whether it be on social media, from a stage, on a podcast, or in person, broadbrushing is a lazy attempt to deal with an issue that may be a seriously troubling area, but requires careful thinking and careful response.

## 4. PLEASING JESUS IS MOST IMPORTANT

The Christian landscape can sometimes look like a series of camps. In each camp are leaders, commonly held beliefs, written and unwritten rules, and a sense of identity. Camps can be helpful for bringing likeminded people together, establishing schools and seminaries, creating an ecosystem of support, and providing clarity for our doctrinal distinctives. Camps can also be problematic because they may foster secrecy, cover up sin, and destroy those who stand up for truth at the cost of key leaders in the camp. Nothing is more important than unity with Christ. He is the one we ought to be most concerned about pleasing.

If you're a charismatic who is concerned about certain abuses, do not be afraid to speak up. Please Jesus, even it means you walk the plank alone. If you're Baptist or Reformed and are concerned about boundaries and rules made by men and not Scripture, do not be afraid to lead your ministry in a way that pleases Jesus, no matter the cost. In life and ministry, there will be those who expect you to fly their flag, be loyal to their camp, and be a "company man." Those types are usually the most frustrated when they find out you're loyal only to Christ. When attacked, misunderstood, or even ostracized, root your confidence in the fact that if you have upset some people but pleased the Lord, you have done what is right. If you've done well for the camp but not pleased the Lord, repent. If you've upset some folks but pleased the Lord, rejoice.

## CONCENTRIC CIRCLES OF DOCTRINAL DISTINCTION

With these principles as our foundation, we need to answer the most important questions: What doctrines should we consider essential? What doctrines may impact our church membership but not our global-church partnership? All Christians have a responsibility to think deeply about what isn't worth dividing over. This monumental task requires prayer, study, and wise counsel because it dictates how we will worship and with whom we will worship. What makes this task even more difficult is that our immaturity can lead us to draw lines where the Bible does not, or not to draw lines where the Bible does. Sorting through the stack of key doctrines from the Bible is no small matter, so pastors and church leaders do well to spend weeks, months, and even years revisiting this topic. The gospel is worth defending and even dividing over, and yet the bride of Christ should reflect the love and unity God calls us to. When do you pull out the sword to fight the good fight, and when do you put your sword away lest you foolishly wound

## Figure II.I: Concentric Circles of Doctrinal Distinction

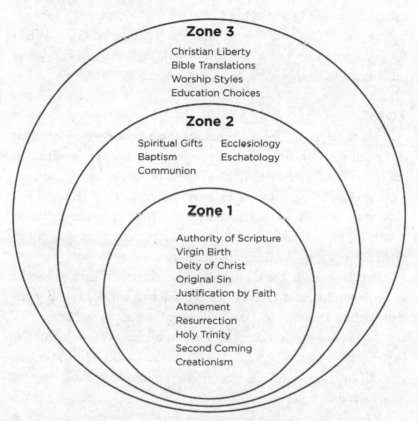

**Zone 3**

Christian Liberty
Bible Translations
Worship Styles
Education Choices

**Zone 2**

Spiritual Gifts    Ecclesiology
Baptism            Eschatology
Communion

**Zone 1**

Authority of Scripture
Virgin Birth
Deity of Christ
Original Sin
Justification by Faith
Atonement
Resurrection
Holy Trinity
Second Coming
Creationism

brothers and sisters in Christ? Figure 11.1 is a visual aid that we use in our church and to guide our staff discussions on doctrinal fences. My staff team often teases me about my love for concentric circles, diagrams, and charts, and this one is a favorite! Some readers will think I am being too open, others will find me to be too narrow-minded. Please note that these lists are not exhaustive. At any rate, I hope it gives you a starting point from which to work.

In the figure, there are three zones:

## ZONE 1

These doctrines are of primary importance for salvation and for being considered as part of the Christian faith. If someone does not believe the same about these things, there can be no unity. When these doctrines are being misrepresented, then the gospel is being undermined and should be defended at all costs.

## ZONE 2

These doctrines are important to the practice of our faith but do not directly impact someone's eternal salvation. If we differ on these subjects, we may limit the extent of fellowship or partnership, sticking to gospel work that keeps zone 1 at the center of our collective effort. Even though zone 2 doctrines are not essential to salvation, they should be taken seriously because they impact our practices and shape us in significant ways.

Ecclesiology is the doctrine of the church. There are some incredibly important aspects that we want to get right, and some that faithful churches will do differently from one another.

Eschatology is the doctrine of the end times. We should not be indifferent to what Scripture says about the Lord's return, yet two faithful believers can come to different conclusion about how to interpret various passages.

Zone 2 matters, but we must be careful how far we separate ourselves from those who differ from us in these positions. We tend to choose where to place our church membership based on these doctrines, but we may experience great joy, friendship, and gospel partnership with believers who differ with us on zone 2 matters. Notice that spiritual gifts are in zone 2. This means that many beloved believers may hold different views but can still experience unity in the faith. When it comes to baptism, Lutherans who sprinkle and Baptists who immerse should still find great unity in the faith in zone 1 matters, though they may insist on being a member of a church where they align in zone 2.

Different churches will add or subtract things from zone 2 based on their denominational or leadership convictions, but this general framework will help us to be thoughtful and cause us to be increasingly more careful of calling family in Christ by any other label.

## ZONE 3

These doctrines should have little bearing on our unity, though we do not dismiss them as altogether unimportant. We may be passionate about them because of our study and convictions, or because of regional experiences where the church is clashing with the culture and so we've chosen to take a strong stance. In zone 3, our personal convictions cannot become public commands. A pastor may prefer traditional worship styles over modern ones, or a contemporary music director may lower the lighting during a worship set. One may prefer one Bible translation over another, yet both are still faithful to the original manuscripts. Various Christians will exercise their liberties in different ways, or not exercise them at all. These preferences matter in our churches to some degree and there may be wisdom in making certain decisions regarding them, but they should not have bearing on our gospel unity. Respected theologians and wise pastors have long counseled Christians against causing needless division over these issues.

# A WORD TO "REFORMED BAPTIST TYPES"

I fit into this category and have made my fair share of hasty generalizations about those I differ with on matters of pneumatology (doctrine of the Holy Spirit). One of the most humbling experiences is meeting people with whom I have had strong differences only to find that they are Jesus-loving, gospel-preaching family in Christ who see things differently than I do on certain matters.

There are legitimate concerns in the charismatic movement that should be addressed, and even my friends who are in the movement express those concerns. In our critiques, though, let us not forget the Great Commission (Matt. 28:16–20) and our collective duty to see the gospel go forth. While there are false teachers whom we need to call out for their gospel-twisting ministries, we must keep that in a different category from concerns over secondary differences. For example, there may be important conversations and even debate to be had with charismatic brothers and sisters over the use of tongues in certain ways, but we must take great care in these matters so as not to conflate false teachers who trample on the gospel with our family in Christ who see the gifts of the Spirit differently than we do.

When we express concerns about certain aspects of the charismatic movement, let us be careful not to merely seek a reaction from our audiences or to paint the movement at its worst and leave it at that. Faithfully call out errors, but graciously highlight the truth. Perhaps as people see the genuine care we have for them *and* the truth, they will be more receptive to constructive criticism and meaningful dialogue. Even if they do not agree, we will have pleased Christ, whom both we and those we are criticizing call Lord, and we may find friends who sharpen us as well.

## A WORD TO CHARISMATICS

To my charismatic friends (and my critics who find me to be too dogmatic on certain doctrinal positions), I hope that you have found this book to be charitable, or at least reasonable in the areas in which we differ. There is much good that you bring to the table by way of passion, evangelism, and strong optimism that the Spirit is going to move in power to bring revival in our churches. I commend you for this.

I know many charismatics and Pentecostals who love the Word of God but because they want to experience the power of God in tangible ways have found themselves drawn to experiences rather than the simple truth of the Word. I encourage all of us to be cautious of spending more time chasing an experience than the power of God's Word. The Word is living, active, and sharper than any two-edged sword (Heb. 4:12). The people in our churches do not *always* need a Sunday filled with experiences, but rather they need to be fed the pure milk of the Word (1 Peter 2:2). Give more time to preaching, teaching, and going deeper into doctrine and I believe you will find balance in ways you never imagined. My goal is to encourage you right where you are to fortify the flock of God and your life with doctrine that acts as a rudder, steering the ship as the Spirit of God fills the sails.

## CLOSING THOUGHT ON UNITY

My sincerest prayer and hope is that this book has helped you grow to a greater understanding of the Spirit's work. If you find yourself aligned with some of the debated positions I've presented, I praise God for you and hope you'll glorify Jesus with every breath he gives you. If you find yourself appreciative of the book but not in complete agreement with some of the debated positions I've presented, I praise God for you and hope you'll glorify Jesus with every breath he gives you.

In all things, let us never veer off course from the gospel, and may we "press on toward the goal for the prize of the upward call of God in Christ Jesus" (Phil. 3:14).

# A FINAL WORD OF COMMISSIONING

I WANT TO LEAVE YOU WITH SEVERAL FINAL thoughts as you reach the conclusion of this book. Depending on your background or reason for reading the book, you've learned many truths, studied many truths, or perhaps were challenged by or disagreed with various sections. Whatever the case, well done. You made it! But the journey continues and I pray for the following outcomes.

First, *let's be biblical.* In our relationship with the Holy Spirit and our study of any theological topic, devoting ourselves to rooting our thoughts, arguments, conclusions, and applications in Scripture is going to always be more fruitful than arguing primarily from experience or unstudied opinion.

Second, *let's be humble.* Spiritual pride is a constant danger when we've studied a topic and feel that we have a grasp on it. Any confidence we have in the truth should be wielded with humility. We have the Bible, and that is enough to know our God and relish who he is. But there is nothing more prideful than using our knowledge of God as a weapon for power and arrogance. The more we know the Bible, the more awestruck we should be of how holy and righteous God is. How, then, can we respond to such understanding without falling before him in humility and thanksgiving? His mercy is undeserved, his ways unfathomable, his holiness unattainable, yet he has made himself knowable.

Third, *let's be respectful.* I need to take these words to heart as much as anyone when it comes to those with whom I disagree on certain things. Yet even in the midst of sharp disagreement or healthy debate, when the Jesus of the Bible is our common Lord, we are one (Eph. 4:1–6), and we need to walk in a manner worthy of our calling. Respect those with whom you disagree by doing your best to represent their positions with fairness and by seeing them as image bearers even though you think they are wrong about something.

Fourth, *let's be teachable.* God is in the business of teaching us, growing us, and sanctifying us from the day we are saved to the moment we die. I am of the mind that the worst form of spiritual arrogance is a lack of teachability. When someone thinks they know it all, the downgrading of their spiritual vitality has begun. When we are not teachable, we are prideful, and God opposes that (James 4:6).

Fifth, *let's be hopeful.* God the Father is drawing his sheep home, Jesus is building his church, and the Spirit is sanctifying us day by day. Maybe you're frustrated with certain sins in your life and wish you were growing faster. Maybe you're sick and tired of the abuses revolving around the Spirit's works. Maybe you wish Reformed types would stop broad-brushing Pentecostals or that Pentecostals would stop saying that Reformed types don't believe in the power of the Spirit. Don't give up hope! Keep praying, keep dialoguing, keep asking big questions, and keep trusting that the Lord will do his work in all of us and adorn his bride, preparing her for that glorious day when he returns to make all things new: "I saw the Holy City, the new Jerusalem, coming down out of heaven from God, prepared as a bride beautifully dressed for her husband. And I heard a loud voice from the throne saying, 'Look! God's dwelling place is now among the people, and he will dwell with them. They will be his people, and God himself will be with them and be their God'" (Rev. 21:2–4).

May the Spirit work in us and through us as we seek to bring glory and honor to Jesus Christ until that great day!

APPENDIX 1

# Common Questions about Tongues, Quenching, Grieving, and Blaspheming the Holy Spirit

THE FOLLOWING ARE QUESTIONS THAT WERE SENT in to our ministry at For the Gospel and from beloved people who have attended Shepherd's House Bible Church.

## 1. WHAT DO YOU THINK ABOUT SOMEONE HAVING A PRIVATE PRAYER LANGUAGE?

There are those who say that Paul's reference in 1 Corinthians 14:4 to anyone who speaks in tongues as edifying themselves and not others is sarcastic, because he employed sarcasm at multiple points in 1 Corinthians to drive home his rebukes (4:8–10; 14:16). They say that he is saying that the Corinthians' private use of tongues isn't even useful and is nothing more than self-satisfaction that puffs up their pride. Another interpretation sees Paul as having no issue with the private use of tongues so long as they are interpreted (presumably by the tongue speaker). Some believe this can be edifying between the speaker and God in private. One thing to note is that, as we discussed, all tongues were known languages. Therefore, regardless of which interpretation one lands on, there is no room for an ecstatic utterance that comes out as gibberish. If that has happened to you, it may be a false spirit or an experience that was emotionally manipulated by someone who taught you to do that. Use discernment and seek the Lord for wisdom.

## 2. I HAVE HEARD OF PEOPLE WHO WENT TO THE JUNGLES OF PAPUA NEW GUINEA AND SPOKE IN TONGUES; WHAT WOULD YOU SAY TO THAT?

God is the sovereign giver of the gifts and it is his sovereign prerogative to do as he pleases (Ps. 115:3). No one can say "Lies!" to this question because no one can say what God would or wouldn't do in a jungle where they don't live, but the gift of tongues is a gift, and the gifts of God are not revoked. One is not given the gift of teaching during a trip in a jungle but then returns home to the USA and cannot teach ever again. The stories often told about these experiences usually involve someone randomly speaking a language, then not ever doing it again. One could argue that this is the providence of God to bring the gospel in a local language, but I believe that the gift of tongues would be ongoing for someone who possessed it. Furthermore, I am not at all convinced that American churches speaking in tongues *en masse* like many do is the same thing as those who claim they spoke in tongues to advance the gospel on the mission field.

## 3. CAN TONGUES BE DEMONIC?

Yes. The Kundalini practices of Hinduism include speaking in tongues (ecstatic utterance) and Mormons speak in tongues as well. Both of these are false belief systems that are at odds with Christianity, so I believe without a doubt that there are demonic counterfeits within these systems that the devil uses to confuse and deceive people. One of the reasons that I am cautious of the extreme convulsions in the charismatic movement, and of the wild animal noises at the Toronto Blessing revival in the 1990s, and of the meetings of teachers like Kenneth Hagin is because they are very similar to the manifestations of Kundalini practices. A documentary video by Andrew Strom is worth watching—at your discretion—and serves to encourage us to be discerning and to do research.[1] This video gives me pause and makes me want to pray for discernment with any movement that produces such manifestations. It is important to test all things.

### 4. WHAT DOES IT MEAN TO QUENCH THE SPIRIT?

The subject of quenching the Spirit comes up in 1 Thessalonians 5:20 with regard to prophecy. The Thessalonians were told not to despise prophetic utterances, which would be quenching the Spirit. Some people might think that when I say there are no more prophets today, I am quenching the Spirit. But this text is referring to the Thessalonians' not despising or rejecting genuine prophecy that was given at that time. To quench the Spirit, one would have to have a 100 percent-trustworthy revelatory prophecy from God and either refuse to share it or refuse to listen to it. D. Michael Martin explains the issue that could result in the Thessalonian context: "The person with the gift of prophecy proclaimed the word of the Lord to the congregation for its 'strengthening, encouragement and comfort' (1 Cor 14:3, 6–7, 22). A word of prophecy could also be evangelistic, leading to the conviction and conversion of unbelievers (1 Cor 14:24–25). The Spirit might be quenched by the prophet himself if he refused to speak the word the Spirit gave to him. But

---

1. One of the most disturbing and sobering comparisons between the manifestations in Hinduism's Kundalini practices and modern charismatic extremism is presented in this video: Andrew Strom, "Shocking Documentary 1: False Spirits Invade the Church—Kundalini Warning—Andrew Strom—Part 1," July 6, 2010, www.youtube.com/watch?v=eBpw2oQrvMM.

the exhortations in vv. 21–22 indicate that it was the community of faith that was evaluating the worth of the prophecy and determining whether to accept or reject it, not the prophet himself. The church as a body might quench the Spirit by refusing to hear the word of the prophet."[2]

## 5. WHAT IS BLASPHEMING THE HOLY SPIRIT?

In Matthew 12:22 Jesus heals a man who was demon possessed, blind, and dumb (unable to speak). The Pharisees are looking on and hear the people wondering whether Jesus is the Messiah. They are filled with jealousy, as usual. They declare to the crowds, "This man [Jesus] casts out demons only by Beelzebul the ruler of the demons [Satan]" (Matt. 12:24). Jesus rebukes them and explains that the "blasphemy against the Spirit" is the one unpardonable sin. He says, "Whoever is not with me is against me, and whoever does not gather with me scatters. Therefore I tell you, every sin and blasphemy will be forgiven people, but the blasphemy against the Spirit will not be forgiven. And whoever speaks a word against the Son of Man will be forgiven, but whoever speaks against the Holy Spirit will not be forgiven, either in this age or in the age to come" (Matt. 12:30–32 ESV).

Notice that Jesus says "every sin," including blasphemy will be forgiven, which means that there is only one sin that will be linked to damnation. Since there is only one thing that can damn someone to hell, which is to reject Christ and live in unbelief, Jesus is referring to the sin of unbelief and rejection of God. Jesus, the Son of God and Savior, was right in front of the Pharisees, yet their blind eyes could not see that he was the promised Messiah. Instead of believing in him by faith, they called him a demonic agent of Satan. They refused to receive him, but even more so, they accused him.

---

2. D. Michael Martin, *1, 2 Thessalonians*, vol. 33, New American Commentary (Nashville: Broadman and Holman, 1995), 184–85.

No one today can commit blasphemy against the Holy Spirit unless they do the same thing and reject Christ, calling him nothing more than the agent of Satan.

Some people are afraid to call out anything that labels itself Christian or to speak about the deception of darkness masquerading as the work of the Spirit because they fear they might be committing the unforgivable sin. They even claim that I have committed that sin by calling certain things like "slaying in the Spirit" *potentially* demonic in some cases. My claim does not fit into the category of blasphemy against the Spirit because it has no relation to what Jesus was doing and because I am not rejecting the genuine work of Christ, as the Pharisees were. I am showing that there is no instance in the Bible of people barking like dogs, crawling around like animals, convulsing, screaming, or touching each other inappropriately, so I call that behavior *potentially* demonic. Should someone do the genuine works of Christ and be the Messiah, and I outright reject that person and call him or her an agent of Satan, *that* would be the unforgiveable sin, which is what the Pharisees were committing. When people act in ways that are not at all represented in Scripture and we "test the spirits" (1 John 4:1) and those spirits look nothing like the Spirit of God, it is fair to say that the manifestations are of another spirit and not the Spirit of God. Demonic counterfeits are real. Second Corinthians 11:13–15 says that false apostles will appear as workers of righteousness and that they are like the devil, who disguises himself as an angel of light. When something looks nothing like Scripture, it is not the unforgivable sin to call it what it is.

## 6. HOW DOES ONE GRIEVE THE HOLY SPIRIT?

In Ephesians 4:30 Paul warns, "Do not grieve the Holy Spirit of God." A number of errant interpretations of this verse attempt to make more of it than it is. For example, when famous faith healer Kathryn Kuhlman used to see people moving around during one of her services, she would say, "Don't grieve the Holy Spirit!" Countless others have followed suit. I was in a service once where someone got up to use the restroom during a normal part of the service (which would go on for hours) and the preacher shouted, "Don't move! You will grieve the Holy Spirit!" That is not even close to what the apostle Paul is saying in Ephesians 4:30. Those who paint the Spirit to be a fragile, oversensitive, timid deity are treading on dangerously unbiblical ground. He is God, and yes, he is sensitive to sin just as the Father and the Son are, but we must not go beyond what Scripture teaches and create abusive and fear-driven environments where everyone is afraid to "grieve the Spirit" by upsetting the preacher. The Spirit is grieved when we revel in our sin, when we walk in the worldly ways of our old nature, when we use unwholesome language, when we are filled with wrath, anger, quarrelling, evil, and malice (Eph. 4:25–31). He is not grieved when we get up to use the restroom during a three-hour-long charismatic service. Deliberate disobedience grieves him, and we should repent to close the gap in our fellowship with him if that's our situation (1 John 1:9).

For more answers and to send in questions, subscribe to
the *For the Gospel Podcast* on YouTube or your favorite
podcast platform, and go to www.forthegospel.org for free
video teachings, articles, interviews, and more.

# APPENDIX 2

# Are There Still Apostles Today?

ARE THERE STILL APOSTLES TODAY? YOU NEED
answers to this doctrinal issue because it's a prevalent teaching.
Leaders around the world are claiming to be apostles and that the
Spirit has reopened the apostolic era.

For the discerning believer, Scripture is the final authority. So
are there still apostles? Can you be an apostle?

No.

Here are three simple reasons why.

## 1. APOSTLES WERE THE FOUNDATION OF
## THE CHURCH

Ephesians 2:19–22 says, "You are no longer foreigners and
strangers, but fellow citizens with God's people and also members
of his household, built on the foundation of the apostles and prophets, with Christ Jesus himself as the chief cornerstone. In him, the
whole building is joined together and rises to become a holy temple
in the Lord. And in him you too are being built together to become
a dwelling in which God lives by his Spirit" (NIV).

In this passage, the apostle Paul explains to the Ephesians how they are being built up as the church and how the church at large is being built and established. The apostles and prophets played a foundational role by providing new revelation directly from God, and Christ is the chief cornerstone that the church is built on and around. The apostles and prophets were, much like Christ, a one-time foundational part of establishing the church. Do you relay a foundation with more Christs? Never! Do you add new apostles and prophets suddenly in the twenty-first century because of some supposed word from the Lord? No. Does the church ever get torn down like an old house and rebuilt? No. Likewise, there are no new apostles or prophets today. The foundation was laid once and for all.

## 2. APOSTLES WERE EYEWITNESSES TO CHRIST

Acts 1:21–22 gives us evidence of how the early church viewed apostleship. In this passage we see the apostles select the man to replace Judas as the twelfth apostle. Peter proclaims, "It is necessary that of the men who have accompanied us all the time that the Lord Jesus went in and out among us—beginning with the baptism of John until the day that He was taken up from us—one of these must become a witness with us of His resurrection."

According to Peter, the new apostle needed to be someone who was associated with Christ, who had consistently sat under his teaching, and who had witnessed firsthand his life and ministry. You may agree with this but immediately think of two people who don't fit this description, so let's answer two key questions:

1. *What about Paul? He wasn't with Christ like that.* But Paul was visited by Christ and called as an apostle in a supernatural way, verifying his call to apostleship from Jesus himself (Acts 9:1–19; Gal. 1:1–12). Furthermore, the twelve apostles, including Peter, unanimously affirmed that Paul

was called by Christ himself and verified him to be counted among them (Gal. 1:18).

2. *What about Barnabas? He wasn't one of the twelve or like Paul.* Barnabas was not one of the twelve, nor was he like Paul in the sense that Jesus appeared to him in a vision and called him to be an apostle. There are two possibilities (both are reasonable) for Barnabas's being called an apostle in Acts 14:14:

- *Possibility 1:* Luke is using the term *apostolos*, which can mean simply "messenger." Luke may be using this term to describe the nature of Paul and Barnabas's mission in that situation, while not labeling him as an apostle in the sense of his office.
- *Possibility 2:* Luke is describing Barnabas in kind with Paul, leading to the possibility that Paul, as a true apostle, had the power to impart (or bestow) apostolic authority and ability to Barnabas. This could be the reason for Barnabas's being the one to introduce Paul to the twelve (Acts 9:27), but this is not explicit evidence. This possibility does not open the door for apostolic succession because all of this takes place with men who were alive while Jesus was on the earth or had direct contact with the twelve for the purpose of being confirmed, and even the disciples of John (like Polycarp) did not refer to themselves as apostles nor receive apostleship. The term *bishop* or *pastor* became more prevalent after the apostles were dead.

Whatever the case, Barnabas's being an apostle is hardly evidential reasoning for modern-day apostleship. Anyone who claims to be an apostle now would have a hard time pulling off the next evidence for true apostleship.

## 3. APOSTLES DID IMPOSSIBLE SIGNS
## AND WONDERS

In 2 Corinthians 12:12 Paul tells the church that the "marks of a true apostle" had been done among them through signs, wonders, and miracles. What signs and wonders did Paul perform?

- Acts 13:11: Paul commanded blindness to come upon a man to show his power.
- Acts 14:10: Paul commanded a man who had been lame from birth to stand up on his feet, and he jumped up and began to walk.
- Acts 16:18: Paul commanded a demon to come out immediately, not during a three-hour-long exorcism like people try to do today.
- Acts 19:11–12: God performed miracles through Paul so that even aprons and handkerchiefs he had touched were used to heal people.
- Acts 20:10–12: Paul raised Eutychus from the dead.

Apostles performed signs and wonders that no modern-day faith healers or so-called apostles can pull off. The apostolic gifts were for the establishment of the apostles' authority. They had been with Christ and wielded the power of Christ.

So are there apostles today? No. God used them as part of the body of Christ to lay the foundation of the church.

# ABOUT THE AUTHOR

COSTI W. HINN (@COSTIWHINN) IS THE TEACHING pastor at Shepherd's House Bible Church in Chandler, Arizona. His weekly sermons are available at www.shepherdsaz.org. In addition to being a pastor and an author, Costi is the founder and president of For the Gospel, a resource ministry that provides sound doctrine for everyday people. FTG now reaches more than one million people every month in more than 180 countries through videos, teaching series, podcasts, and social media. Costi hosts the *For the Gospel* podcast, which releases a new episode every week. You can subscribe on YouTube and listen on Apple, Spotify, Google, or wherever you listen to podcasts. Visit www.forthegospel .org and follow @forthegospelmin for sharable content on all social media outlets, including Instagram, TikTok, Facebook, Twitter, and YouTube.

# More Than a Healer

## Not the Jesus You Want, but the Jesus You Need

*Costi W. Hinn*

Find hope that lasts beyond earthly pain and spiritual encouragement to lead you into a deep relationship with the Healer himself.

Our hearts, our bodies, and our world are desperate for healing. Whether we are experiencing physical, emotional, or financial brokenness, we rightfully look to Jesus to perform a masterful restoration. But how does healing fit into God's will, especially when God doesn't heal? And how do we catch ourselves from slipping into the trap of seeking God for what he can do for us, and not for who he really is?

Author, pastor, and frequently sought speaker Costi Hinn provides clarity through thoughtful answers and biblical truths about Jesus and his healing ministry. Growing up immersed in one of the world's leading faith-healing dynasties, Costi witnessed the tragedy of people chasing after healing more than the Healer. And now he shares with others the true power and hope that come from a genuine relationship with God.

With captivating stories—beginning with the vivid memory of the night he discovered his son's cancer diagnosis—Costi empathetically unpacks the layered feelings and questions we have about God and his healing power and provides practical principles for growing close to Jesus. With gentle clarity and biblical wisdom, Costi explains how to pray for healing while submitting to God's sovereignty, navigate tough conversations about the topic, and hold on to faith even in the most painful trials.

More than chasing after the Jesus we want, this hopeful and encouraging book will guide us to discovering the Jesus we truly need.

Available in stores and online!

# God, Greed, and the (Prosperity) Gospel

## How Truth Overwhelms a Life Built on Lies

*Costi W. Hinn*

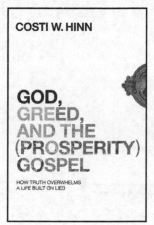

A captivating first-person look at one of the world's most powerful prosperity dynasties that offers a unique perspective on greed, the church, and the journey toward truth.

Millions desperate for hope and solutions are enticed by the promise of the prosperity gospel—that God will do whatever they need with just a little faith and a financial gift. All the while, prosperity preachers exploit the poor and needy to stockpile their riches. What can followers of the true gospel do to combat the deception?

Through a remarkable and fascinating journey, Costi Hinn went from a next-generation prosperity preacher to the first to abandon the family faith and share the true gospel. Nephew of world-famous televangelist Benny Hinn, Costi had a front-row seat to the inner workings and theology of the prosperity gospel. But as Costi's faith deepened, so did his questions about prosperity teaching. As the deceptions in his past were exposed, Costi came face to face with the hypocrisy and devastation caused by his belief system, and the overwhelming truth about the real Jesus Christ.

This captivating look into the daily lives of one of the world's leading prosperity dynasties offers a thoughtful perspective on the perils of greed, the power of the true gospel, and hope for the future of the global church. Through real-life stories, Costi challenges and equips readers to be living lights pointing the way to the true gospel and the saving grace of Christ. *God, Greed, and the (Prosperity) Gospel* will bolster your faith and encourage your journey toward the truth.

Spanish edition also available.

Available in stores and online!